On the Edge of the Cliff

Parallax **Re-visions of Culture and Society**

Stephen G. Nichols, Gerald Prince, and Wendy Steiner, Series Editors

ON THE
EDGE
History, Language, and Practices
OF THE

ROGER CHARTIER
CLIFF

Translated by Lydia G. Cochrane

The Johns Hopkins University Press

Baltimore and London

© 1997 The Johns Hopkins University Press
All rights reserved. Published 1997
Printed in the United States of America on acid-free recycled paper

06 05 04 03 02 01 00 99 98 97   5 4 3 2 1

The Johns Hopkins University Press
2715 North Charles Street
Baltimore, Maryland 21218-4319
The Johns Hopkins Press Ltd., London

Library of Congress Cataloging-in-Publication Data will be found
at the end of this book.

A catalog record for this book is available from the British Library.

ISBN 0-8018-5435-0
ISBN 0-8018-5436-9 (pbk.)

Contents

Acknowledgments

Chapter 1 is translated from "L'histoire entre récit et connaissance," *Modern Language Notes* 109 (1994): 583–600. © Copyright 1994 by The Johns Hopkins University Press.

Chapter 2 is translated from "Quatre questions à Hayden White," *Storia della Storiografia* 24 (1993): 133–42. © Copyright 1993 by *Storia della Storiografia*.

Chapter 3 is translated from "L'histoire ou le savoir de l'autre," in *Michel de Certeau,* ed. Luce Giard (Paris: Editions Centre Georges Pompidou 1987), 155–67. © Copyright 1987 by Editions Centre Georges Pompidou. Portions of this essay appeared in *Libération,* 11–12 January 1986, soon after the death of Michel de Certeau, and in a paper presented to the colloquy "Ecriture et pratiques historiennes avec Michel de Certeau," Centre de Recherches Historiques, Ecole des Hautes Etudes en Sciences Sociales, Paris, 9–10 February 1987.

Chapter 4 appeared in *Foucault and the Writing of History,* ed. Jan Goldstein (London: Basil Blackwell, 1994), 167–86 and 291–94. © Copyright 1994 by Basil Blackwell.

Chapter 5 is translated from "Les historiens et les mythologies," *Liber: Revue Européenne des Livres* 11 (September 1992), "Actes de la Recherche en Sciences Sociales," 94, supp. © Copyright 1992 by *Liber*.

Chapter 6 is translated from the foreword, "Textes, formes, interprétations," in D. F. McKenzie, *La bibliographie et la sociologie des textes,* translated from the English by Marc Amfreville, (Paris: Editions du Cercle de la Librairie, 1991) 5–18. © Copyright 1991 by Editions du Cercle de la Librairie.

Chapter 7 is translated from "Pouvoirs et limites de la représentation: Sur l'oeuvre de Louis Marin," *Annales: Histoire, Sciences Sociales* 2 (March–April 1994): 407–18. © Copyright 1994 by Librairie Armand Colin. A preliminary version of this essay was presented at the colloquy "Limits of Representation: An Interdisciplinary Symposium, in Memory of Louis Marin," Johns Hopkins University, Baltimore, 12–13 November 1993.

Chapter 8 is translated from the foreword, "Conscience de soi et lien social," in Norbert Elias, *La société des individus,* translated from the German by Jeanne Etoré (Paris: Fayard, 1991), 7–29. © Copyright 1987 by Suhrkamp Verlag, Frankfurt am Main. French translation © Copyright 1991 by Librairie Arthème Fayard.

Chapter 9 is translated from the foreword, "Double lien et distanciation," in Norbert Elias, *Engagement et distanciation: Contributions à la sociologie de la connaissance,* translated from the German by Michèle Hulin (Paris: Fayard, 1993), i–x. © Copyright 1983 by Norbert Elias. French translation and foreword © Copyright 1993 by Librairie Arthème Fayard.

Chapter 10 is translated from the foreword, "Le sport ou la libération contrôlée des émotions," in Norbert Elias and Eric Dunning, *Sport et civilisation: La violence maîtrisée,* translated from the English by Josette Chicheportiche and Fabienne Duvigneau (Paris: Fayard, 1994), 7–24. Original edition © Copyright 1986 by Norbert Elias and Eric Dunning. French translation and foreword © Copyright 1994 by Librairie Arthème Fayard.

The epilogue is translated from the foreword, "L'amitié de l'histoire," in Philippe Ariès, *Le temps de l'histoire,* 2d ed. (Paris: Editions du Seuil, 1986), 9–31. © Copyright 1986 by Editions du Seuil.

Introduction

"On the edge of the cliff": this image, which Michel de Certeau used to describe the work of Michel Foucault,[1] seems to me appropriate for all intellectual approaches having at their heart relations between the products of discourse and social practices. Rendering intelligible practices that are not governed by the laws of the formation of discourses is a difficult, unstable enterprise poised at the edge of the void. It is always threatened by the temptation to do away with all difference between heteronomous but nonetheless interconnected forms of logic— the ones that organize utterances and the ones that command action and behavior.

That distinction is one of the fundamental themes of this book, which pleads the cause of a history capable of inscribing the diverse modalities of the discursive construction of the social world within the objective constraints that both limit the production of discourse and make it possible. To do so this work, a collection of eleven essays that appeared between 1986 and 1994, proceeds in a different way than other works of mine that have appeared in English and that address a specific historical problem—the study of the forms, uses, and effects of print culture in the societies of the early modern age, from the sixteenth century to the eighteenth, in particular in ancien régime France.[2] This book departs from research in the usual sense of the term to concentrate on reading.

Most of the essays gathered here return to the time-honored genre of a conversation with and among the dead. The texts devoted to Michel Foucault, Michel de Certeau, Louis Marin, Norbert Elias, and Philippe Ariès were all written after their deaths. Frequenting their works has long been a major source of inspiration for all (and I count myself among them) who have tried, in these past fifteen years, to shift cultural history's lines of questioning and its approaches. When death came to interrupt the work of these five authors, it seemed to me necessary and proper to acknowledge my debts.

My goal in proposing this series of readings is neither to construct a sociology of the contemporary intellectual field (a task that would require other inquiries and other tools) nor to suggest that the authors assembled here furnish a homogeneous corpus of notions and perspectives. They seldom cite one another (even when, as do Norbert Elias and Philippe Ariès, they treat closely related topics), and they differ profoundly both in the concepts they treat and in their ways of treating them. Still, reading their works provided intersecting paths that supported the trajectory of a cultural history that, once emancipated from the traditional definition of the history of mentalities, came to pay more attention to the modalities of appropriation than to statistical distributions, more to processes for constructing meaning than to the unequal circulation of objects, and more to seeing connections among practices and representations than to inventorying mental tools. These shifts (one, for example, changed the history of the production and diffusion of the book into a history of the practices of reading) were based on parallels and comparisons that historians borrowed from the works of the authors discussed here, all of whom "did" history but none of whom was, either by training or by intellectual practice, an "ordinary" historian. They shared an emphasis on the historicity of social forms, intellectual categories, systems of representations, fields of discourse and objects, and the basic structures of personality. Hence the centrality of the notion of discontinuity, which for Foucault, who had read Nietzsche, meant emergences without origin and for Elias meant the succession of differentiated figurations that engender one another within a long-term process. It is that radical rupture with all forms of projecting to universality categories held to be unvarying—and along with them, all the formalistic conceptions identifying structures and formulas that are supposed to remain unchanged in very different historical contexts—that constitutes the fundamental kinship among the authors whose work is presented and commented on in this book.

Walking awhile in their company helps us formulate more clearly the crisis (or at least the uncertainty) of history often announced today.[3] The optimistic and all-conquering enthusiasm of the "new history" was followed by a time of doubt and interrogation. There are several reasons for such an anxious, often gloomy mood: a loss of confidence in the infalli- [REASONS FOR UNCERTAINTY] bility of quantification, an abandonment of the traditional classifications (geographical divisions at the head of the list) of historical objects, and—again—a questioning of notions ("mentalities," "popular culture," etc.), categories (social classes, socioprofessional classifications, etc.), and models of interpretation (structuralist, Marxist, demographic, etc.) that had been those of triumphant historiography.

The crisis of history's intelligibility was felt all the more strongly because it occurred just when the number of professional historians and their publications had grown immensely. The crisis had two effects. First, [① FEDERATING DISCIPLINE ??] history lost its position as a federating discipline within the social sciences. In France, but also in Europe in general, the two successive programs of the *Annales*—the first, in the 1930s, guided by the primacy of economic and social history, the second, in the 1970s, identified with historical anthropology—provided a focus, if not for the unification of the science of society that Emile Durkheim's sociology and Henri Berr's historical synthesis had dreamed of at the beginning of this century, at least for an interdisciplinary approach with history as its keystone. This is [NO LONGER INTERDISCIPLINARY?] hardly the case today. Second, the time of the challenge to accepted ideas was also a time of dispersion: all the great historiographical traditions [② TRADITIONS LOST UNITY] lost their unity; they shattered into different and often contradictory propositions that produced a multiplicity of objects, methods, and "histories."

In the face of the retreat of the great explicative models, a first, strong temptation was to return to the archives and to the raw document that registers the upwelling of singular instances of speech, which are always richer and more complex that what the historian has to say about them. By disappearing behind the words of the "other," the historian attempted to escape the posture, inherited from Jules Michelet, that consists, as Jacques Rancière put it, in "the art of making the poor speak by keeping them silent, of making them speak as silent people."[4]

This attempt to withdraw behind the words of the actors in history— [HISTORIANS ESCAPED BEHIND WORDS OF HISTORICAL ACTORS] words to be read in their intrinsic literality—might seem paradoxical at a time when, quite to the contrary, history was inhabited by a demand (at times loudly proclaimed) for the historian's subjectivity, the affirmation of the rights of the "I" in historical discourse, and the temptations of *ego-histoire*.[5] The contradiction is only apparent. Offering old texts for reading is not, in Arlette Farge's words, "recopying reality." By their choices and comparisons, historians assign new meaning to speech pulled out of the silence of the archives. "Apprehension of speech responds to an in-

terest in reintroducing existences and singularities into historical discourse, in using words to draw scenes that are as many events."[6] This totally changed the meaning of the presence of quotation in a historical
text. No longer the illustration of a regularity established by series and
measure, henceforth the quotation indicates the irruption of a difference
and a gap.

The return to the archives raises a second problem—the relation between the categories manipulated by the actors in history and the notions
put into operation in the process of analysis. A break between the two has
long seemed the very precondition of scientific discourse about the social
world. That certainty is no longer acceptable. For one thing, the traditional criteria and classifications that long underlay social history (socioprofessional classification, for instance, or classification by position within
production relations) have lost their force as evidence. Historians have
become aware that the categories they manipulated also had a history and
that social history was necessarily the history of the construction and uses
of those categories.[7] For another thing, the habitual hierarchies founded
on a fixed and univocal conception of professional activity or social interests seemed to account only poorly for the lability of the relations and
trajectories that define identities.

Hence the importance historians have accorded to the categories and
the lexicon of history's actors and their emphasis on the interactions and
networks that show solidarities and antagonisms. Hence also, in the radical formulations of the American "linguistic turn," the dangerous reduction of the social world to a purely discursive construction and to
pure language games. The challenge to create a new history of societies
(Italian *microstoria* could be considered exemplary here) thus consisted
in finding a necessary articulation between describing the perceptions,
representations, and rationalities of history's actors and identifying the
unconscious interdependencies that both limit and inform the strategies
of those actors. That articulation makes it possible to bypass the classical opposition between subjective singularities and collective determinations. This is why special attention is given here to the group of notions
("figuration," "social habitus," "society of individuals") that enabled
Norbert Elias to think about the relations between the individual and the
social world in a new way, detached from the heritage of traditional philosophy.

Making the connection between objective social properties and their
internalization in individuals in the form of a social habitus commanding

[margin note: PROBLEM W/ LOOKING TO LANGUAGE ??]

thoughts and actions leads to considering conflicts (or negotiations) among groups as struggles among representations in which the stakes are always the capacity of the groups or the individuals to ensure recognition of their identity.[8] The affirmation (or negation) of a community's social being depends on the credit accorded (or refused) the image—the "perceived being"—of itself that the community produces. This explains the importance of the notion of *representation* (treated here in relation to the work of Louis Marin), a notion that pertains on three levels of reality: first, on the level of collective representations that embody, within individuals, the divisions of the social world and organize the schemes of perception by which individuals classify, judge, and act; second, on the level of forms of exhibition and stylization of the identity that those individuals or groups hope will be recognized; third, on the level of the delegation to representatives (single individuals, institutions, or abstract instances) of the coherence and stability of the identity thus affirmed.

The history of the construction of social identities thus becomes a history of relations of symbolic force. It defines the construction of the social world as the success (or failure) of the work that groups perform on themselves—and on others—to transform the objective properties common to their members into a "belonging" that is perceived, demonstrated, and recognized (or denied). It understands symbolic domination as the process by which the dominated accept or reject the identities imposed on them with a view to ensuring and perpetuating their subjection. It inscribes within the long-term process of the reduction of violence and the containment of affect described by Elias the growing importance taken on in the modern age by confrontations whose stakes and instruments are symbolic forms.

The historians' return to the archives is part of the broader movement of renewed interest in the text. Historians lost much of their timidity (and their naïveté) about the canonical texts of their colleagues in neighboring disciplines—historians of literature, science, and philosophy—just as those "other" histories were finding new vigor in sociohistorical or contextualist approaches after the decline of the total domination of structuralist and formalist approaches.

To take only one example, the traditional and dominant postulates in the history of philosophy (to wit, the definition of the legitimacy of questions and authors based on their relevance for contemporary philosophical activity; the existence of a common fund of problems and responses independent of all specific formulation; the autonomy of that *philosophia*

[margin notes: IDEA OF SOCIAL BEING; ✳ REPRESENTATION; RENEWED INTEREST IN TEXT; ??]

perennis from any inscription in history) today seem discomfited by other, equally legitimate ways of thinking about the relation of philosophy to history. In a typology that has become classic, Richard Rorty contrasts the rational, deliberately anachronistic and a historical reconstructions of analytical philosophy with three other ways to write the history of philosophy—all three fully historical, and all three held to be pertinent. First, *Geistesgeschichte,* defined as the history of strictly "philosophical" questions and of the constitution of the canon of the "philosophers" who formulated them; second, "intellectual history," understood as a history of the very preconditions of philosophical activity; third, historical reconstructions that relate the meaning of texts to the context in which they were elaborated and to their conditions of possibility.[9] This last perspective is obviously the closest to traditional historical practices in that it accentuates the discontinuity of philosophical practices, which are differentiated by the social place or institution of learning where they are exercised, by changes in the questions and styles of inquiry that are considered legitimate, by genres and forms of discourse, and by the intellectual configurations that give the same concepts different meanings.[10]

These three ways of viewing the history of philosophy have their equivalents in the history of science, the history of art, and the history of literature. They illustrate a form of return to the texts (or more generally to the works) that inscribes them within the places and milieus of their elaboration, situates them within the specific repertory of the genres, questions, and conventions proper to a given time, and concentrates on the forms of their circulation and their appropriation. In that they clearly show that just when doubts had invaded the discipline of history, historical approaches claimed their rights elsewhere, in philosophy, literary criticism, and aesthetics.

Among historians, one of the effects of a renewed interest in texts was to return the disciplines of erudition to the central role they once played. Long relegated to the level of ancillary sciences, these technical skills, which propose rigorous and formalized descriptions of objects and forms, became (or became again) essential once documents were no longer considered solely for the information they furnish but were also studied in themselves for their discursive and material organization, their conditions of production, and their strategic utilization. In this manner paleography and diplomatics were transformed as a history of the social uses of writing, brilliantly illustrated by the works of Armando Petrucci and his students.[11] The "analytical bibliography" practiced especially, but not exclusively, in the Anglo-Saxon world was enlarged to become an ambitious "sociology of texts," in D. F. McKenzie's terms. The chapter in this book devoted to McKenzie is a reminder (against the tyranny of strictly linguistic approaches) that the determinations at work in the process of constructing meaning are plural. They depend on strategies of writing and publishing, but also on the possibilities and constraints inherent in each of the material forms that carry discourse and on the competencies, practices, and expectations of each community of readers (or spectators).[12] The "sociology of texts," thus understood, is not incompatible with recent thinking on the notion of representation, since, following the distinction proposed by Louis Marin, the very forms given to texts (oral or written, in manuscript or in print) belong to the "reflexive" dimension of all representations by which a material device is presented as representing something—here, a text.

Historians today are well aware that they too produce texts. The writing of history, even the most quantitative or the most structural history, belongs to the genre of the narrative, whose fundamental categories it shares. Narratives of fiction and narratives of history share the way they make their "characters" act, the way they construct temporality, and the way they conceive of causality. These are familiar notions, thanks to the works of Michel de Certeau and Paul Ricoeur.[13] They recall, first of all, that given the fundamental dependency of all history of any sort on the techniques of "emplotment," the repudiation of "event-oriented" history by no means meant abandoning the narrative. This is a good way of saying that historians, like other people, do not always do what they think they are doing and that proudly proclaimed ruptures often mask misunderstood continuities.

But the most essential problem lies elsewhere. It can be formulated thus: Why was history so long unaware that it belonged to the class of narrative?[14] Narrative was necessarily hidden in all the regimes of historicity that postulated a close coincidence between historical events and the discourses whose task it was to render an account of them. Whether it offered a collection of examples in the manner of classical antiquity, presented itself as knowledge of itself in the historicist and romantic German tradition, or thought of itself as "scientific," history could not avoid refusing to think of itself as a narrative. Narration, in fact, had no status of its own the minute—according to the case at hand—it was subject to the dispositions and the figures of the art of rhetoric, was considered the place where events themselves deployed, or was perceived as a major ob-

THERE IS
TRUTH IN
HISTORY
?

stacle to true knowledge. It was only when that epistemology of coincidence was cast into doubt and when historians became aware of the gap that exists between the past and its representation (or to use Ricoeur's expression, between "ce qui, un jour, fut"—what once was and is no more—and the discursive constructions that function as a *représentance*, "standing for," or *lieutenance*, "taking the place," of that past)[15] that reflection could develop concerning the modalities (both shared and specific) of historical narrative.

This acute awareness of the narrative dimension of history offered a serious challenge to all historians who refused to take a relativist position à la Hayden White and see historical discourse as merely a free play of rhetorical figures and as one mode of fictional invention among others. Against that dissolution of the status of history as a specific knowledge (a stance often taken as a figure of postmodernism), one must insist forcefully that history is commanded by an intention and a principle of truth, that the past history has taken as its object is a reality external to discourse, and that knowledge of it can be verified.

This reminder is highly useful at a moment when the strong temptations of identitarian history risk muddying all distinction between a universally acceptable, verified knowledge and the mythical reconstructions that sustain particular memories and aspirations. As Eric Hobsbawm has written, "Reading the desires of the present into the past, or, in technical terms, anachronism, is the most common and convenient technique of creating a history satisfying the needs of what Benedict Anderson has called 'imagined communities' or collectives, which are by no means only national ones."[16]

But can one resist drifting off course in this fashion, which is fatal to the referential function of history, simply by reaffirming—necessary as this may be—the demands, disciplines, and virtues of exercising the critical function? Now that knowledge, historical or not, can no longer be thought of as a pure coincidence or a simple equivalence between an object and a discourse, do we not have to seek a more essential refounding? This is the direction Joyce Appleby, Lynn Hunt, and Margaret Jacob are going in when they plead for a "new theory of objectivity" (understood as "an interactive relationship between an inquiring subject and an external object" and thought of as not excluding a plurality of interpretations) and when they adopt an epistemological position they call "practical realism," in which "people's perceptions of the world have some correspondence with that world and . . . standards, even though they are historical products, can be made to discriminate between valid and invalid assertions."[17]

From a different perspective, Paul Ricoeur specifies the conditions of possibility of a "critical realism of historical knowledge." For Ricoeur, those conditions come from the inscription of the historical subject and the historical object within the same temporal field: "The very same system is used to date the three temporal events that constitute the period under consideration; that is, the beginning of the period under consideration, its end or conclusion, and the present of the historian (more precisely, of the historical enunciation)." They also come from the fact that both historians and the actors whose history they are writing share a field of sufficiently common practices and experiences to provide a foundation for the "historian's dependence on the 'making' of real historical actors for his own history 'making.'" Ricoeur adds, "Before presenting themselves as master craftsmen of stories made out of the past, historians must first stand as heirs to the past. This idea of inheritance presupposes that the past in some sense lives in the present and therefore affects it."[18]

It is perhaps paradoxical to evoke Paul Ricoeur's hermeneutic and phenomenological approach at the end of the introduction to a book that accentuates historical thinking about rupture and difference. But perhaps it is only within that tension that we can think about and comprehend the past or the "other" and can get beyond the discontinuities that separate historical configurations. From Norbert Elias to Michel de Certeau, the figures of that possible intelligibility circulate throughout this book.

HISTORICAL THINKING ABOUT RUPTURE AND DIFFERENCE

This is not enough, however, to endow history with the status of true knowledge. One question remains, which it seems to me is not completely resolved either by the attempts to found a "new theory of objectivity" or by the propositions that aim at ensuring the "critical realism of historical knowledge." What are the criteria by which a historical discourse—always a knowledge based on traces and signs—can be held to be a valid and explicative reconstruction (or at least more valid and more explicative than others) of the past reality it has defined as its object? There is no easy answer to this question, even more so today than was true when the deep-rooted certitudes of critical objectivity and an epistemology of a coincidence between the real and knowledge of the real protected history from all anxiety about its regime of truth. This is no longer the case. To found the discipline of history on its dimension of knowledge, and a knowledge that is other than the one furnished by works of fiction, is in a certain manner to walk along the edge of the cliff. Historians have lost

✳ QUESTION

a good deal of their naïveté and their illusions. They know now that respect for the rules and operations proper to their discipline is a necessary but not sufficient condition for establishing history as a specific kind of knowledge. It is perhaps by following the path traced in this introduction, which leads from the archive to the text, from the text to writing, and from writing to knowledge, that they can take up the challenge facing them today. And they can do so by practicing their craft, but also thanks to a familiarity with strong works that oblige them to question all they hold as evident and all they have inherited. This is the reason for—and, who knows, the usefulness of—the series of readings offered in this book.

PART 1

Fiction and Knowledge

ONE

History between Narrative
and Knowledge

A time of uncertainty and of epistemological crisis; a critical turning point: such are the diagnoses, mostly apprehensive, given of history in recent years. Two statements in particular have opened the way to widespread discussion. The first was an editorial in the *Annales* for March and April 1988:

Today the time for incertitude seems at hand. A reclassification of disciplines is transforming the scholarly landscape, challenging established priorities and reshaping the ways innovation has traditionally circulated. The dominant paradigms that once were sought in the various Marxisms and structuralisms and in a confident use of quantification are losing their structuring force. . . . History, a good part of whose dynamism was founded in a federative ambition, has not been spared by this general crisis in the social sciences.[1]

The second statement differed in its motivation but reached similar conclusions. It was made in 1989 by David Harlan, in an article in the *American Historical Review* that launched a debate that continues to this day. As Harlan put it, "The return of literature has plunged historical studies into an extended epistemological crisis. It has questioned our belief in a fixed and determinable past, compromised the possibility of historical representation, and undermined our ability to locate ourselves in time."[2]

What do such pronouncements mean? They seem somewhat paradoxical at a time when history publishing displays admirable vitality and consistent inventiveness, to judge by the continuing success of great collective ventures, the launching of European collections, increasing numbers of translations, and the intellectual repercussions of some major books. What such statements point to, in my opinion, is a highly important change brought about by the weakening of models of comprehension and principles of intelligibility once commonly accepted by most or all post-1960 historians.

In the 1960s and 1970s, all-conquering history had two basic projects. The first was to apply the structuralist paradigm, openly acknowledged or implicit in practice, to the study of ancient or contemporary societies. Historians' task was to identify the structures and relations that operated, independent of the perceptions and intentions of individuals, to govern economic mechanisms, organize social relations, and engender forms of discourse. Hence the affirmation of a radical separation between the object of historical knowledge and the subjective consciousness of the actors in history.

In the second project, history was subjected to the procedures of number and series; it was inscribed within a paradigm of knowledge that Carlo Ginzburg, in a famous article,[3] designated "Galilean." This involved the quantification of phenomena, the construction of serial data, and the use of statistical techniques to draw up a rigorous formulation of the structural relations that were the very object of history. Borrowing from Galileo in *Il Saggiatore (The Assayer),* historians supposed that the social world was "written in mathematical language," and they set out to establish its laws.

The effects of that dual revolution in history—the structuralist and the Galilean—were vast. Thanks to it, the discipline of history abandoned a pure cartography of particularities and a simple (and always incomplete) inventory of individual cases and single facts. History thus reestablished contact with the founding ambition of the social sciences at the beginning of this century (particularly in their sociological and Durkheimian versions) to identify structures and regularities that permitted the formulation of general relationships.

At the same time, history broke free of the "highly meager idea of the real," to use Michel Foucault's expression, that had long inhabited it because it took the systems of relations that organize the social world to be just as "real" as material, physical, and corporeal things grasped in the immediacy of sense experience. Beyond the diversity of its objects, territories, and manners, the "new history" was thus strongly anchored in the very principles that supported the ambitions and conquests of the other social sciences.

During the past ten years precisely those certitudes, once so widely shared, have been shaken. There are a number of reasons for this. Historians, sensitive to new anthropological or sociological approaches, worked to restore the role of individuals in the construction of social bonds. This move led to several fundamental shifts: from structures to networks, from systems of positions to lived situations, from collective norms to individual strategies. "Microhistory," first in Italy, then in Spain,[4] gave a particularly striking translation of this change in historiography, based on recourse to interactive models and ethnomethodology. Quite unlike the traditional historical monograph, each *microstoria* took a particular situation (normal because exceptional) and attempted to reconstruct the way individuals use alliances and confrontations to produce the social world through the ties of dependency that link them or set them apart. Hence the object of history was not—or was no longer—the structures and mechanisms, lying beyond all subjective grasp, that govern social relations but rather the multiple rationalities and strategies put into operation by communities, kinship groups, families, and individuals.

This new form of social and cultural history focused on the gaps and discordances that exist both between one system of societal norms and another and within each of those systems. Historians' gaze shifted from the imposed rules to the inventive uses of those rules; from obligatory behaviors to the decisions each individual's resources permitted—resources that included social power, economic opportunities, and access to information. The history of societies, which had formerly drawn up hierarchies and constructed collectivities (socioprofessional categories, classes, groups), took on new objects, studied on a smaller scale. The biography of ordinary people was one of these, since, as Giovanni Levi wrote,

No normative system is de facto sufficiently structured to eliminate all possibility of conscious choice, of manipulation or interpretation of the rules, or of negotiation. It seems to me that this makes biography an ideal place for verifying the interstitial—but important—nature of the liberty available to agents and for observing the concrete operations of normative systems, which are never totally free of contradictions.[5]

Hence the reconstitution of the dynamic processes (negotiations, transactions, exchanges, conflicts, etc.) that provide a mobile, unstable picture of social relations and, at the same time, define areas where individual strategies can operate. Jaime Contreras expresses this notion exceptionally well in a recent book, *Sotos contra Riquelmes:*

Groups did not obliterate individuals; the objective existence of group forces did not prevent the exercise of a personal trajectory. Families . . . deployed their strategies to widen their spheres of solidarity and influence, but their men also played their roles individually. If the call of blood and the pull of lineage were intense, so too were the desire and the opportunity to create individual spaces. In the drama created by the specter of heresy—the "brainchild" of an ambitious inquisitor—collective interests and different conceptions of the world clashed, but at the same time each individual could react personally, following his own, original scenario [*tramazón*].[6]

Old certitudes were shaken for another, more deep-seated reason. Historians became aware that their discourse, whatever its form, was always a narrative. The pioneering reflections of Michel de Certeau, followed by a major work of Paul Ricoeur[7] and more recently the application to history of a "poetics of knowledge" that Jacques Rancière has defined as "the set of literary procedures by which a discourse escapes literature, gives itself the status of a science, and signifies this status,"[8] have forced historians to recognize, willingly or not, that history belongs to the literary genre of the narrative, understood in the Aristotelian sense of "the emplotment of represented actions." This was not particularly easy for the historians who thought that when they had rejected "events history"—*l'histoire événementielle*—in favor of a structural and quantified history, they had seen the last of the sham of narration and the perennial but highly dubious proximity of history and fable. The rupture between the two had seemed definitive: the "new history" had replaced the personages and heroes of the old narratives with anonymous and abstract entities; the spontaneous time of consciousness had given way to a constructed, hierarchically organized, neatly articulated temporality; self-explanatory narration had been rejected in favor of the explicative capacity of a knowledge that could be confirmed and verified.

In *Temps et récit (Time and Narrative)* Paul Ricoeur showed how illusory this proclaimed break was. All history, even the least "narrative," even the most structural, is always constructed according to the same formulas that govern the production of narratives. The entities that historians manipulate (society, classes, mentalities, etc.) are "quasi characters" implicitly endowed with the properties of the singular heroes and the ordinary individuals who make up the collectivities designated by the abstract categories. Moreover, historical temporalities remain largely subservient to subjective time. Ricoeur shows (in a superb passage) how Fernand Braudel's *La Méditerranée au temps de Philippe II (The Mediterranean and the Mediterranean World in the Age of Philip II)* is ultimately based on an analogy between the sea's time and the king's time, and how the long time span—*la longue durée*—is simply a particular and derived modality of the emplotment of the event. Finally Ricoeur shows that the explanatory procedures of history continue to be solidly anchored in the logic of the singular causal imputation; that is, in the model of comprehension that, both in daily life and in fiction, permits an account of the decisions and actions of individuals.

[margin handwritten: ALL HISTORY, NO MATTER HOW STRUCTURAL IS NARRATIVE]

This analysis, which inscribes history within the class of narrative and identifies the underlying kinship uniting *all* narratives, historical or fictional, has several consequences. First, we can consider the debate about the supposed "return of the narrative" that some scholars have seen as characteristic of history in recent years to be a question poorly stated. How, indeed, could there have been any "return" or rediscovery where there had been no departure and no abandonment? There was a change, but it was of another order. It had to do with the preference accorded lately to certain forms of narration at the expense of other, more classical, forms. For example, the interwoven biographical narratives of microhistory do not deal with the same figures or the same constructions as the great structural narratives of global history or the statistical narratives of quantitative history.

[margin handwritten: ① "RETURN" OF NARRATIVE IS POORLY STATED]

Hence a second proposition, the need to point out the properties specific to the historical narrative as it relates to all the other sorts of narrative. Chief among these properties is the "split" or "laminated" organization (Michel de Certeau's terms are *clivé* and *feuilleté*) of a discourse that contains, in the form of quotations that are as many references to reality, the materials on which it is based and of which it hopes to produce understanding. Those properties also include the specific procedures of accreditation by which history displays and guarantees its status as genuine knowledge. A number of works have been devoted to identifying the forms in which historical discourse is cast—an enterprise that has led to a variety of projects, some aimed at establishing universal taxonomies and typologies, others focused on recognizing localized and individual differences.

Hayden White's attempt to identify the rhetorical figures that command and constrain all the possible modes of historical narration and explication—that is, the four classical tropes of metaphor, metonymy, synecdoche, and (with a special, "metatropological" status) irony—belongs in the first of these two groups.[9] A similar search for constants—anthropological constants (which constitute the temporal structures of experience) and formal constants (which govern the modes of the representation and narration of historical experiences)—led Reinhart Koselleck to distinguish three types of history: notation history *(Aufschreiben)*, cumulative history *(Fortschreiben)*, and history as rewriting *(Umschreiben)*.[10]

The second group, comprising projects involving a poetics of knowledge sensitive to gaps and differences, includes such works as Philippe Carrard's *Poetics of the New History*.[11] Carrard describes how various historians, members of the same "school" or group, found quite different ways to mobilize the figures of the enunciation, projection, or disappearance of the "I" in scholarly discourse, the system of verb tenses, the personification of abstract entities, and modalities of proof (citations, tables, graphs, quantitative serial data, etc.).

[margin note: DISAPPEARANCE OF THE "I"]

In the past ten years, history not only has been shaken in its deepest certitudes, it also has faced a number of challenges. The first of these, which was launched in different and even contradictory ways on the two sides of the Atlantic, set out to break all connection between history and the social sciences. In the United States the assault took the form of the "linguistic turn," which held language, in strict Saussurean orthodoxy, to be a closed system of signs whose relations autonomously produce signification. Thus the construction of meaning is detached from all subjective intention or control and assigned to an automatic and impersonal linguistic function. In this view reality is no longer to be thought of as an objective referent, exterior to discourse, because it is constituted by and within language. John Toews has given a clear description of this radical position (which he does not share): "Language is conceived of as a self-contained system of 'signs' whose meanings are determined by their relations to each other, rather than by their relation to some 'transcendental' or extralinguistic object or subject." Hence "the creation of meaning is impersonal, operating 'behind the backs' of language users whose linguistic actions can merely exemplify the rules and procedures of languages they inhabit but do not control."[12]

[margin note: LINGUISTIC TURN]

[margin note: CREATION OF MEANING IS IMPERSONAL]

This approach makes the most customary historiographical operations pointless, beginning with the basic distinctions between text and context, between social realities and symbolic expressions, between discourse and nondiscursive practices. Keith Baker, to cite one example, applies the "linguistic turn" to problems relating to the origins of the French Revolution, arriving at a double postulate. On the one hand, social interests have no exteriority in relation to discourse because they constitute "a symbolic and political construction," not "a preexisting reality." On the other hand, all practices should be included in the order of discourse, because "claims to delimit the field of discourse in relation to nondiscursive social realities that lie beyond it invariably point to a domain of action that is itself discursively constituted. They distinguish, in effect, between different discursive practices—different language games—rather than between discursive and nondiscursive phenomena."[13]   *?*

Among French historians the challenge, as it crystallized in debates about the interpretation of the French Revolution, has taken an inverse shape. Far from postulating that the production of meaning is automatic and lies above or beyond the will of individuals, they have focused on the liberty of the subject, on the part reflection plays in action, and on conceptual constructions. This impugns the classic operations of a social history that aimed at identifying the unconscious determinations commanding thought and behavior. It also affirms the primacy of the political, understood as the most all-embracing and most revelatory level of any society. This is the connection that Marcel Gauchet puts at the center of the recent change of paradigm that he sees in the social sciences:

What seems to be taking shape at the end point of the problemizing of the originality of the West in modern times is a recomposition of the outline of a total history. On two axes: by accession, through the political, to a new key to the architecture of the whole; and by absorption, in function of that opening, of the reflective part of human action, [ranging] from the most fully elaborated philosophies to the most broadly based systems of representation.[14]

The historians (and I am one of them) for whom it is still essential that *THINKS HISTORY IS A SOCIAL SCIENCE* history remain among the social sciences have attempted to respond to this dual, and at times harsh, call to account. Unlike the proponents of the "linguistic turn" or the "semiotic challenge" (Gabrielle Spiegel's term),[15] these historians believe it is not legitimate to reduce the practices *✳* that constitute the social world to the principles that command discourse. Recognizing that past reality is usually accessible only through texts intent on organizing it, dominating it, or representing it is not the same thing as postulating that the logocentric and hermeneutic logic governing the production of discourse is identical to the practical logic ruling conduct and actions. All historical stances must take it into account that experience is not reducible to discourse, and all need to guard against unconstrained use of the category of the "text"—a term too often inappropriately applied to practices (ordinary or ritualized) whose tactics and procedures bear no resemblance to discursive strategies. Maintaining the distinction between the two is the only way to avoid "giving as the principle of the practice of agents the theory that must be constructed to understand it," as Pierre Bourdieu put it.[16]

Moreover, we need to note that the construction of interests by means of discourse is itself socially determined and limited by the unequal resources (linguistic, conceptual, material, etc.) available to those who produce that discourse. Discursive construction thus necessarily refers back to the objective social positions and properties external to discourse that characterize the various groups, communities, and classes making up the social world.

Consequently the fundamental object of a history that aims at recognizing the way social actors make sense of their practices and their discourse seems to me to reside in the tension between the inventive capacities of individuals or communities and the constraints, norms, and conventions that limit (more or less strongly according to their position within relations of domination) what it is possible for them to think, say, and do. This also holds true for a history of literary works and of aesthetic productions, which are always inscribed within the field of possibilities that make them thinkable, communicable, and comprehensible. I would have to agree with Stephen Greenblatt when he states that "the work of art is the product of a negotiation between a creator or a class of creators and the institutions and practices of society."[17] The same statement applies equally well to a history of practices, which are also inventions of meaning limited by the multiple determinations that define, for every community, legitimate behavior and the embodied norms.

As an alternative to a "return to the political," conceived as radically autonomous, it seems to me that historians should place two things at the center of their work: first, the complex and variable relations established among the divers modes of organizing and exercising power in a given society; and second, the social configurations that make such political forms possible and are engendered by them. In this manner the construction of the absolutist state supposes a strong and previous differentiation of social functions, but it also demands the perpetuation (thanks to a number of mechanisms, chief among them court society) of a balance of tensions among competing dominant social groups.

As an alternative to a return to the philosophy of the subject that accompanies or underlies the return to the political, history understood as a social science recalls that individuals are always connected by reciprocal ties of dependence—perceived or invisible—that fashion and structure their personalities and that, as one modality succeeds another, define forms of affectivity and rationality. Hence the importance many historians accord to the lifework of Norbert Elias, an oeuvre that long remained insufficiently appreciated and whose basic thrust was precisely to connect, over the long term, the construction of the modern state, modalities of social interdependence, and figures of psychic economy.[18]

Elias's works permit us, in particular, to articulate the two significations that always overlap when historians use the term "culture." The first designates the works and the acts that, in a given society, concern aesthetic or intellectual judgment; the second aims at the ordinary practices—the ones "with no qualities"—that weave the fabric of daily relations and express the way a community lives and reflects its relation with the world and with the past. To think historically about cultural forms and practices is thus necessarily to elucidate the relations between these two definitions.

Works have no stable, universal, fixed meaning. They are invested with **NO STABLE UNIVERSAL MEANING** plural and mobile meanings constructed in the negotiation that takes place between a proposal and a reception, in the encounter between the forms and patterns that give them their structure and the competencies or expectations of the various publics that make use of them. Admittedly, the creators of a work, the authorities, or the "clerics" (in and outside the church) always aspire to fix the work's meaning and to proclaim a "correct" interpretation that will constrain reading (or viewing). It is just as true, however, that reception always invents, shifts things about, and distorts. Works produced in a specific sphere, within a field that has its rules, conventions, and hierarchies, escape that sphere and take on a certain density in their pilgrimage—at times over a very long time span—through the social world. Deciphered based on mental and affective schemes that constitute the culture (in the anthropological sense) of the communities that receive them, such works become in turn a resource for thinking the essential: the construction of the social bond, of self-awareness, and of the relation with the sacred.

Inversely, any creative act inscribes in its forms and its themes a relation to the fundamental structures that, at a given moment and place, fashion the distribution of power, the organization of society, and the economy of personality. Thought of (and thinking of himself) as a demiurge, the artist, the philosopher, or the scholar nonetheless invents within constraint—constraint concerning the rules (of the client-patron relationship, of patronage, of the market, etc.) that define his condition. Even more fundamental is constraint concerning the disregarded determinations that inhabit every work and make it conceivable, transmissible, and comprehensible. What any history must think about is thus the *difference* that all societies bring into play (using varying figures) to separate a particular domain of human activity from daily routine and, indissociably linked to that difference, the *dependencies* that inscribe (in multiple ways) aesthetic and intellectual inventions within their conditions of possibility.

DIFFERENCES

Even when it is firmly reconnected with the social sciences, history cannot avoid another challenge, which is to surmount the clash (ultimately a sterile clash) between the study of positions and relations and the analysis of actions and interactions. Getting beyond this opposition between "social physics" and "social phenomenology" requires the construction of new areas of investigation in which the very definition of the questions to be posed obliges us to put clear thoughts, individual intentions, and particular wills within the systems of collective constraints that both make them possible and rein them in. There are a number of examples of such new categorizations that necessarily involve articulating objective structures and subjective representations. One such is the intellectual domain that combines textual criticism, the history of the book, and cultural sociology. This new cross between very different scholarly and national traditions (literary history in its various definitions, the Anglo-Saxon bibliographical tradition, the social history of writing practiced by the Italian paleographers, sociocultural history in the *Annales* vein) has the fundamental aim of understanding how the particular, inventive reading of the individual reader fits into a number of determinations—the effects of meaning targeted by the texts through the devices of their writing, constraints imposed by the forms that transmit those texts to their readers (or listeners), and the competencies or reading conventions proper to each community of interpretation.

We find this sort of approach, whose prime characteristic is that it upsets canonical frontiers, in many other domains of investigation—among them studies of the city, of educative processes, and of the construction of scientific knowledge. It is an approach that reminds us that intellectual and aesthetic productions, mental representations, and social practices are always governed by mechanisms and dependencies the subjects themselves are unaware of. It is from this perspective that we can understand contemporary historians' interest in rereading the classics of the social sciences (Elias, but also Weber, Durkheim, Mauss, and Halbwachs) and that we can grasp the renewed importance of the concept of "representation" over customary notions from the history of mentalities. That concept in fact permits the designation and connection of three areas of reality: first, the collective representations that embody, within individuals, the divisions of the social world and that organize the schemes of perception and appreciation by which individuals classify, judge, and act; second, the forms in which social identity or political power is exhibited, as seen in signs and such symbolic "performances" as images, rites, or what Max Weber called the "stylization of life"; third, the "presentification" within a representative (individual or collective, concrete or abstract) of an identity or a power, a process that endows that identity or power with continuity and stability.

A good many recent historical works make use of that triple definition of representation, for two reasons. On the one hand, the lessening of violence that was characteristic of Western societies between the Middle Ages and the eighteenth century and that grew out of the seizure (at least the potential seizure) by the state of a monopoly on the legitimate use of force made social conflict (previously expressed in direct, brutal, and bloody confrontations) give way, more and more often, to struggles in which the weapons and the stakes were representations. On the other hand, the authority of a constituted power or the power of a group depended (and depends today) on the credit given to (or withheld from) the representations they proposed of themselves. A history of modalities for shaping belief and of the various forms of belief has thus appeared on the terrain of the representations of power with Louis Marin, on that of the construction of social and cultural identities with Bronislaw Geremek and Carlo Ginzburg.[19] Such a history is primarily one of symbolic relations of force and of the acceptance or rejection, by the dominated, of inculcated principles and imposed identities that are aimed at guaranteeing and perpetuating their subjection.

A similar question lies at the center of a history of women that gives a large place to the mechanisms of symbolic violence—a violence, as Pierre Bourdieu wrote, "that succeeds only to the extent that the person subjected to it contributes to its efficacy; that constrains only inasmuch as he [or she] is predisposed by previous apprenticeship to *recognize* it."[20] The construction of female identity was durably rooted in women's internalization of norms stated in male discourse. One major objective of the history of women is thus to study the varied mechanisms, on every level, that guaranteed (or were calculated to guarantee) that women would consent to the dominant representations of the difference between the sexes in such matters as women's juridical inferiority, the schools' inculcation of gender roles, the division of tasks and spaces, and the exclusion of women from the public sphere. Far from leading away from reality or indicating mere figments of the male imagination, representations of female inferiority, tirelessly repeated and demonstrated, were inscribed in the thoughts and the bodies of men and women alike. But such an incorporation of domination did not exclude—far from it—possible deviations or manipulations that occurred when female appropriation of male models and norms transformed representations that had been forged to ensure women's dependence and submission into instruments of resistance and affirmations of women's identity.

Recognizing the mechanisms, the limits, and above all the uses of consent is a good strategy for correcting the privilege that history has long accorded to the view of women as "victims or rebels"—as "active, or [as] actresses of their destiny," to the detriment of "passive women, judged to consent too easily to their condition, although, precisely, the question of consent is utterly central in the functioning of a system of power, be it social or (or social and) sexual."[21] Not all the cracks invading male domination took the form of spectacular breaks, nor were they always expressed by the eruption of a discourse of refusal and rebellion. They often arose within consent itself, employing the language of domination to strengthen a refusal to submit.

When the domination imposed on women is defined as symbolic violence, it helps us understand how the relation of domination (which is historically and culturally constructed) was always asserted to reflect an irreducible and universal difference rooted in nature. What is essential is thus not to carry out a term-by-term opposition of a biological definition and a historical definition of the male/female dichotomy, but rather to identify the mechanisms that proclaim and represent as "natural" (hence biological) the social (hence historical) division of roles and functions. Moreover, the "natural" reading of the difference between the male and the female is itself historically dated, since it relies on the decline of medical representations of the similarity between the sexes and the replacement of that notion by an open-ended inventory of their biological differences. As Thomas Laqueur states, beginning in the late eighteenth century the "the old model [of one sex] in which men and women were arranged according to their degree of metaphysical perfection, their vital heat, along an axis whose telos was male" gave way to "an anatomy and physiology of incommensurability."[22] Sexual difference, as it is embodied in practices and events and as it organizes reality and daily life, is always constructed by the discourses that found and legitimate it. But those practices and events are in turn rooted in social positions and interests calculated to guarantee the subjection of women and the domination of men. The history of women, formulated in terms of a history of relations between the sexes, is a good illustration of the challenge facing historians today: to link the discursive construction of the social to the social construction of discourse.

There is a final challenge, and it is not the least formidable one. Some historians, faced with the (well-founded) assertion that all history, of whatever sort, is always a narrative organized by figures and formulas identical to the ones that put imaginary narrations in motion, have concluded that all distinction between history and fiction must be swept aside, since history is merely a "fiction-making operation," as Hayden White put it. History brings a truthful acquaintance with reality no more (and no less) than the novel does, and it is totally illusory to attempt to classify and hierarchize the works of historians according to epistemological criteria evaluating how well they achieve the account of past reality that is their object.[23] For White, the only criteria that permit differentiation among varieties of historical discourse arise out of the formal properties of such discourse: "A semiological approach to the study of texts permits us . . . to shift hermeneutic interest from the content of the texts being investigated to their formal properties."[24]

Against an approach (or a "shift") of this sort, we need to recall that the aim of knowledge is what constitutes historical intentionality. That aim founds the specific operations of the discipline of history: the compilation, organization, and treatment of data, the production of hypotheses, the critique and verification of results, the validation of the adequacy of historical discourse to its object. Even when they write in a "literary" form, historians are not making literature. This is because the historian is dependent on two things: first, the archive and the past of which the archive is a trace. As Pierre Vidal-Naquet has said,

> The historian *writes,* and that writing is neither neutral nor transparent. It is rooted in literary forms, even rhetorical figures. . . . Who can regret the historian's loss of innocence, the fact that he has been taken as an object or that he takes himself as an object of study? It remains the case nonetheless that if historical discourse is not connected—by as many intermediate links as one likes—to what may be called, for lack of a better term, reality, we may still be immersed in discourse, but such discourse would no longer be historical.[25]

Historians are also dependent on the "scientific" criteria and technical operations that are part of their métier. Recognizing variations among them (Braudel's history is not Michelet's) does not necessarily warrant concluding that such constraints and criteria do not exist or that the only demands on the writing of history are the same as the ones that govern the writing of fiction.

When historians have set out to define the "scientific" regime proper to their discipline—which is the only way to fulfill their ambition to state what was—they have chosen different paths. Some have concentrated on the study of what made possible (and still makes possible) the production and the acceptance of historical forgeries. As Anthony Grafton and Julio Caro Baroja have shown,[26] there is a close and reciprocal relation between forgery and philology; between the rules forgers must submit to and the progress of documentary criticism. This means that the work of ✳ historians in analyzing and unmasking forgeries, which intersects that of historians of science interested in the Moulin-Quignon jaw or the Piltdown skull, is a paradoxical and ironic way of reasserting the capacity of history to establish true knowledge. Thanks to its unique techniques, the discipline of history is skilled at recognizing fakes for what they are and, by that token, at denouncing forgers. It is by returning to its own deviations and perversions that history demonstrates that the discrete knowledge it produces is inscribed within the order of a confirmable, verifiable knowledge. This means that history has weapons to resist what Carlo Ginzburg has called "the skeptical war machine" that denies it any chance of speaking about past reality or of separating truth from falsehood, and also to resist the mythical reconstructions of the past governed by the needs of communities, imagined or real, national or not, that create or accept historical narratives to suit their desires and expectations.[27]

Nonetheless one cannot—or can no longer—think of historical knowledge as fitting into the order of truth within the categories of a mathematical and deductive "Galilean paradigm." And one cannot—or can no longer—accept an epistemology of the correspondence or duplication between the historical discourse and the events or realities that are its objects, as if the discourse were mere cartography, a faithful copy of the past. Historians today are fully aware of the gap that exists between the past and its representation, between the vanished realities and the discursive form that aims at representing and understanding them. Narrow is the way, therefore, for anyone who refuses to reduce history to an untrammeled literary activity open to chance and worthy only of curiosity, yet also refuses to define its scientific character based on the one model of knowledge concerning the physical world. In a fundamental text Michel de Certeau gave expression to that underlying tension in history. History is a "scientific" practice that produces instances of knowledge, but a practice whose modalities depend on variations in its technical procedures and on constraints imposed by the social arena and the institution of learning where it is practiced and by the rules that necessarily command its writing. One might also turn that statement around: history is a discourse that puts into operation constructions, compositions, and figures that are those of all narrative writing—hence also of fable—but at the same time it also produces a body of "scientific" statements, if the term "scientific" is understood as "the possibility of conceiving an ensemble of *rules* allowing control of operations adapted to the production of specific objects or ends."[28]

Michel de Certeau invites us to think about what is unique to historical comprehension. Under what conditions can one hold as coherent, plausible, and explicative the relations instituted between the historiographic operation and the referential reality to which that operation attempts to give adequate "representation"? The answer is not easy, but it ✳ is certain that the historian's special task is to give an appropriate account of the "population of the dead" (de Certeau's words)—individuals, mentalities, or prices—that are its object. If we give up striving for truth, an ambition that may be out of all measure but that is surely fundamental, we leave the field open to all manner of falsification and to all the forgers who betray knowledge and therefore hurt memory. It is only by giving new foundations to the critical realism of historical knowledge that historians will be able to resist the possible perversion of their discipline.

TWO

Four Questions for
Hayden White

1   Hayden White's *Metahistory* was published in 1973.[1]
The book made no stir in France. Ignored, it failed to find the place it deserved within the discussion on history inaugurated two years before by Paul Veyne's provocative *Comment on écrit l'histoire (Writing History)* and advanced by the publication of Michel de Certeau's "L'opération historique" in 1974.[2]

A missed opportunity, then, if we recall what Paul Veyne had to say. He challenged, one by one, the axioms that provided a scientific base for the quantitative, serial history held at the time to be a veritable "revolution in historiographic consciousness."[3] For Veyne, history cannot shed the traditional literary forms: the explanations it produces are "nothing but the way in which the account is arranged in a comprehensible plot,"[4] and in the last analysis, history serves ends of pure curiosity.

The sharpest response came from Michel de Certeau, first in a review of Veyne's book in the *Annales,* then in an essay seemingly endorsed by the *Annales* community, given that Jacques Le Goff and Pierre Nora used it to lead off their *Faire de l'histoire.* The complete text of de Certeau's piece was reprinted the following year in a collection of his essays titled *L'écriture de l'histoire (The Writing of History).*[5] Like Paul Veyne, de Certeau stressed that all historical writing, whatever its form, is a narration that constructs its discourse according to processes of "narrativization" that reorganize and reorder investigative operations. He suggested, however, two displacements of Veyne's perspectives. First, for him what determines historians' choices (as they group objects, favor one or another form of work, and pick one mode of writing) is much more their place within an "institution of learning" than their subjective preference. Second, what gives coherence to their discourse is not, or not only, a respect for the rules of the literary genres they are borrowing but specific practices determined by the techniques of their discipline.

*[margin note: * THE DISCIPLINE HAS TECHNIQUES]*

Why recall this discussion here? Perhaps only to show the depth that might have been brought to it had Paul Veyne, Michel de Certeau, and others been aware of the works of Hayden White, who was investigating the terms of their debate in his own manner. The thrust of White's *Metahistory* was not (or not uniquely) to describe the discursive formalities of history, even though he defines history, with Veyne and de Certeau, as a "a verbal structure in the form of a narrative prose discourse" (*Metahistory*, ix). White had a higher ambition: to understand "the deep structure of the historical imagination" (ix) that commands the possible combinations among the various archetypes of emplotment ("Romance, Comedy, Tragedy, Satire"), the different paradigms of historical explanation ("Formism, Organicism, Mechanism, Contextualism"), and a number of ideological implications (Anarchism, Conservatism, Radicalism, Liberalism). The various types of association among these twelve elements (which in theory give sixty-four possible combinations but in reality yield fewer, since some are logically impossible) define coherent historiographical styles, each with its own aesthetic perception, cognitive operation, and ideological commitment. The basic objective of White's "poetics of history" was thus to identify the "deep structures" that are the matrices of such associations.

*[margin note: * AMBITION OF METAHISTORY]*

For Hayden White, these associations must be located in the linguistic and poetic prefigurations of the historical field itself; that is, in the way the historian "both creates his object of analysis and predetermines the modality of the conceptual strategies he will use to explain it" (31). The four principal modalities of that prefiguration are designated and described by the four classical tropes of poetic language: metaphor, metonymy, synecdoche, and with a special, "metatropological" status, irony. White states: "In short, it is my view that the dominant tropological mode and its attendant linguistic protocol comprise the irreducibly 'metahistorical' basis of every historical work" (xi).

[margin note: 4 TROPES ↓ METAPHOR, METONYMY, SYNECDOCHE, IRONY]

In seeking to identify this "metahistorical basis," White went much further in *Metahistory* than the French historians of the time had gone in their descriptions of the nature of "historical writing"—or, in White's terms, all that goes into "emplotment." From the outset, however, White's argument contained an ambiguity. How was one to understand those "deep structural forms of the historical imagination" (31)? The very use of the term "deep structure" leads quite naturally to thinking of the prefigurations of historical discourse as following a strict linguistic and structuralist model, and thus to believing they operate automatically and impersonally to regulate historiographical preferences. Hayden White encouraged just such an interpretation of his thought by using oppositions dear to structural linguistics (surface and depth, the manifest and the implicit, language and thought) to define his approach: "I have tried first to identify the manifest—epistemological, aesthetic, and moral—dimensions of the historical work and then to penetrate to the deeper level on which these theoretical operations found their implicit, precritical sanctions" (x). Furthermore, it is with the same categories that he designates the constraining force of language, presenting as "the essential point" of his demonstration "that, in any field of study not yet reduced (or elevated) to the status of a genuine science, thought remains the captive of the linguistic mode in which it seeks to grasp the outline of objects inhabiting its field of perception" (xi). Precritical and precognitive, the tropological matrices of historical discourses can thus be interpreted as imposed, unrecognized structures that command the "choices" of historians irrespective of their will and their consciousness.

This is the way Hayden White's work has most often been understood when it has been granted a place of prime importance, by its proponents and detractors alike, among works that subject history to the "linguistic turn." Gabrielle Spiegel, one of its critics, remarked that "no one has been more forceful in articulating the implications of post-Saussureian linguistics for the practice of history than Hayden White." One of its proponents, David Harlan, credits Hayden White for his "acute sensitivity to the ways in which language both constitutes and dissolves the subject."[6]

But to return to the preface of *Metahistory,* the vocabulary White employs ("deep structure," "understructure," "deeper level") is not uniquely that of structuralism, linguistic or other. White also uses a repertory of terms from a quite different tradition: "historical consciousness" (four times); "choice" or "to choose" (three times). Thus historians seem to decide freely, consciously (or according to a less affirmative formula, "more or less self-consciously" [xi]), from among the historiographical styles White recognizes. Tropological prefigurations thus make up a collection of possible forms historians can choose among according to their moral or ideological inclinations. Hayden White illustrates the reality of this freedom of choice by citing his own decision: "It may not go unnoticed that this book is itself cast in an Ironic mode. But the Irony which informs it is a conscious one, and it therefore represents a turning of the Ironic consciousness against Irony itself" (xii).

The latent contradiction between the two perspectives has not escaped the notice of commentators—in particular those who rally most fervently to the defense of applying the linguistic model to history. Hans Kellner puts the question this way: "If language is irreducible, a 'sacred' beginning, then human freedom is sacrificed. If men are free to choose their linguistic protocols, then some deeper, prior, force must be posited. White asserts as an existential paradox that men *are* free, and that language *is* irreducible."[7] David Harlan notes the same dilemma. After recognizing White's sensitivity toward the way language both constitutes and dissolves the subject, Harlan notes "on the other hand, [his] deep commitment to liberal humanism, to the human subject and epistemological freedom," which leads Harlan, somewhat surprisingly, to link Hayden White and J. G. A. Pocock.[8]

In an article in which he responded to objections to his tropological theory of historical discourse, Hayden White returned to this potential tension, stressing his distance from all forms of linguistic determinism. Against his critics—but also perhaps against some overzealous disciples— he reaffirms that the choice between one strategy of argumentation and discourse and another is a decision made in full liberty and consciousness: "Until . . . a Copernican Revolution occurs, historical studies will remain a field of inquiry in which the choice of a method for investigating the past and a mode of discourse for writing about it will remain free, rather than constrained."[9] In the same article he says that "although [tropology] assumes that figuration cannot be avoided in discourse, the theory, far from implying linguistic determinism, seeks to provide the knowledge necessary for a free choice among different strategies of figuration" (34). White thus totally safeguards the liberty of the thinking and writing subject by shifting the free choice that classical intellectual history held so dear from philosophical arguments to tropological preferences.

But that leaves the problem of the compatibility between that position and White's adoption of a theory of language, borrowed from structural linguistics, based on two postulates: first, that for every utterance there is a previous code; for every *parole,* a previous *langue:* "Language . . . is itself in the world as one 'thing' among others and is already freighted with figurative, tropological, and generic contents before it is actualized in any given utterance" (23); and second, that all language always operates unknown to those who use it, beyond their control or their will, to produce unexpected and unstable meanings: "Historical discourse . . . like metaphoric speech, symbolic language, and allegorical representation, always means more than it literally says, says something other than what it seems to mean, and reveals something about the world only at the cost of concealing something else" (25).

This leads to my first question: Is it possible to link, without serious contradiction, post-Saussurean linguistics and the freedom of the historian as a literary creator?

QUESTION

2   My second question concerns tropology as a theory of discourse. On several occasions Hayden White has pointed to its two sources, Vico and Nietzsche. Thus White is not attempting to describe or make use of the rules of classical rhetoric, and in my opinion those who reproach him for simplifying or betraying that rhetoric do so unfairly. He is after something else: identifying the fundamental structures through which all possible figurative discourses can be produced; that is, the four tropes of classical and neoclassical rhetoric.

In the preface to *Tropics of Discourse* White limits the area of pertinence of the "pattern of tropological prefiguration": "I claim for it only the force of a convention in the discourse about consciousness and, secondarily, the discourse about discourse itself, in the modern Western cultural tradition" (13). Hence the recurrent use of such a pattern: in Vico to characterize stages in the passage from barbarity to civilization; in Piaget to qualify the four moments in cognitive development; in Freud to designate the four mechanisms at work in dreams. Hayden White thus transforms into a generic matrix for the production of discourses, hence of modes of comprehension, categories that had traditionally been restricted to describing figures of style.

A displacement of this sort suggests that the four fundamental tropes (metaphor, metonymy, synecdoche, and irony) are to be understood as a priori categories in Western understanding (since White limits their validity to the Western cultural tradition). He states explicitly, "My method, in short, is formalist" (*Metahistory*, 3), postulating the existence of invariable mental structures that can be identified in works, once their cultural space has been defined, independent of their time and their milieu of production. In this sense the tropological constitution of the historical imagination, and more generally of all the operations of figuration, is totally dissociated from the historical forms of rhetoric, understood as the art of discourse and persuasion.

Nonetheless, Hayden White himself cannot avoid the question of the relation between a given author's use of a tropological model and the place rhetoric occupies in that author's intellectual formation and particular configuration of knowledge. Thus, on the subject of Freud and dream theory White states:

> I am interested here, obviously, in the mechanisms which Freud identifies as effecting the mediations between the manifest dream contents and the latent dream thoughts. These seem to correspond, as Jakobson has suggested, to the tropes systematized as the classes of figuration in modern rhetorical theory (a theory with which, incidentally, insofar as it classifies figures into the four tropes of metaphor, metonymy, synecdoche, and irony, Freud would have been acquainted, as a component of the educational cursus of gymnasia and colleges of his time). (*Tropics of Discourse*, 13–14).

The parenthetical remark here seems to me to reflect a certain indecision. Either tropological structure is inherent to the imagination of modern Western men and women, in which case it matters little whether Freud's education had made him familiar with classical rhetoric, or the statement pertains to an understanding of how Freud transfers a model of comprehension from one domain (discourse) to another (dreams), in which case the pertinence of the tropological characterization depends greatly on variations in the status and importance of rhetoric in the successive historical configurations that make up the "Western tradition." Hayden White clearly seems to prefer the first of these views. Still, his remarks on Freud's schooling has the ring of doubt, which puts historical contextualizing back into a systemization aimed at identifying generic structures.

Hence my second question: Is it legitimate to apply the tropological model of poetic and linguistic prefiguration without taking into account the place of rhetoric (which varied widely from one historical situation to another) and without measuring how closely various authors adhered to that mode of codifying discourse, which was neither consistent nor stable between the Renaissance and the twentieth century?

3   The most frequent criticism of Hayden White's works has to do with his refusal to grant history the status of a form of knowledge different in nature from the knowledge brought by fiction. Historians as varied as Arnaldo Momigliano and Carlo Ginzburg or as Gabrielle Spiegel and Russell Jacoby[10] have raised the same objection: by holding history to be "a form of fiction-making" (*Tropics of Discourse*, 122), Hayden White chooses to champion an absolute (and highly dangerous) relativism that denies all possibility of establishing "scientific" knowledge concerning the past. When it is disarmed in this manner, history loses all capacity to choose between the true and the false, to tell what happened, and to denounce falsifications and forgers.

Several passages in White's work lend themselves to such a reading. For him, history as the historian writes it is dependent neither on the reality of the past nor on operations proper to the discipline. The choice the historian makes of a tropological matrix, a mode of emplotment, and an explicative strategy is in all ways similar to that of the novelist. White reaffirms this position with constancy, *ne varietur*. In 1974 he wrote, "In general there has been a reluctance to consider historical narratives as what they most manifestly are: verbal fictions, the contents of which are as much *invented* as *found* and the forms of which have more in common with their counterparts in literature than they have with those in the sciences" (*Tropics of Discourse*, 82). And in 1982, "One must face the fact that when it comes to apprehending the historical record, there are no grounds to be found in the historical record itself for preferring one way of construing its meaning over another" (*The Content of the Form*, 75). Thus it is totally illusory to hope to classify the works of historians (and philosophers of history) or to institute any hierarchy among them based on their greater or lesser ability to achieve the object of giving an account of past reality. The only criteria for differentiating among historians are purely formal and internal to discourse, whether they apply to the coherence and the completeness of the narrative or to the historians' awareness of the range of possibilities offered by tropological models and competing narratives.

Hayden White's response to criticism of his position as destructive of all knowledge was to point out that to consider history as a fiction and as participating in the same strategies and procedures as literature does not deny it all value as knowledge; it simply considers history as not having a regime of truth all its own. Myth and literature are forms of knowledge: "Does anyone seriously believe that myth and literary fiction do *not* refer to the real world, tell truths about it, and provide useful knowledge of it?"[11] Engendered by the same matrix as fiction, historical narration displays the same sort of knowledge as fictional constructions. White is not among those who oppose rhetoric and truth.[12]

Still, there is something about his response that leaves us unsatisfied. How indeed can history be thought of without ever (or hardly ever) referring to the operations proper to the discipline—the construction and treatment of data, the production of hypotheses, the critical verification of results, the validation of the coherence and the plausibility of interpretation? It is here, it seems to me, that Michel de Certeau's thoughts have more to offer than Hayden White's. For de Certeau history is indeed a narrative, but it is a specific narrative that produces bodies of "scientific" statements, if what we mean by "scientific" is the construction of specific objects according to verifiable rules.[13] Starting from a definition of "science" less narrow and less rigid than White's, de Certeau invites us to consider history a "scientific" practice that, like all other scientific practices, depends on variations in its technical procedures, on constraints imposed by the social setting and the institution of learning where it is exercised, and on the rules that necessarily govern its writing. To define the "scientific" nature of history in this manner—as the best possible, most nearly adequate rendering of the referential reality it aims at—is neither to deny its fundamentally narrative nature nor to think of historical thought within the "Galilean paradigm" of the mathematical sciences.

Which leads to my third question to Hayden White: If history produces a knowledge identical to that provided by fiction—no more, no less—how are we to consider (and why should we perpetuate) the weighty, highly demanding operations of gathering a documentary corpus, verifying information and testing hypotheses, and constructing an interpretation? If it is true that "historical discourse resembles and indeed converges with fictional narrative, both in the strategies it uses to endow events with meanings and in the kind of truth in which it deals,"[14] if the reality of the events emplotted is of no importance for the nature of the knowledge produced, is not the "historiographical operation" a waste of time and effort?

4   Hayden White states in *The Content of the Form:*

It is often alleged that "formalists" such as myself, who hold that any historical object can sustain a number of equally plausible descriptions or narratives of its processes, effectively deny the reality of the referent, promote a debilitating relativism that permits any manipulation of the evidence as long as the account produced is structurally coherent, and thereby allow the kind of perspectivism that permits even a Nazi version of Nazism's history to claim a certain minimal credibility. (76)

What better summary could there be of the major criticism of White's work? On several occasions he has attempted to respond to this accusation of "relativism," an accusation that takes on particular gravity when it concerns historical events such as crimes committed by tyrannies or, even more, the Shoah.

The first response, which we have already seen, was to emphasize the truth of fiction. To hold the historical narrative to be "a fiction-making operation" is not to reduce it to a simple, arbitrary, and derisory game but, on the contrary, is to consider it capable of the force and lucidity shown in the most powerful works of the imagination. This is the vein in which White responded to Gene Bell-Villada, who maintained that the only reaction of the "U.S. 'critical establishment'" to brutal dictatorships in Latin America was "its wars on referentiality and its preachments that 'History is Fiction, Trope and Discourse.'" White replied, alluding to South American novelists, "Would he [Bell-Villada] wish to say that their works do not teach us about real history because they are fictions? Or that being fictions *about history,* they are devoid of tropisms and discursivity? Are their novels less true for being fictional? Could any history be as true as these novels without availing itself of the kind of poetic tropes found in the work of Mario Vargas Llosa, Alejo Carpentier, José Donoso and Julio Cortázar?"[15]

White elaborated a second response after the emergence of the "revisionist" (more accurately, "negationist") historians who proposed a narrative—an "emplotment"—of the history of Nazism and World War II based on a list of notions that Pierre Vidal-Naquet summarized thus: (1) the gas chambers never existed and the Germans perpetrated no genocide; (2) the "final solution" was merely the expulsion of the Jews toward Eastern Europe; (3) the total number of the Jewish victims of Nazism is much lower than has been claimed; (4) genocide is an invention of Allied propaganda, principally of Jewish, more particularly Zionist, propaganda; (5) Hitler's Germany did not bear the greatest responsibility for World War II; and (6) during the 1930s and 1940s, the principal threat to humanity was the Soviet regime.[16] These elements, separately or recombined in various forms and varying proportions, provided a basis for a radical rewriting of contemporary history. Can it be taken as plausible, acceptable? And if not, why not?

In order to reject the revisionist view without abandoning the principles that underlay his entire work, Hayden White was led to propose a distinction I find somewhat problematic. About the "competing narratives" offered of the Nazi regime and the extermination of Jews and Gypsies he remarks,

Obviously, considered as accounts of events already established as facts, "competing narratives" can be assessed, criticized, and ranked on the basis of their fidelity to the factual record, their comprehensiveness, and the coherence of whatever arguments they may contain. But narrative accounts do not consist only of factual statements (singular existential propositions) and arguments: they consist as well of poetic and rhetorical elements by which what would otherwise be a list of facts is transformed into a story. Among these elements are those generic story patterns we recognize as providing the "plots." . . . Here the conflict between "competing narratives" has less to do with the facts of the matter in question than with the different story-meanings with which the facts can be endowed by emplotment.[17]

A distinction of this sort seems to me to raise two questions. On the one hand, it reintroduces a thoroughly traditional conception of the attested, certain, and identifiable historical event; for instance, the existence of the gas chambers. The problem here is one of the compatibility of a proposition of this kind and Hayden White's overall perspective. How can one reconcile the evidence of the factual event with the quotation from Roland Barthes that White places in an epigraph to *The Content of the Form:* "Le fait n'a jamais qu'une existence linguistique"? And on what basis, starting from what operations, using what techniques, can the historian establish the reality of the fact or verify whether a historical discourse is faithful to the "factual record"? It must be admitted that by systematically ignoring the procedures proper to history, understood as a discipline of knowledge, White leaves us powerless to answer such questions.

On the other hand, by restricting his definition of the "facts" the historian can treat to "singular existential propositions," Hayden White severely limits the domain in which history can operate to discern between the true and the false. It is hard to see what criteria one could use to discriminate among competing historical narratives that construct their plots with the use of "factual statements" alone. Not all historical narratives are equal, either in their mode of discourse or in their internal coherence; nor are they equal in their pertinence and their accuracy in giving an account of the referential reality they hope to represent. Gauging the differential truth of historical discourses is not an easy task, but to consider the effort to do so vain and useless is to deny all possibility of assigning even a minimal specificity to history, since neither its tropological prefigurations nor its narrative modalities, or even the fact that its discourse bears on the past, are uniquely its own.[18]

This remark leads me to a fourth and final question, which is fitting when dealing with works so profoundly attached to the principle of a "fourfold analysis." My question goes back to *Metahistory*. Without doubt this book liberated historiography from the inflexible boundaries of a classical approach totally insensible to the modalities and figures of discourse. It should be congratulated and thanked for doing so. Still, is it possible, and is it intellectually desirable, to adhere to a "semiological approach to the study of texts" that "permits us to moot the question of the text's reliability as witness to events or phenomena extrinsic to it, to pass over the question of the text's 'honesty,' its objectivity" (*Content of the Form*, 192)? Isn't it the very object of the history of history to understand how, in each particular historical configuration, historians put into operation research techniques and critical procedures that give their discourses (in unequal measure) just such an "honesty" and "objectivity"?

THREE

Michel de Certeau

History, or Knowledge of the Other

Michel de Certeau was not fond of defining who he was, nor did he like hemming in what he did to fit within the sort of disciplinary categories that university professors, as if to reassure themselves, claim as their own. Nonetheless, he described his intellectual career in *La prise de la parole,* a slim book written in the immediate aftermath of the "symbolic revolution" of 1968 that is still among the most acute analyses of that event: "I discovered in the movement that shook the underside of the country the very question that experience as a historian, a traveler, and a Christian raised in me. Elucidating it was for me a necessity."[1] The distance between the three (historian, traveler, and Christian) is not as great as it may seem. For de Certeau, of all the humane sciences history was the most apt, by its heritage or by its program, to represent difference and portray otherness. Hence it retained something of the quest for the word of the other that was the passion, to the point of despair, of the ancient Christians whose historian he had become, and something of the encounter with foreignness he had felt with each discovery of a new world, from Brazil to California. This may be why de Certeau, a man of wide-ranging knowledge, proclaimed himself a historian first, and why, on his election to the Ecole des Hautes Etudes en Sciences Sociales in 1983, he chose to join the Centre de Recherches Historiques, the center within the Ecole that brings together people who, in various ways, do history.

A widely read man (as the seventeenth century put it), Michel de Certeau was not an ordinary historian. Travel had taken him throughout the world and led him across disciplines. Writing a work of history was for him submitting to critical experimentation models—sociological, economic, psychological, or cultural—forged elsewhere and, at the same time, attempting to understand the meaning of the signs concealed in archival documents by bringing to bear on them the skills of the semiotician, ethnologist, and psychoanalyst. Out of unexpected, free, and paradoxical combinations born of a mastery of these sciences, he created a unique writing style in which professional historians recognize a superb respect for the rules of their craft but also a gauge of where they themselves fall short. At times his unconfined intelligence disquieted or irritated minds too narrow to comprehend it; and there were enough of them (not only among historians) that two scholarly institutions in France (the Centre National de la Recherche Scientifique and the Fifth Section of the Ecole Pratique des Hautes Etudes) failed to open their doors to him.

One basic question runs through Michel de Certeau's work as a historian: how to explain the words and the actions of a spirituality that remained outside ecclesiastical institutions and that challenged the clergy's exclusive appropriation of the sacred. From his earliest books on Pierre Favre and Jean-Joseph Surin to *La fable mystique*, from *La possession de Loudun* to the nearly complete manuscript on bodily experiences in mysticism he left at his death,[2] his work profoundly changed our comprehension of Christianity in the age of religious reform. Thanks to him, we have a better understanding of how a number of men and women of the sixteenth and seventeenth centuries lived their faith and proclaimed it, with no legitimate place in which to speak of it, living out a hazardous, errant, and marginal existence authorized uniquely by their certitude that they heard God's word within themselves.

This question, pursued in one book after another, provided a needed corrective to the perspectives of an overly short-sighted religious history: de Certeau signaled distinctions that had not been clearly perceived (for example, between sorcery and possession)[3] and proposed comparisons that some found scandalous, as between mystical speech and the speech of the possessed, both forms of speech inhabited by the other and each in its own way inscribed within a discourse that imposed on it the categories of a theological or demonological order.[4] He set up these two modes of speech—the inhabited speech wrung out of the possessed and the dialogued, voluntary speech of the mystic—as experiences at the limits that provide an opportunity to observe a vacillation among the shaping influences of doctrinal authority, the new science, and the power of the crown. Possession and the mystical (de Certeau's English translator coins the term "mystics," on the model of "physics" or "optics"), both resisting explanation by tradition or reason and both connoting an upwelling of the strange in its most menacing mode, put all disciplines and rationalities to the test. For Michel de Certeau, this was what gave them their heuristic value and what led him into a lifetime of research.

His research on that central question was always accompanied by other projects and other inquiries. De Certeau enjoyed working with others on a dossier constructed and deciphered in common in the fraternity of shared discovery. Hence he turned to sixteenth-century accounts of voyages to the Americas that elicited the dual question of a discourse on the foreign and the writing down of oral materials. Similarly, in 1975 he worked with two friends and historians, Dominique Julia and Jacques Revel, on a book about Abbé Grégoire's survey of French patois, which gave him an opportunity to work on the same dual problem with other materials.[5] In a university environment often narrow and at times fiercely individualistic, he gave a precious example of boundless enthusiasm, a tireless desire to learn, and a generous willingness to share.

If we want to comprehend how Michel de Certeau conceived of the historian's task, we need to return to one of his most often cited and most commented on texts. It was titled "L'opération historique" when it served at the opening essay in the 1974 collective work *Faire de l'histoire (Constructing the Past)*, edited by Jacques Le Goff and Pierre Nora. The same text appeared the following year with a slightly different title, "L'opération historiographique," in de Certeau's *L'écriture de l'histoire (The Writing of History)*, this time with a third part on historical writing that had been cut from *Faire de l'histoire* for lack of space.[6]

Michel de Certeau builds this text around a tension between thinking of history as a "scientific" practice and, at the same time, identifying variations in its technical procedures, constraints imposed by the social setting and the institution of learning where it is produced, and the rules obligatory to its writing.[7] That tension, maintained throughout the text and basic to it, must first be understood in the context of the historiographic moment when it was written. Two major events stand out. The first was the epistemological challenge—one might say provocation—of Paul Veyne's *Comment on écrit l'histoire (Writing History)*, published in 1971.[8] De Certeau discussed some of Veyne's sharpest thrusts in a critique written for the *Annales:*[9] hence "The Historiographical Operation" should be read as a continuation of this critical dialogue between de

Certeau and Veyne, whose book had caused quite a stir among historians. In that essay de Certeau returns to two of Veyne's pronouncements but totally reformulates them. History, says de Certeau, is indeed a discourse, but a discourse whose determinations are to be sought not in the conventions perpetuated by a literary genre but in the practices determined by the technical institutions of a discipline, which differ according to time and place and are subject to varying ways of separating truth from falsehood and to contrasting definitions of what constitutes historical proof. Moreover, if all historical writing returns to the "I" who produces it, that "I" should be constructed not on the curiosity principle (an ahistorical manifestation of the pleasure principle), but rather in terms of the position each historian occupies in the historical institution of the time.

If Veyne's questions bore such weight, it was perhaps because they implied a complete break with the practice of historians (at least the more inventive and the most favored among them) who had created a new paradigm of historical science based on the use of the computer and the techniques it made possible. Such historians held the quantitative treatment of large amounts of homogeneous data to be a real revolution. As François Furet put it, "Serial history, therefore, is not only, nor indeed predominantly, a transformation of historical materials. It is a revolution in historiographic consciousness."[10] It replaced history-as-narrative, lulled by the recitation of events, with history-as-problem, obliged to construct its own object, state its hypotheses explicitly, and be clear about its procedures. It countered uncertain judgments backed by no standards for discrimination with the rigor of numbers and the certainty of the "scientifically measurable." The enthusiasm of those days is understandable: Emmanuel Le Roy Ladurie declared, "Tomorrow's historian will have to be able to programme a computer to survive."[11]

But these historians were not alone in perceiving that their task had changed. In the early 1970s Michel Foucault noted the same change as he set about analyzing discourse, contrasting, term for term, the "effective work of historians" in "the great change in their discipline" with the philosophy of history (the "history no one does any more") of philosophers imbued with Hegelianism.[12] By practicing history as a "certain use of discontinuity for the analysis of temporal series," historians broke decisively with the major concepts of "philosophical history" postulating the unity of the spirit through successive and necessary historical particularizations.

In "The Historiographical Operation" Michel de Certeau agrees and disagrees with Foucault's analysis. On the one hand, de Certeau points out the results of a recourse to the "current techniques of information retrieval" that had precipitated the redefinition of the historian's task. Such techniques brought new ways to select among sources, henceforth sifted according to their capacity for furnishing serial, homogeneous, and repeated data. They separated operations that once were mingled: the construction of an object of study, the collection and accumulation of information, its treatment and interpretation. They modified the very function of history: "Historians . . . create laboratories of epistemological experimentation" to test the validity of models borrowed from the social sciences. It was clear that there were new strategies in historical practice whose use produced "a theorization that conforms better to the possibilities offered by the sciences of information."

Still, if we replace de Certeau's text within the context of the "defense and illustration" of quantitative history, it has a different ring to it. Nowhere in it does he state that comprehension by means of numbers, backed by the massive treatment of quantitative data, is a radical epistemological break presumed to mark history's entry into the age of Science with a capital S. What he sees as essential still is to understand how a new "apparatus" and new techniques permit new responses and new questions. For de Certeau, the most interesting questions that quantitative history raises come precisely from its inverse and are connected to the welling up of the singular, the exception, and the gap: "If historical 'comprehension' is not enclosed within the tautology of legend or has not taken flight into ideology, its primary characteristic is not making series of data understandable (although that may be its 'basis'), but rather *never denying* the relation that these 'regularities' keep with the 'particularities' which escape them."[13] Even while setting in motion the machines of the time, the historian remains a prowler *(rôdeur)* who haunts the margins and the marches. Throughout de Certeau's lifetime, these frontier zones took the dazzling form of past religious experiences situated outside the ordinary routine of the ecclesiastical institution.

Although de Certeau was sensitive to the results of crossing a methodological revolution (quantitative data) with a technological revolution (the computer), he nonetheless remained aloof from the scientific illusions, so strong in the 1960s, brought on by the conquests of the numerical approach. At a time when the notion had almost been forgotten, he recalled that if history is an institution and a practice, it is also, and perhaps above all, writing. The third part of his "Historiographical Operation" is devoted to that notion; without it the piece is unbalanced and out of plumb. The first of two fundamental propositions in this section states that all historical writing is *récit*—narrative—and is necessarily constructed according to rules that reverse the approach of research, which puts things in chronological order, establishes a tight demonstration, and constructs a seamless discourse out of materials that are always open and full of holes. With this statement, Michel de Certeau opened the way for all the others who, like Paul Ricoeur in *Temps et récit (Time and Narrative),*[14] reflected that all forms of history—even the most structural, even the least event-based—belong to the field of the narrative. Because it is "narrativization," history continues to be dependent on formulas for the "emplotment of represented actions," to use an Aristotelian term, and it shares the laws that underlie all narratives: in particular the obligation of temporal succession.

When we read "The Historiographical Operation" carefully, it is clear that the pronouncement a few years later that the very latest changes in history moved in the direction of a "revival of narrative" was by and large illusory.[15] Whatever else it might be, history is always narrative, but it is a particular narrative, since it aims at producing true knowledge: "Historical discourse claims to provide a true content (which pertains to verifiability), but in the form of a narration."[16] This leads de Certeau to formulate explicitly or point to a broad range of questions. The first regards what distinguishes historical narration from other narrative modes, a particularity to be sought in the "laminated" *(feuilleté)* or "split" *(clivé)* structure of the historiographical text. Because it comprehends within itself, in the form of citations, the materials that provide its foundation and that it explains, historical discourse has a specific way of organizing both its strategies of accreditation (the document standing for the real) and its rhetorical operation (knowledge being written in the very language of its object). A second question concerns differing modes of intelligibility implied by the choice of one form or another of the narrative. Biography, for example, affords an opportunity to stress difference in relation to the global constructions given in the form of a structural narrative. *The Mystic Fable,* written eight years later, retained something of the same tension that had appeared in this earlier work when, in its fourth section, it treated "Figures of the Wildman" as destinies standing apart from the regularities of the mystical discourse.

De Certeau's essay "The Historiographical Operation" also contains something like a response to Hayden White (whose *Metahistory* was published in 1973).[17] History, de Certeau states, cannot be taken for a pure rhetoric or a tropology that makes it into a "form of fiction-making" just like other forms. History claims to be a discourse about truth; it constructs a relationship with what it posits as its referent (the past "reality" to be recalled and understood), which can in principle be verified. Thus historians need to ponder the truth status of historical discourse—and they need to think of that truth status not as something that emerges from the past, rising intact to the surface in archival materials, but rather as the result of establishing relations among data arranged by the operation of knowing: "One thus passes from a historical reality (History, or *Geschichte*) 'received' in a text to a textual reality (historiography, or *Historie*) 'produced' by an operation whose norms are fixed in advance."[18]

[margin note: DETERMINE "TRUTH STATUS" OF HISTORY]

Historical discourse is thus articulated according to a regime of truth that is neither that of literature nor that of philological certitude. The verification of facts that Arnaldo Momigliano insisted on—that is, the renewable, verifiable, technical operations that make up documentary criticism—is not sufficient as a foundation for history as an objective reconstitution of the past, confident of its truth status.

In "The Historiographical Operation" Michel de Certeau opened up new vistas at a key moment in the evolution of the discipline of history, torn between quantitative techniques (the sign of a hard-won scientific validity) and Roland Barthes's and Paul Veyne's descriptions of its nature as a literary genre. By shifting the terms of the antinomy, de Certeau attempted to establish under what conditions a discourse built by means of the procedures specific to historical work could be accepted as an adequate representation of the historical configuration that was its object. This obviously supposes a repudiation of any epistemology of immediate coincidence or transparency between knowledge and the true, between discourse and the real. But it also supposes thinking of the historical operation as a knowledge (which others might call evidential or conjectural), as an operation that is "scientific" in that it "means changing something which had its own definite status and role [here, the document, the archive], into *something else* which functions differently [the historical text]." It is because it succeeds in maintaining that primary tension that de Certeau's essay formulates—and anticipates—the terms of the debates on the organizing paradigms of historical discourse that have flourished in recent years.

[margin note: TO WHAT EXTENT?]

*[margin note: *]*

In loyalty to that epistemology of difference, all of de Certeau's work as a historian was centered on the precise, careful analysis of the practices by which men and women of past times appropriated, each in his or her own way, the codes and the places that were imposed on them, or else subverted the accepted rules to create new formalities. The practices proper to the language of the mystical are emblematic of these "arts of doing" or "doing with" that make use of the materials at hand and turn them to new purposes. In passing from one language to another, and by using metaphor (a way to muddle the canonical borders between fields of knowledge) and stripping words of their conventional meanings, mystical discourse institutes the conditions of a communication that is like no other. Thus fashioned by reuse and displacement, it is capable of expressing a totally novel experience—of relating, in the first person, the internal speech that occurs on hearing, finally, "the One who speaks."

At a time when historians necessarily privileged the description of the mechanisms by which power, in all its forms, worked to produce control and constraint and to manufacture authority and conformity, Michel de Certeau recalled that "the ordinary man" is not without ruse or refuge in face of all the forces that attempt to dispossess and domesticate him:

In a word, one might say that the mystical is a reaction against the appropriation of truth by the clerics, who started to become professionalized in the thirteenth century. It favored the illuminations of the illiterate, the experience of women, the wisdom of fools, the silence of the child; it opted for the vernacular languages against the Latin of the schools. It maintained that the ignorant have competence in matters of faith. . . . The mystical is the authority of the crowd, a figure of the anonymous, that makes an indiscreet return in the field of the academic authorities.[19]

From *L'invention du quotidien (The Practice of Everyday Life)*[20] to *The Mystic Fable*, de Certeau pursued the same quest in his search for the operative procedures of a creativity that institutions are powerless to check.

Penser, c'est passer: To think is to pass through.[21] Michel de Certeau thought much and passed through much. He was a traveler and a historian, which are perhaps one and the same. But his journey never lacked coherence, and its detours were not really detours. For him, making history always demanded elucidation of the relation between the discourse of knowledge and the body social that produced that discourse and in which it was inscribed. Far from making his history less "scientific," that lucidity was its very condition of being. Hence the sharply focused reflections on the discipline that have been examined here, which saw history simultaneously as a place and as a practice, as science and as writing.

Hence also de Certeau's emphasis, in recognition of the discontinuities of history, on the tensions between the discourses of authority and rebel wills, tensions that permeate our present just as they did societies now dead. History is a place of experimentation, a way of bringing out differences. It is knowledge of the other, hence of the self.

PART 2

Discursive and Social Practices

FOUR

The Chimera of the Origin

Archaeology of Knowledge, Cultural

History, and the French Revolution

1   In this chapter, taking Michel Foucault's work as a starting point, I propose an interpretation of the French Revolution that will
relate the origins of that event not only to the new political discourses
that appeared in France after the mid-eighteenth century but also (and
more fundamentally) to the connections between discursive practices and
other practices—deployed in registers different from the order of discourse and not reducible to it. That Foucault's work refers so frequently
to the French Revolution justifies this approach. One preliminary question cannot be avoided, however: Is it so easy to enlist Foucault's work in
the service of a historian's investigation aimed at rendering intelligible the
motivations that, in the late eighteenth century, made a radical and sudden rupture with the Old Regime thinkable, and hence possible?
    In fact, Foucault's work does not readily lend itself to practical appli-
cation by historians. Such a project supposes that a certain number of
texts (books, articles, lectures, interviews, etc.) are to be considered as
forming a body of works ("Foucault's work"); that such a body of works
can be assigned to an "author" whose proper name ("Foucault") refers
to a specific individual endowed with a unique life history; and that,
based on the reading of this primary text ("Foucault's work"), it is legitimate to produce another discourse in the form of a commentary. According to Foucault, however, those three operations are not as evident
or as unmediated as they long seemed in the "traditional history of ideas."[1]

To begin with, Foucault removed the supposed universality of these operations by restoring their variability. Thus, by specifying the particular historical conditions (juridical and political) that made the proper name a fundamental category in the classification of works (he calls this the "author-function"), he invites consideration of the reasons behind and the results of such an operation, which are to guarantee the unity of a body of works by ascribing it to one sole font of expression; to resolve the eventual contradictions between texts of the same "author," explained by changes undergone as his or her life evolved; to establish a relation between the works and the social world by setting the author, as an individual, in his or her time.

Moreover, for Foucault, all the operations that designate and assign works must always be considered operations of selection and exclusion. How can a work be extracted from "the millions of traces left by an individual after his death"? The answer to this question required a decision to separate (following criteria with neither stability nor universality) the texts constituting the work ("Foucault's work") from other texts, written or spoken, "without quality," and thus not assignable to the "author-function."

Finally, for Foucault those various operations—delimiting the works, attributing them to an author, and producing a commentary—are not neutral operations; they are borne along by the same function, a restrictive and constraining function that aims at controlling discourses by classifying, ordering, and distributing them.

Foucault's first and formidable challenge to his readers consists of undermining the foundations of the intelligibility and interpretation of any works (including Foucault's own) in our configuration of knowledge. This creates a dizzying and unique tension in which any reading of a text of Foucault's is always—simultaneously and necessarily—a question of that reading and of the ordinary concepts ("author," "work" [oeuvre], "commentary") that govern relations with texts in our society. In a remark in "The Discourse on Language," perhaps confessing something about himself, Foucault does not exempt the author from subjection to the categories governing the regime of discourse production at a particular historical moment:

I think that, for some time, at least, the individual who sits down to write a text, at the edge of which lurks a possible oeuvre, resumes the functions of the author. What he writes and does not write, what he sketches out, even preliminary sketches for the work, and what he drops as simple mundane remarks, all this interplay of differences is prescribed by the author-function. It is from his new position, as an author, that he will fashion—from all he might have said, from all he says daily, at any time—the still shaky profile of his *oeuvre*.[2]

The author's assimilation of those categories that account for works in the common order of discourse is what makes possible the articulation between writing, understood as a free, fecund, and contingent practice, and the procedures that aim at controlling, organizing, and selecting discourses. Still, that the interpreter and the author both accept the conventions commanding the mode of assignment and classification of works does not mean those conventions can be considered neutral or universal.

Foucault adds a second challenge. His entire project for critical and historical analysis of discourses is founded on an explicit objection to the concepts used in the "traditional history of ideas," the most immediately mobilizable resource for understanding or helping others understand a text, a body of works, or an author. For Foucault, the postulate of the unity and coherence of a body of works, the attempt to show creative originality, and the inscription of meaning into discourse are all categories that must be countered by constructing a different and indeed contrary approach attentive to the discontinuities and regularities that constrain the production of discourses. Understanding a set of statements thus supposes recourse to principles of intelligibility that challenge the old notions (which have hardly been spruced up in recent years) of the history of ideas.

This raises a difficult question: Under what conditions is it possible to produce a "Foucauldian" reading of Foucault? That is, how can we read his works by starting from that "slender wedge" (as he writes ironically) that "consists not in dealing with meanings possibly lying behind this or that discourse, but with discourse as regular series and distinct events" and that permits "the introduction, into the very roots of thought, of notions of *chance, discontinuity,* and *materiality*"? Must we oppose Foucault to Foucault and place his efforts in the very categories he considered powerless to render an adequate account of discourses? Or should we submit his works to the procedures of critical and genealogical analysis that they proposed and, by that token, reject what permits us to delimit their uniqueness and singularity? Foucault was undoubtedly delighted to have fabricated this "tiny (odious, too, perhaps) device" that insinuates a vexing doubt into the very heart of commentary that claims to pronounce on the meaning or the truth of his works. We can almost hear the metallic, lightning-swift laughter of Michel Foucault in this good joke on all—and they have been and will continue to be many— who attempt to read him.[3]

2   That laughter has an even more caustic tone to the historian who hopes to make intelligible the origins of the French Revolution (or any other phenomenon). In one of his few texts explicitly devoted to the works of Nietzsche, probably his fundamental philosophical reference, Foucault presents a devastating critique of the very notion of origin as historians are accustomed to using the term.[4] Because it justifies an endless quest for beginnings, and because it denies the originality of the events, which is supposed to be already present even before it occurs, the category of "origins" masks both the radical discontinuity of "emergences" (irreducible to any prefiguration) and the discordances separating different series of discourse or practice. When history succumbs to "chimeras of the origin," it purveys several presuppositions (without always being aware of doing so): that every historical moment is a homogeneous totality endowed with an ideal and unique significance present in each of its manifestations; that historical development *(devenir)* is organized like a necessary continuity; that events are linked together, the one engendering the other in an uninterrupted flow that permits decreeing one the "cause" or "origin" of the other.

For Foucault, "genealogy" must part company with precisely these classic notions (totality, continuity, causality) if it strives for an adequate comprehension of ruptures and divergences. The first of the "particular traits of historical meaning, as Nietzsche understood it—the sense which opposes 'wirkliche Historie' to traditional history" is thus to transpose "the relationship ordinarily established between the eruption of an event and necessary continuity. An entire historical tradition (theological or nationalistic) aims at dissolving the singular event into an ideal continuity— as a teleological movement or a natural process. 'Effective' history, however, deals with events in terms of their most unique characteristics, their most acute manifestations."

With a radicality permitted by the form he has chosen—a "commentary" on texts of Neitzsche's—Foucault gives a totally paradoxical definition of the event, paradoxical because it situates the contingent not among the accidents of the course of history or the choices of individuals, but in

[margin note: CRITIQUE OF ORIGINS]

transformations in relations of domination, which is what seems to historians the most determined aspect of events and the one least open to change:

An event . . . is not a decision, a treaty, a reign, or a battle, but the reversal of a relationship of forces, the usurpation of power, the appropriation of a vocabulary turned against those who had once used it, a feeble domination that poisons itself as it grows lax, the entry of a masked "other." The forces operating in history are not controlled by destiny or regulative mechanisms but respond to *haphazard conflicts*. They do not manifest the successive forms of a primordial intention and their attraction is not that of a conclusion, for they always appear through *the singular randomness of events*. [My emphases]

Teeming facts, multiple intentions, and interlocking actions thus cannot be ascribed to any system of determination capable of giving a rational interpretation of them, that is, of pronouncing on their meaning and their causes. Only by accepting this renunciation will "the historical sense free itself from the demands of a suprahistorical history." For traditional historians the price to be paid is not small, since it is the abandonment of all claim to universality, a universality they hold as the condition of possibility and the very object of historical comprehension. Foucault says, commenting on Nietzsche:

"Effective" history differs from traditional history in being without constants. Nothing in man—not even his body—is sufficiently stable to serve as the basis for self-recognition or for understanding other men. The traditional devices for constructing a comprehensive view of history and for retracing the past as a patient and continuous development must be systematically dismantled. Necessarily, we must dismiss those tendencies that encourage the consoling play of recognitions.

3   On the ruins of what Foucault calls the "history no one does any more" (or should do), what is to be constructed? In several texts published from 1968 to 1970, at a turning point in his intellectual development, Foucault often refers to the practice of historians, an essential characteristic of which ("a certain use of discontinuity for the analysis of temporal series") could be used to shore up intellectually his own project of a critical and genealogical description of discourse and to legitimize its strategy. The essence of "the effective work of historians" lies not in the invention of new objects but in a "systematic putting into play of the discontinuous" that breaks in fundamental ways with the sort of history imagined or consecrated by philosophy, which was a recital of continuities and an affirmation of the sovereignty of consciousness. Foucault says that "attempting to make historical analysis the discourse of the continuous and to make the human consciousness the original subject of all knowledge and all practice are two aspects of the same system of thought. Time is conceived in terms of totalization, and revolution is never anything but reaching awareness."[5]

Contrary to this "system of thought," what Foucault calls "history as it is practiced today"—the history of economic conjunctures, demographic shifts, and social change that dominated the historical scene in the 1960s, following the leads of Fernand Braudel and Ernest Labrousse—considers multiple and articulated series each commanded by a specific principle of regularity, each tied to its own conditions of possibility. Contrary to what historians think they are doing (or say they are doing), this approach in no way banishes the event, any more than its preference for the long time span implies the identification of immobile structures. Quite the contrary: it is by constructing homogeneous and distinct series that discontinuities can be identified and emergences situated. At a certain distance from both "philosophical history" and structural analysis, the history that deals in the serial treatment of massive archival materials (in "The Discourse on Language" Foucault mentions "official price-lists [mercuriales], title deeds, parish registers [and] harbor archives") is neither the ongoing narration of ideal history, nor history in the Hegelian or Marxist manner, nor a structural description without events:

History has long since abandoned its attempts to understand events in terms of cause and effect in the formless unity of some great evolutionary process, whether vaguely homogeneous or rigidly hierarchized. It did not do this in order to seek out structures anterior to, alien or hostile to the event. It was rather to establish those diverse converging, and sometimes divergent, but never autonomous series that enable us to circumscribe the "locus" of an event, the limits of its fluidity and the conditions of its emergence.[6]

One can thus imagine a connection between the contingent singularity of emergences, as designated by "effective history," and the regularities that govern temporal series, discursive or nondiscursive, that are the object of the historians' empirical work.

This leads Foucault to a dual conclusion, paradoxical in light of the naively antieventalized definition of *Annales* history, which associates the series and the event and detaches the latter from any reference to a philosophy of the subject:

The fundamental notions now imposed upon us are no longer those of consciousness and continuity (with their correlative problems of liberty and causality), nor are they those of sign and structure. They are notions, rather, of events and of series, with the group of notions linked to these; it is around such an ensemble that this analysis of discourse I am thinking of is articulated, certainly not upon those traditional themes which the philosophers of the past took for "living" history, but on the effective work of historians.[7]

4   Often Foucault opposed, term by term, his analysis aimed at discerning "discursive formations" and the history of ideas, that "old patch of ground cultivated to the point of exhaustion."[8] To counter the traditional criteria for classifying and identifying discourses ("author," "text," "work," "discipline"), archaeological description relies on less immediately visible principles of delimitation. To quote from the "Réponse au Cercle d'épistémologie": "When, in a group of statements, one can discern and describe *one* system of dispersion, *one* type of enunciative distance, *one* theoretical network, *one* field of strategic possibilities, one can be sure that they belong to what might be called a *discursive formation.*"[9] We need to be on guard here for the differences between these notions and the apparently closely related or identical notions that seem appropriate for individualizing groups of utterances. The *référentiel*—principle of dispersion—of a series of discourses is not the stable, unique, and exterior "object" that is its supposed aim. It is defined by the rules of formation and transformation of the mobile and multiple objects that those discourses construct and posit as their referents. The *écart énonciatif*—enunciative distance—designates not one unique and codified form of enunciation considered inherent to a set of discourses but rather a *régime d'énonciation*—an enunciative pattern—that displays dispersed and heterogeneous statements related by a similar discursive practice. The *réseau théorique*—theoretical network—operates in the same fashion on the conceptual level, aiming at the rules of formation of notions (including their possible contradictions) rather than the presence of a system of permanent and coherent concepts. Finally, the *champ des possibilités stratégiques*—field of strategic possibilities—challenges any individualization of discourses based on the nature of their themes or their opinions. What it designates is a similarity of theoretical choices, which can quite easily express contrary opinions or, inversely, differences in those choices short of a common set of themes.

I have two reasons for recalling these four notions, which Foucault presents as fundamental to his archaeological description of discourses in 1968 and 1969, although they no longer figure explicitly either in "The Discourse on Language" or in later works. First, just when he was inaugurating a new way of working, Foucault used these various stages of analysis to give retrospective coherence to his past works. He characterizes each of his previous books as exploring, through the study of a particular discursive formation, one specific problem in archaeological analysis: "the emergence of a whole group of highly complex, interwoven objects" in his *Histoire de la folie* (1961); the forms of enunciation of discourse in *The Birth of the Clinic* (1963); "the networks of concepts and their rules of formation" in *The Order of Things* (1966).[10] Admittedly, in this reading Foucault describes his own labors with the aid of criteria (unity, coherence, meaning) that belong more to the history of ideas than to the archaeology he proposes. Nonetheless, it designates a fundamental departure from traditional approaches by considering discourses as practices that obey rules of formation and operation.

Hence—and this is a second reason for paying heed to the notions opposed to the classical concepts of intellectual history—the need to consider how discursive practices are articulated with other practices of a different nature. This theme, which was to become central in Foucault's work after *Discipline and Punish,* is sketched on several occasions in *The Archaeology of Knowledge.* Unlike direct and reductive causality, but also unlike the postulate of the "sovereign, sole independence of discourse,"

archaeology . . . reveals relations between discursive formations and non-discursive domains (institutions, political events, economic practices and processes). These *rapprochements* are not intended to uncover great cultural continuities, nor to isolate mechanisms of causality. Before a set of enunciative facts, archaeology does not ask what could have motivated them (the search for contexts of formulation) nor does it seek to rediscover what is expressed in them (the task of hermeneutics); it tries to determine how the rules of formation that govern it—and which characterize the positivity to which it belongs—may be linked to non-discursive systems: it seeks to define specific forms of articulation.[11]

This projected archaeology is particularly pertinent to reflection on the French Revolution and its origins. It maintains the exteriority and the specificity of practices that are not in themselves of a discursive nature in relation to the discourses that, in many ways, are articulated based on those practices. Recognizing that access to such nondiscursive practices is possible only by deciphering the texts that describe them, prescribe them, prohibit them, and so on does not in itself imply equating the logic that commands them or the "rationality" that informs them with the practices governing the production of discourses. Discursive practice is thus a specific practice (Foucault calls it "strange") that does not reduce all other "rules of practice" to its own strategies, regularities, and reasons. In this sense I must take issue with the current positions that assimilate social realities to discursive practices.[12] Such positions cancel out— wrongly, in my opinion—the radical difference separating "the formality of practices" (to cite a category of Michel de Certeau's) and the rules organizing the positivity of discourses.

Maintaining the irreducibility of that gap leads us to question two ideas that recur throughout all strictly political history of the French Revolution: first, that it is possible to deduce the practices from the discourses that serve as their foundation and justification; second, that it is possible to translate the latent meaning of social operations into the terms of an explicit ideology. The first operation, classic in all the literature devoted to the connections between the Enlightenment and the Revolution, credits the diffusion of "philosophical" ideas with the acts of rupture from the established authorities, thus supposing a direct, automatic, and transparent engendering of actions by thoughts. The second leads to the conclusion that the sociability of the voluntary associations (clubs, literary societies, Masonic lodges) that proliferated during the eighteenth century was implicitly Jacobin, or that political practice during the first months of the Revolution already arose out of a terrorist ideology.

Against these two operations of deduction and translation, a different articulation between sets of discourses and patterns of practice can and must be proposed. There is neither continuity nor necessity between the one and the other. If they are connected, it is not through causality or equivalence but through difference—through the gap that exists between the singular specificity of discursive practices and all other practices. Thus, with respect to the eighteenth century, we should stress the gap between the (competing) discourses that, in representing the social world, proposed to refound it and the (multiple) practices that, as they came into being, were inventing new ways of dividing things up.

This perspective can easily lead to characterizing the Enlightenment somewhat differently. Instead of accepting the classic definition of the Enlightenment as a corpus of specific statements or a set of clear and distinct ideas, should we not rather see that term as covering a set of multiple and intermingled practices guided by a concern for common utility, which aimed at a new management of spaces and populations and whose mechanisms (intellectual, institutional, social, and so on) imposed a complete reorganization of the systems for the perception and organization of the social world? Accepting this view leads to a profound reevaluation of the relation between the Enlightenment and the monarchy, since the latter, the target par excellence of philosophic discourse, was doubtless the most vigorous source of practices instituting reforms. Tocqueville clearly states this notion in book 3, chapter 6, of *The Ancien Régime and the Revolution,* which he titles "How Certain *Practices* [my emphasis] of the Central Power Completed the Revolutionary Education of the Masses." Thinking of the Enlightenment as a sheaf of practices without discourse (or outside discourse)—in any event, of practices irreducible to the ideological affirmations intended to justify them—is perhaps the surest way to avoid teleological readings of the French eighteenth century (which are more persistent than one might think) that view it from the standpoint of its necessary end point, the Revolution, and retain in it only what led to that supposedly necessary outcome: the Enlightenment.

5   To establish a firm distinction between discursive practices and nondiscursive practices is not to consider only the latter as belonging to "reality" or to the "social." Against those (historians, in particular) who have "a very impoverished notion of the real," Foucault states:

We have to demystify the global instance of *the* real as a totality to be restored. There is no such thing as "the" real that can be reached by speaking about everything, or about certain things that are more "real" than others and that one would fail to grasp, to the profit of inconsistent abstractions, if one kept to showing other elements and other relations. One must perhaps also ask about the principle, often admitted implicitly, that the only *reality* history should lay claim to is *society* itself. A type of rationality, a way of thinking, a program, a technology, a set of rational and coordinated efforts, of definite and actively pursued objectives, instruments to attain this goal—all that is of reality, even if it does not claim to be "reality" itself or the whole of "society."[13]

Thus Foucault breaks down the division, long held to be fundamental to historical practice, between living experience, institutions, and relations of domination on the one hand and texts, representations, and intellectual constructs on the other. The real weighs equally on either side: all such elements constitute "fragments of reality" whose arrangement we must grasp in order to "see the interplay and the development of diverse realities that articulate with one another: a program, the connection that explains it, the law that gives it constraining force, and so on, are just as much realities (although in another mode) as the institutions that give it body or the comportments more or less faithfully added to it."[14]

6   "What is the status of the reality that rationality represents in modern Western societies?"[15] Foucault's question helps us understand why he gives the Enlightenment central importance, and also why his historical analysis of the formation and the functions of rationality is not a critique of reason. To recognize the contradiction between the emancipating philosophy of the Enlightenment and the dispositions, reliant on Enlightenment ideas, that multiplied constraints and controls is not a denunciation of the rationalist ideology as the matrix of the repressive practices characteristic of contemporary societies. As Foucault puts it, "What reader will I surprise by stating that analysis of the disciplinary practices of the eighteenth century is not a way of making Beccaria responsible for the Gulag?"[16] Establishing such a connection would be doubly mistaken: first, by constituting ideology as the determining instance of social operations, whereas all regimes of practices are endowed with a regularity, logic, and reason of their own, irreducible to the discourses that justify them; second, by ascribing the mobile and problematic figures of the division between the true and the false to a referential, original rationality, given, once and for all, as "the" rationality. Ten years before the bicentennial of the French Revolution, Foucault wrote (perhaps imprudently): "As for the *Aufklärung,* I know no one among those who do historical analyses who sees it as *the* factor responsible for totalitarianism. I think, what is more, that posing the problem in such a fashion would not be of any interest."[17] His warning seems to me another way of stressing the oversimplification of any analysis of the Revolution that plays the game of retrospective dovetailing to inscribe 1793 in 1789, Jacobinism in the decisions of the National Assembly, and terrorist violence in the theory of the general will.

7   The French Revolution is present in all of Foucault's major books from the *Histoire de la folie* to *Discipline and Punish*. In none of them, however, is it considered a time of total and global rupture reorganizing all intellectual disciplines, discourses, and practices. What is essential lies elsewhere, in the disparities that run throughout the Revolution and in the continuities that place it within longer time spans. When, in *The Archaeology of Knowledge*, Foucault sums up the analysis of the discursive formations identified in his earlier books, he stresses disparities:

> The idea of a single break suddenly, at a given moment, dividing all discursive formations, interrupting them in a single moment and reconstituting them in accordance with the same rules—such an idea cannot be sustained. . . . Thus the French Revolution—since up to now all archaeological analyses have been centered on it—does not play the role of an event exterior to discourse, whose divisive effect one is under some kind of obligation to discover in all discourses; it functions as a complex, articulated, describable group of transformations that left a number of positivities intact, fixed for a number of others rules that are still with us, and also established positivities that have recently disappeared or are still disappearing before our eyes.[18]

"Let the friends of the Weltanschauung be disappointed" by this removal of the event from all possibility for a noncontradictory totalization.

Unlike the certitude of a radical accession to power or an absolute inauguration, which suffuses the words and decisions of the actors in the event, Foucault's insistence on the discordances that separate the various discursive series (the ones invented or transformed with the Revolution or the ones in no way affected by it) recalls forcefully that the reflective and voluntary portion of human action does not necessarily provide the meaning of historical processes. Tocqueville and Cochin—the two authors usually hailed by the historians who plead most forcefully for a return to the primacy of politics, of the idea, and of consciousness—demonstrate this point by stressing that in reality the men of the Revolution did the opposite of what they said and thought they were doing. The revolutionaries proclaimed an absolute rupture with the Old Regime, but they strengthened and completed its work of centralization. The enlightened elites claimed to contribute to the common good within peaceful *sociétés de pensée* loyal to their king, but they invented the terrorist mechanisms of Jacobin democracy.

The point here is not whether these two analyses are accurate but that they refuse to conceive of the Revolution according to its own categories—beginning with the proclamation of a radical discontinuity between the new political era and the old society. The intelligibility of the event supposes, to the contrary, a gap between it and the awareness its actors had of it. That the revolutionaries believed in the absolute efficacy of politics, invested with the dual task of refounding the body social and regenerating the individual, does not oblige us to share their illusion. That the Revolution can be characterized above all as "a political phenomenon, a profound transformation of political discourse involving powerful new forms of political symbolization, experientially elaborated in radically novel modes of political action that were as unprecedented as they were unanticipated,"[19] does not mean the history of the event need be written in its own language.

With *Discipline and Punish* and the texts that prepared or surrounded it, analysis seems to encroach on the Revolution. In no way does Foucault consider its chronological stages or the succession of political events germane to resolving the question he poses, which is, "Why did the physical exercise of punishment (which is not torture) replace, with the prison that is its institutional support, the social play of the signs of punishment and the prolix festival that circulated them?"[20] An attempt to understand why incarceration was placed at the center of the modern punitive system (the aim of *Discipline and Punish*) leads Foucault to determine a specific domain of objects and to construct a temporality of his own that bears little resemblance to the usual periodizations. Indeed, he situates the formation of the "disciplinary society" that invented the technologies of subjection and the methods of surveillance the prison both inherits and exemplifies between the age of French classicism and the mid-nineteenth century.

As Foucault's analysis advances, he establishes a number of temporal divisions: from the late eighteenth century to the early nineteenth for the shift to a penal policy of detention; the decades from 1760 to 1840 for the reduction of torture and the transformation of the economy of illegalism; the period from the latter half of the seventeenth century to the nineteenth century for perfecting disciplinary techniques in military, medical, and educational institutions and manufacturing concerns. He assigns to the "conjuncture" of the eighteenth century the fundamental fact of the universalizing of disciplines made necessary by an enormous population increase, the growth of the mechanisms (not only the economic mechanisms) of production, and the domination of the bourgeoisie. For

Foucault, in fact, modes of discipline and liberties, "everyday panopticisms" and juridical norms, are indissociable mechanisms that ensured and perpetuated a new and socially designated hegemony:

Historically, the process by which the bourgeoisie became in the course of the eighteenth century the politically dominant class was masked by the establishment of an explicit, coded, and formally egalitarian juridical framework, made possible by the organization of a parliamentary, representative regime. But the development and the generalization of disciplinary mechanisms constituted the other, dark side of these processes. . . . The real, corporal disciplines constituted the foundation of the formal, juridical liberties.[21]

Foucault's analysis, which he repeats elsewhere,[22] seems surprising today for its borrowings from the most rudimentary sort of Marxism of the unified concept of a bourgeoisie, the category of formal liberties, and a model of historical development that substitutes one dominant class for another. What interests me here is not those highly debatable interpretations but that Foucault inscribes the revolutionary period, as he does the periodizations organizing his demonstration, within a longer time span, hence eliminating its singularity.

Thus Foucault traces a perspective for historical comprehension that uncouples the significance of the event from the consciousness of individuals. This makes it possible to consider the Revolution and the Enlightenment as belonging—together—to a long-term process that embraces them and reaches beyond and to see them both, although with different modalities, as tending toward the same ends and inhabited by similar expectations. Alphonse Dupront expressed this notion forcefully (but without sociological oversimplification):

The world of the Enlightenment and the French Revolution stand like two manifestations (or epiphenomena) of a greater process—the definition of a society of independent men without myths or religions (in the traditional sense of the term); a "modern" society; a society with no past and no traditions; [a society] of the present, wholly open toward the future. The true connections of cause and effect between the one and the other are those of this common dependence on a broader and more whole historical phenomenon than their own.[23]

The "veritable Revolution," as Dupront writes, is not the complex of events that the actors—and often the historians—have designated as such, but "a broader historical development . . . that is essentially the passage from a traditional mythology (a mythology of religion, of sacralities, of religious and political authority) to a new mythology, or renewed common faith, one of whose most vehement affirmations is that it does not care to be or know itself to be mythical."[24]

8   The relation between the Revolution and the Enlightenment is central to Foucault's commentary, in 1983, on two texts of Kant's: "What Is Enlightenment?" (1784) and the second dissertation of *The Conflict of the Faculties* (1798).[25] In his analysis of the latter text, Foucault follows Kant's demonstration step by step as Kant attempts to show how the French Revolution constituted an indisputable "historical sign" of the existence of a permanent cause guaranteeing the constant progress of the human race. To do so, Kant distinguishes between the Revolution as a grandiose event and voluntary enterprise and the Revolution as producing among all peoples "a wishful participation that borders closely on enthusiasm." As a historical process the Revolution, which accumulated miseries and atrocities, could just as easily have failed as succeeded, and in any event its price was so high that it dissuaded imitations forever. Thus it cannot be held as a demonstration of the ineluctable progress of the human race—one might say quite the contrary. On the other hand, the welcome given to that event attests to the force of the "moral tendency of the human race," which urges men to give themselves a freely chosen constitution in harmony with natural law ("one, namely, in which the citizens obedient to the law, besides being united, ought also to be legislative") and "created in such a way as to avoid, by its very nature, principles permitting offensive war."

The Revolution, or more accurately the reactions it set loose, revealed a "predisposition" in human nature that "permits people to hope for Progress" more fundamental than the hazards of the event in which it is manifest. Hence Kant states, "Now I claim to be able to predict to the human race—even without prophetic insight—according to the aspects and omens of our day, the attainment of this goal. That is, I predict its progress toward the better which, from now on, turns out to be no longer completely regressive." In itself, neither the course nor the outcome of the Revolution counts; its importance lies in its giving spectacular visibility to the virtualities underlying both the *Aufklärung* and the philosopher's task:

Enlightenment of the masses is the public instruction of the people in its duties and rights vis-à-vis the state to which they belong. Since only natural rights and rights arising out of the common human understanding are concerned here, then the natural heralds and expositors of these among the people are not officially appointed by the state but are free professors of law, that is philosophers who, precisely because this freedom is allowed to them, are objectionable to the state, which always desires to rule alone; and they are decried, under the name of enlighteners, as persons dangerous to the state.[26]

With the commentary on these texts that opened his course at the Collège de France in 1983–84, Foucault intended to show that Kant not only originated the philosophical tradition that holds as central the question of the conditions of possibility of true knowledge (which Foucault calls an "analytic of the truth") but was also the first to constitute the present as an object of philosophical interrogation. In both of Kant's texts (1784 and 1798), "discourse has to return to a consideration of its actuality: first, to find its own place in it; second, to say what it means; finally, to specify the mode of action it is capable of exerting within that actuality."[27] This reference to the basis of a critical tradition that considers "the question of the present as a philosophical event to which the philosopher who speaks of it belongs" seems to me to characterize the work of Foucault even better than the formula so often cited: "My books aren't treatises in philosophy or studies of history; at most, they are philosophical fragments put to work in a historical field of problems."

9

In the last years of the eighteenth century, European culture outlined a structure that has not yet been unraveled; we are only just beginning to disentangle a few of the threads, which are still so unknown to us that we immediately assume them to be either marvelously new or absolutely archaic, whereas for two hundred years (no less, yet not much more) they have constituted the dark, but firm web of our experience.[28]

In *The Birth of the Clinic* as later in *Discipline and Punish,* Foucault situates the constitution of the discourses and practices that provide the basis for "modernity" in the half century (roughly speaking) from 1770–80 to 1830–40, which included the Revolution.

Foucault's characterization of that decisive period has often been badly misunderstood. Although it was indeed the moment in which disciplinary procedures, the technologies of surveillance, and panoptical mechanisms were constituted as the essential methods for organizing and controlling social space, that does not mean they actually gridded, policed, and disciplined the social world. Their proliferation shows their weakness, not their efficacy: "When I speak of a 'disciplinary' society, that does not imply a 'disciplined society.' When I speak of the diffusion of discipline, it is not to assert that 'the French are obedient'! In the analysis of the procedures put into effect for instituting norms there is no 'thesis of a normalization.' As if, precisely, all those developments were not on the scale of a perpetual lack of success."[29] There is thus a "reverse" side to the history of disciplinary measures—a reverse of interwoven resistances, deviations, and illegalities. To combat oversimplified readings of his work, Foucault recalls the force of rebellious practices that respond in various ways to the microtechniques of constraint:

Resistances to the Panopticon will have to be analysed in tactical and strategic terms, positing that each offensive from the one side serves as leverage for a counter-offensive from the other. The analysis of power-mechanisms has no built-in tendency to show power as being at once anonymous and always victorious. It is a matter rather of establishing the positions occupied and modes of action used by each of the forces at work, the possibilities of resistance and counter-attack on either side.[30]

"Strategy," "tactics," "offensive," counteroffensive," "positions," "counterattack": the military vocabulary indicates that even if it is not equal, the battle between the procedures of subjection and the comportment of the "subjected" always takes the form of confrontation, not enslavement. It is in that confrontation that "we must hear the distant roar of battle."[31]

The late eighteenth and early nineteenth centuries were fundamental also because they constructed a new figure of power, anonymous, autonomous, and operating through practices that are not accompanied or legitimated by any discourse. That conception of power, which inhabits all the measures that aim at rendering it both constraining and hidden, widely disseminated and coherent, managed and automatic, must by no means be confused with Foucault's concept of power. Here again Foucault reacts vigorously to a misinterpretation frequently committed by the critics (and the adepts) of *Discipline and Punish*:

The automaticity of power, the mechanical nature of the devices in which it takes shape, is absolutely not the *thesis* of the book. It is rather the idea in the eighteenth century that such a power would be possible and desirable; it is the theoretical and practical search for such mechanisms; it is the desire to organize such devices, ceaselessly manifested at the time, that constitutes the *object* of analysis. Studying the way people attempted to rationalize power—for which a new "economy" of the relations of power was conceived in the eighteenth century—and showing the important role that the themes of the machine, of the gaze, of surveillance, of transparency, and so on, played in them, is not to say either that power is a machine or that an idea of the sort was born mechanically.[32]

Confusion between the "thesis" and the "object" has been one of the major and recurrent reasons for misunderstanding Foucault's work. It marked the readings given to the famous lecture "Qu'est-ce qu'un auteur?" which Foucault gave on 22 February 1969 to the Société Française de Philosophie, readings that have often (and wrongly) equated the question posed (the conditions of the emergence and distribution of the "author-function," defined as the mode of classifying discourses that assigns them to a proper name) and the theme of the "death of the author," which bases the meaning of works on the impersonal and automatic functioning of language.[33] Foucault corrects just such a mistaken view of the intentions of his work in his reply to Lucien Goldmann's objections during the debate that followed his lecture:

The death of man is a theme that allows light to be shed on the way the concept of man has functioned in knowledge. . . . It is not a matter of affirming that man is dead; it is a matter of seeing, based on the theme—which is not of my invention [and] has been repeated incessantly since the late nineteenth century—that man is dead (or that he is about to disappear, or that he will be replaced by the superman), in what manner and according to what rules the concept of man has been formed and has functioned. I have done the same thing with the notion of the author. Let us hold back our tears.[34]

10   When Foucault distinguishes, as in *The Archaeology of Knowledge,* between discursive formations and practices that "are not themselves of a discursive nature," when he shows, as in *Discipline and Punish,* how practices without discourse come to contradict, invalidate, or "vampirize" (the word is Michel de Certeau's)[35] the proclamations of ideology, Foucault's work retains all its critical pertinence today, regarding both the "semiological challenge" and the "return to politics."

We all know of the "linguistic turn" proposed to historians of texts and practices: to hold language as a closed system of signs that produce meaning merely by the way their relations function; to think of social reality as being constituted by language, independent of any objective reference.[36] In contrast to these formulations, Foucault (perhaps paradoxically for those who made a structuralist of him, a label he always vehemently rejected)[37] helps us recall that one cannot reduce the practices that make up the social world to the "rationality" that governs discourses. The logic commanding the operations that construct institutions, dominations, and relations is not the same hermeneutic, logocentric, scriptural logic that produces discourses. That practices, articulated with but not homologous to discourses, are not reducible to discourses can be considered the fundamental partitioning principle in all cultural history, which is by that token invited to avoid unguarded use of the category of "text," too often used to designate practices whose procedures in no way obey the "order of discourse."

The theme of the "return to politics" often (though not always, as Keith Baker's work proves) figures as the inverse of the "linguistic turn." Far from postulating that the production of meaning is automatic, it stresses the liberty of the subject, the part reflection plays in action, and the autonomy of decisions. Hence it rejects all initiatives that aim at establishing determinations individuals are not conscious of, while it affirms the primacy of the political, held to be the most comprehensive and most significant level in all societies.[38] Here too Foucault helps define a perspective opposed, term by term, to that proposition—first, by considering the individual not in the supposed liberty of his or her own separate "I" but as constructed by the configurations, discursive or social, that determine its historical figures; and second, by postulating not the absolute autonomy of politics but, at each particular historical moment, its dependence on the balance of tensions that both fashions its devices and results from its efficacy.

11   Foucault revolutionized history in two ways. First, after him it has become impossible to consider the objects whose history the historian claims to write as "natural objects," as universal categories whose historical variations (be they madness, medicine, state, or sexuality) the historian simply notes. Behind the lazy convenience of vocabulary, what we need to recognize are singular demarcations, specific distributions, and particular "positivities" produced by differentiated practices that construct figures (of knowledge or of power) irreducible to one another. As Paul Veyne has written,

Foucault's philosophy is not a philosophy of the "discourse," but a philosophy of relation. For "relation" is the name of what some have designated as "structure." Instead of a world made of subjects or of objects or of their dialectic, of a world in which consciousness knows its objects in advance or is itself what the objects make of it, we have a world in which relation is primary; it is structures that give their objective faces to matter. In this world we do not play chess with eternal figures like the king and the fool [the bishop]; the figures are what the successive configurations on the playing board make of them.[39]

Thus there are no historical objects that predate the relations that constitute them; there is no field of discourse or of reality delimited in a stable and unmediated fashion: "Things are only the objectivations of determinate practices, the determinants of which must be brought to light, since consciousness does not conceive them." Thus it is by identifying the demarcations and exclusions constituting the objects history gives itself that history can conceive of them not as the circumstantial expressions of a universal category but, quite the contrary, as "individual and even singular constellations."[40]

To transform the definition of the object of history is necessarily to modify the forms of writing. In his commentary on *Discipline and Punish*, Michel de Certeau stressed the rhetorical displacement (and the perils) implied by a history of practices without discourses that constructs these "panoptical fictions":

When theory, instead of being a discourse upon other preexistent discourses, ventures into non-verbal or pre-verbal domains in which there are only practices without accompanying discourse, certain problems arise. There is a sudden shift, and the usually reliable foundation of language is missing. The theoretical operation suddenly finds itself at the limits of its normal terrain, like a car at the edge of a cliff. Beyond, nothing but the sea. Foucault works on this cliff when he attempts to invent a discourse that can speak of non-discursive practices.[41]

Hence in *Discipline and Punish* there is a contradictory *écriture* that organizes the discourse on knowledge according to the very procedures that are its object and, at the same time, constructs "panoptical fictions" to exhibit and subvert the foundations of the punitive rationality established at the end of the eighteenth century. As de Certeau says, "On a first level, Foucault's theoretical text is still organized by the panoptical procedures it elucidates. But on a second level, this panoptical discourse is only a stage where a narrative machinery reverses our triumphant panoptical epistemology."[42]

12   "At the edge of the cliff." The image is a vivid expression of the disquietude appropriate to any history that attempts the operation, at the limit of the possible, of accounting, within the order of discourse, for the "reason" for practices—both the dominant practices that organize norms and institutions and the scattered and minor practices that make up the fabric of daily experience or introduce illegalities.

But there is help for all who draw close to the edge of that cliff: in the work and the thought that were always "situated at the point where an archaeology of problematizations and a genealogy of practices . . . intersect."[43]

FIVE

Discourses and Practices

On the Origins of the French Revolution

After the high waters of 1989, there seemed nothing left to say about the French Revolution, its origins, or its significance. Since then, however, a number of books and articles have returned to the debates that were launched (or should have been raised) during the bicentennial year. At the time, the leading issues historians discussed, in complex and intertwined ways, were the political reading of the French Revolution, the historical interpretation of its causes or its origins, and the very definition of what can and must be the historical intelligibility of an event. A consideration of the works published since that date will provide a clearer focus on a book of mine published in 1990.[1] Critics perceived and understood this book very differently: some found it "strongly idealistic" and wholly inspired by the "linguistic turn" that had been the basis, in the United States, for an analysis of political language; others saw it as grounded in a cultural sociology emphasizing (too strongly for some tastes) practices and mechanisms rather than ideas and theories.

Let us begin with a classical problem—the relation between the Enlightenment and the French Revolution. Some found it excessively provocative to ask, contrary to the traditional formulation (that the Enlightenment produced the Revolution), how the Revolution constructed or "invented" the Enlightenment. Obviously that proposition was not intended as a denial of the existence of the Enlightenment as a major historical event; rather, it was aimed at understanding how the revolutionaries erected a pantheon of authors and a corpus of ideas into which they read an anticipation and a legitimation of that event. The operation supposes, simultaneously, that they selected among all the possible authors and writings and that they reduced to unity an extreme diversity of opinions and positions. Using a broad variety of oratorical, ceremonial, iconographic, and textual devices, the revolutionaries worked to transform a plural ideological heritage into a necessarily unified political genealogy.

Two sorts of remarks arose regarding how the Revolution reworked the Enlightenment. First, some scholars investigated the multiple differentiations that had fragmented the world of the Enlightenment: radical utopian thinkers versus practical reformers (Franco Venturi); "High Enlightenment" versus "Low-Life of Literature" or the "Rousseau du ruisseau" (Robert Darnton); provincial elites versus the men of letters of the capital (Daniel Roche); the generation of the *encyclopédistes* versus the prophet-philosophers of the 1780s (Vincenzo Ferrone); the "intellectual Enlightenment" versus the "popular, nonintellectual Enlightenment" (Aram Vartanian). Such differences of position and stance, of generation, and of epistemological model depicted a more fractured and diverse reality than had long been proposed when the Enlightenment was equated with a body of stable, commonly shared propositions.

Second, other scholars took a harder look at how the French Revolution related to history. A paradox underlies that relation, because although that event can be thought of as a rupture that set off something new—as an absolute beginning—it is also written of in reference to a past that justified and shaped it. In that sense the relation of the Revolution to the Enlightenment cannot be separated from the relation of the Revolution to classical antiquity. The election to the pantheon that was literal in the case of Rousseau and symbolic in that of Mably clearly shows the connection between these two founding references. But the reconstruction of an inspiring or exemplary past was not without tensions or conflicts. Just as the Spartan model and the Roman model were far from being unanimously accepted,[2] the Enlightenment was not the same for everyone who took part in the Revolution. As several German historians have suggested (Thomas Schleich, Rolf Reichardt, Hans-Jürgen Lüsebrink), each of the various revolutionary parties constructed its own "Enlightenment," and tracing the history of this process in which multiple interpretations and conflicting customs clash leads in a quite different direction from a history of ideas moving too hastily to postulate a unity of meaning.

Naturally this approach touches the heart of any history of the cultural origins of the French Revolution. Several things are involved: first, broadening the usual questionnaire of intellectual history to take into account not only conceptual products but also (and especially) collective representations and forms of belief; next, restoring to institutions and forms of sociability their unique dynamism rather than considering them as simply accepting or rejecting ideas and theories; finally, refusing to reduce nondiscursive practices to the discourses that, in a variety of ways, were intended to legitimate, condemn, represent, control, or organize them. By doing all these things, such a perspective also aims at resisting two operations frequent in the historiography of the French Revolution and its origins: on the one hand, deducing practices from thoughts, thoughts from readings, and readings from texts; on the other hand, translating social functions in terms of an explicit ideology.

The first of these two operations lent support to the traditional view that tied the revolutionary rupture to a wider and wider dissemination of philosophical ideas. When this view, stated with prudence and subtlety, was shifted from the great classics of the Enlightenment to the texts that the eighteenth-century book trade called "philosophical books" (critical pamphlets, scandalmongering chronicles, anticlerical satires, pornographic works), it provided Robert Darnton with a basis for evaluating the "subversive violence of clandestine literature." Thanks to the circulation of print works, seditious texts depicting the despotic corruption of the monarchy or the depraved mores of the court engendered a change in thought and in representations, henceforth detached from old loyalties. "This corrosion operated in two ways: at the level of ideas, the writings of Voltaire and d'Holbach openly denounced the falsities of the systems of orthodoxy that supported the church and the crown; at the level of representations, the pamphlets and scandalmongering chronicles desacralized by throwing mud on the monarchy and all the values that structured its political rationality."[3]

Still, if we draw too close a connection between the subversion contained in the texts and the "revolution" worming its way into people's minds, we risk destroying the specificity of the mechanisms by which books and pamphlets acquired meaning. Those mechanisms depended in part on the way the texts themselves organized the plurality of ways they could be understood. This was the case, for example, with the pornographic pamphlets exposing Marie-Antoinette's dissolute sexuality. These works operated on several levels, involving the conventions of erotic literature, means for producing effects taken as true, games of court politics, denunciatory rhetoric, and more.[4] But the intelligibility of clandestine literature also depended on the "horizon of reception" it encountered; hence the hypothesis that some forms of detachment from the sovereign, the monarchy, and the old order should be understood as a condition for the success of such literature rather than as the result of the circulation of "philosophical books." "Sedition was hatching," Darnton writes. "It was instilled in people's minds. . . . We know for certain that it was communicated by a formidable instrument—the book."[5] Why should we not think that the same "sedition" was already present and inhabited actions, emotions, and thoughts that owed nothing to reading the written word in any form?

This is what Arlette Farge suggests in her analysis of the *mauvais propos* or *mauvais discours* aimed at the king that interested both the police spies and the writers of sensational newssheets. She states conclusively, "Popular opinion did not emerge from the cumulative reading of pamphlets and placards; it was not unilinear and did not base arguments on the sum total of what it read."[6] Thus Farge disputes the interpretation that saw the increase in seditious writings in the last two or three decades of the ancien régime as the matrix of a desacralization of the monarchy that opened the way to radical and universal criticism. Statements of disapproval or hatred of the sovereign, attacks on his acts, and expressions of a desire to kill him did not arise from the flourishing clandestine literature. Nor did they start with Damiens's attempt to assassinate Louis XV, which, rather than unleashing a proliferation of regicide discourse, persuaded the authorities of the reality of Jansenist and Jesuit plots and set them in hot pursuit of such literature. For Arlette Farge, "the failed murder of Louis XV had a ready-made public opinion; it tells us more about the monarchy's reactions than about any new and original turn of popular thought."[7] That remark lends support to a second idea: the symbolic and affective disinvestment that transformed relations with authority when it was deprived of all transcendence was manifested (but not caused) by the wide diffusion—even the very wide diffusion—of "philosophical books." The erosion of the founding myths of the monarchy, the desacralization of royal symbols, and the distancing of the person of the king formed a body of representations that was "already there," ready to welcome the radical denunciations of the subversive literature of the 1770s and 1780s.

To think of social practices as autonomous implies a rejection of the operation that translates them into ideological terms. An exemplary illustration of just that sort of approach is the thesis of Augustin Cochin, picked up by François Furet, that the operation of the *sociétés de pensée* in the eighteenth century (Freemasonry in particular) was Jacobin. Independent of the explicit intentions of the Masonic lodges and the *sociétés*, and independent of the particularities of their social recruitment, their egalitarian practice, aimed at producing consensus and eliminating dissent, was seen as constituting the matrix of the pure democracy and the terrorist practice of Jacobinism in both the clubs and the revolutionary government. Fred E. Schrader's book has taken this thesis that detaches from individual wills and consciences the significance of the "social machine" at work in the *sociétés de pensée* and the Masonic lodges and has placed it within the context of Cochin's polemical Durkheimism.[8] For Cochin, making use of Durkheim was above all a way to comprehend democracy in much the same way that republican sociology comprehends religion—as a social fact whose meaning cannot be reduced to the explicit statements it produces, which, indeed, mask the way it really works. Hence the genealogy of the democratic ideology whose terrorist potential is to be identified, on the practical level, in the peaceful societies of the Enlightenment. Social operations thus find their translation in the form of a theory of Jacobinism.

This thesis, although intellectually powerful, fails to take adequate account of the actual practice of the Masonic lodges. For one thing, as Margaret Jacob has stressed, they could hardly have been said to be characterized by the exercise of direct democracy. Quite the contrary, particularly in France, ancien régime practices continued to predominate in their operations—hereditary transfer of prestigious offices; the power of dignitaries; a social exclusiveness that prohibited fraternizing within Masonic circles with people who were not one's own sort in the social world at large. For another thing, if the social mechanisms proper to the Masonic lodges, in and of themselves, followed a democratic, revolutionary, and terrorist logic, how are we to account for the gap between the universality of Freemasonry and the exceptional nature of French Jacobinism? As Jacob says, "If the Masonic lodges were the seedbeds of Jacobinism, then why did they not spawn it in Philadelphia in 1780 or in Brussels and Amsterdam in the 1790s?"[9]

Giving central importance to relations between practice and discourse—between "nondiscursive systems" and "enunciative facts," to quote Foucault in *L'archéologie du savoir (The Archeology of Knowledge)*—leads to a shift of emphasis to detachments not expressed in discourse (or at least not in explanatory, justificative discourse), to the relative independence of systems of representation from the circulation of texts, and to the construction of a political culture built on ordinary experiences and daily conflicts. Putting the question of the cultural origins of the French Revolution in these terms does not imply that its causes were entirely and uniquely of a cultural sort. Far from supposing a "strongly idealistic opinion" that conceives of the Revolution as "purely subjective" (as Paolo Viola states in a review of my book in *L'Indice*), such an approach tries to understand why, at a given moment in the trajectory of the ancien régime, the swift and radical destruction of the foundations of the old order became so easily intelligible, so decipherable, and so broadly accepted. To draw up an inventory of changes in representation and sensitivity that made that break conceivable is not to say that those changes produced that break.

Asking that sort of question of cultural history does not entail subjecting the set of problems connected with the origins of the French Revolution to the "linguistic turn" and the "semiological challenge." That perspective, brilliantly illustrated by Keith Baker, rests on two suppositions. Baker supposes, first, that social interests are in no way external to discourse. Second, he states that one cannot set up any distinction between discursive and nondiscursive practices.[10]

This position, which reflects the most radical formulations of the "linguistic turn" and applies them to intellectual history, seems to me unacceptable. In fact the processes by which discourse constructs interests or events are themselves socially rooted and determined and are limited, in varying degree, by the linguistic, conceptual, and material resources available to their producers. Thus those processes refer to objective social properties external to discourse that are characteristic of each of the groups, communities, and classes that make up the social world. What is more, the logic at work in discourse should not be confused with the logic that commands the "forms of social action." There is a radical difference between the lettered, logocentric, and hermeneutic rationality that organizes the production of discourses and the rationality informing all other regimes of practice.[11]

If, like Baker, we fail to make this distinction, we are led to inscribe the ongoing event within a preexisting discourse—in the French Revolution's choice of one political language (that of general sovereignty) over another (that of the representation of social interests). For Baker the Terror was ineluctable, virtually present in the constitutional decisions of the autumn of 1789 and, before that date, in the theory of the general will elaborated by Rousseau, Mably, and the most radical propagandists in the Parlement. The game was already over when the National Assembly "was opting for the language of political will, rather than of social reason; of unity, rather than of difference; of civic virtue, rather than of commerce; of absolute sovereignty, rather than of government limited by the rights of man—which is to say that, in the long run, it was opting for the Terror." Thus the Revolution was written before it happened: "The revolutionary script was invented . . . from within the political culture of the absolute monarchy,"[12] insofar as it was wholly contained in one of the forms of political discourse developed under absolutism.

For two reasons this thesis, which fits the Terror into the "illiberalism" of 1789[13] and fits that illiberalism into the language of Rousseau, is open to criticism. First, it denies the event any radicality (since the event is already present in discourse before it happens) and any dynamism (since what Maurice Agulhon called the "empirical weight of contingent realities" is refused a role). Second, it makes the historian's interpretation share the illusion of 1789 and 1793. Then, certitude about the absolute efficacy of the political, believed capable of recasting the body politic, refounding society, and regenerating the individual, inspired confidence regarding the power of ideas, the performative word, and the role of individuals. But must that belief mean that the history of the French Revolution has to be written in the language of the event? Paradoxically, perhaps, those who puncture the Jacobin enthusiasms, condemned for their lack of distance from the Revolution, also submit (although in a different fashion) the intelligibility of the event to the historical consciousness of contemporaries. It seems to me that the question of the origins of 1789 necessarily sends us in another direction, toward an elucidation of the determinations that govern the intentions, choices, and discourses of individuals, whether or not they are conscious of the process.

The hypothesis that inscribes the French Revolution within the ancien régime can be understood in quite different terms. Denis Richet provides a basic notion for such a different approach: "The more absolutism brought in reinforcements, the weaker it got."[14] Hence the weakening of the ancien régime (political, social, and cultural) should be sought in the very mechanisms that seemed to ensure its power. For Richet, the definition of the reason of state and the development of a centralized administration laid the foundations for the power of absolutism, but they were also the reasons for its weakness: by rending the social fabric and destroying ideological consensus, they set a coherent body of the king's subjects against him.

This model of interpretation permits us to see how the separation (set in motion by the state itself) of the reason of state, the only check on the actions of the prince, and moral judgment, henceforth relegated to the private or religious conscience of individuals, was eventually turned against the prince, now judged, criticized, and condemned in the name of criteria that had been expelled from the political domain. This is the sense in which one can see "the political structure of absolutism as the precondition of Enlightenment," according to the title of the first chapter in Reinhart Koselleck's *Kritik und Krise (Critique and Crisis)*.[15] Similarly, the institutionalization of the literary field, in which the monarchy initiated and dominated the consecration of works and authors, was the precondition of an autonomous market for opinions and works and for a politicized critical space that eventually became more sovereign than the sovereign. The issue is not so much to postulate that "revolutionary principles and practices were invented in the context of an absolute monarchy"[16] as to understand how the cultural mutations that made the revolutionary rupture conceivable and sapped the authority of the old order were made possible not by signs of growing weakness, but by the monarchy's demonstrations of power.

Its emphasis on the conceptual and social construction of public space gave obligatory authority to Jürgen Habermas's *Die Strukturwandel der Öffentlichkeit (The Structural Transformation of the Public Sphere)*.[17] To many people—in particular to Robert Darnton in an article in the *New York Review of Books* (October 1991)—the work had little relevance. Given that it lacks an empirical base, it is not a book to be read in a historical perspective; rather, it is a philosophical critique of today's society (hence a harbinger of Habermas's later works), in which the critical public sphere is threatened with destruction. The weakness of the book is made all the more evident by Habermas's reintroducing the concept of the bourgeoisie as a category of the "public sphere"—just when that concept had been repudiated in descriptions of both the Enlightenment and the French Revolution. One might make the same remark regarding one possible reading of Koselleck's *Critique and Crisis,* a book subtitled, in the German original, *Eine Studie zur Pathogenese der bürgerlichen Welt* and to which the notion of a "bourgeois elite" is essential. Must we thus accept this surreptitious and Germanic "return of the banished bourgeoisie," as Colin Jones put it in the *Times Literary Supplement* (March 1991)? Or are we to abandon the obligatory reverence accorded Habermas's book, now some thirty years old?

If Habermas's work has become an omnipresent reference, it is perhaps because it offers an alternative to the model of comprehension of the "machine" that Cochin manufactured and Furet reconditioned. A return to the Kant of "What Is Enlightenment?" enables us to stress the articulation between the public and the particular, the necessary link between the circulation of written matter and the public exercise of reason by private persons. It also permits us to go back to the founding of a critical tradition that "considers the question of the present as a philosophical event to which the philosophy that speaks of it belongs."[18] But Habermas's book also makes it possible to give a conceptual framework to a body of studies that aimed at providing a pragmatic history of public opinion, the model for which was Franco Venturi's great *Settecento riformatore*. But these (good) reasons may not be sufficient to save the "bourgeoisie" as a category, except perhaps by redefining it: if it is neither a social designation nor an ideological qualification, the term might refer, irrespective of the social condition of individuals, to a specific modality of the critical relation to the absolutist state that supposed a place for debate outside the sphere of power and that was made up of a "public" that was neither the court nor the people.

This rapid excursion through several works devoted to the history of the origins of the French Revolution should enable us to pose the question that is now central: How are we to make the connection between descriptions of contemporaries' historical consciousness—obsessed as they were in 1789 by a certainty of inaugurating something new and of absolute rupture with the old—with identifying the unrecognized determinations that led those same people to make a history different from the one they thought they were making? We need to restore the radicality of the emerging event, but we also need to rediscover the unrealized, paradoxical continuities that inscribe that event within the long history of the monarchy.

SIX

Texts, Forms,
and Interpretations

D. F. McKenzie's slim book *Bibliography and the Sociology of Texts* already has a history. Its three chapters were originally conceived as lectures given in 1985 to inaugurate the Panizzi Lectures at the British Library. Published the following year by that institution, the book received immediate attention (and at times aroused criticism) from bibliographers, historians of the book, conservators, and librarians.[1] The first edition is already out of print.

Two ideas underlie this work. The first, in a move that runs counter to the established traditions of bibliography in its classical forms, extends the concept of "text" far beyond its ordinary definitions. For McKenzie, we need to undo the connection that the Western literary tradition made between the text and the book. It is in fact true that not all texts are necessarily given in book form: orally produced works and numerical or computer-processed data are "nonbook texts" that mobilize the resources of language without belonging to the class of print objects. There are also texts that presuppose no use of verbal language: the image in all its forms, the geographical map, musical scores, and even landscape can be considered "nonverbal texts." What authorizes calling these various products "texts" is that they are constructed based on signs whose meaning is fixed by convention and that they constitute symbolic systems inviting interpretation. Verbal language, written or oral, is not the only language that operates semantically. This is what makes necessary the extension of the category of "text."

In turn, this broader definition dictates that written texts be considered in a new way. McKenzie's second, and powerful, idea in this book is that forms shape meaning. A text (in the usual sense of the term) is always inscribed within something material—the written object that bears it, the voice that reads or recites it, the representation that makes it available to the understanding. Each of these forms is organized according to structures of its own that have an essential role in the production of meaning. In print writings, for instance, the format of the book, its page layout, the ways the text is divided, and typographical conventions all have an "expressive function" and contribute to the construction of meaning. Organized by an intention, the author's or the publisher's, such formal devices aim at qualifying the text, constraining its reception, and controlling its interpretation. By giving structure to the unconscious in reading (or listening), they support the work of interpretation. Thus, both the imposition and the appropriation of the meaning of a text depend on material forms whose modalities and treatment, long held to be without significance, delimit the intended or possible ways to comprehend the text. "Forms effect meaning": against all the purely semantic definitions of texts, McKenzie forcefully recalls the symbolic value of signs and of material things.

These two connected ideas offer a formidable challenge to habitual notions in several fields of knowledge and practice. First among these is bibliography, McKenzie's own discipline. English-speaking readers may find it somewhat easier than their French counterparts to understand this first aspect of McKenzie's book, thanks to a greater familiarity with works and debates that have shaped a scholarly tradition stronger throughout the Anglo-Saxon world (in Great Britain, the United States, Australia, and New Zealand) than in France. Two postulates define "bibliography" and interconnect its various modalities (systematic, descriptive, analytical, textual): first, the establishment of a text (and eventually its publication) requires a rigorous reconstruction of what took place in the printshop during the work's composition and printing; second, an understanding of the operations involved in producing a book implies description and analysis of the physical characteristics of the extant copies of the edition (or editions) of the text under consideration.

From this perspective, which is that of the major classics of bibliography,[2] analysis of the material aspects of the book is put in the service of studying the text, comparing versions and variants, and in the end establishing an edition that is as accurate as possible. In the broader definition of "analytical bibliography," the most fundamental data are those that help reconstitute the mode of composition of the text—for example, by noting the graphic and orthographic habits of the various compositors who worked on a given work, or by identifying certain peculiarities (damaged letters, initials, ornaments) of their type fonts.[3] The frequency of such elements (clearly recognizable in the printed book) can teach us much about how the print job was organized and the order of its composition and impression, the compositors' decisions regarding the text, the way the text was composed (seriatim, following the page order, or by print forms), and the corrections made as the work was being printed.

Although he is a virtuoso practitioner of such "spelling analyses" and "compositor studies,"[4] McKenzie has nonetheless not limited his lessons on bibliography to the domain of textual criticism. That discipline is for him a fundamental resource for understanding printshop practices and the organization of typographical work during the four centuries stretching from Gutenberg's invention of movable type to the industrialization of printing. When the physical characteristics of extant copies are supplemented with information taken from printshop records (when they exist) and from old printing manuals, they provide the most massive—and perhaps the richest—records for a history of the conditions and habits that governed the production of printed texts.[5]

In his Panizzi Lectures McKenzie went one step further, startling to an extent some who held firmly to traditional bibliography. Defining the discipline as a "study of the sociology of texts," he invited an enlargement of its field of investigation in two ways: first, by establishing protocols of description and techniques of bibliographical verification capable of taking into account the many texts that are not books; second, by including among its objects of study all processes for the production, transmission, and reception of texts of all forms. In its new definition bibliography, far from being a tightly circumscribed and auxiliary form of knowledge focused on inventorying and interpreting formal data in the service of the publication of texts, became a central discipline, essential for reconstructing how a community shapes and formulates its most fundamental experiences by deciphering the many texts it receives, produces, or makes its own. By assigning to bibliography the fundamental task of comprehending the relations between form and meaning, McKenzie obliterated the old divisions between sciences of description and sciences of interpretation, and he made that discipline, based on techniques of its own, central to the study of symbolic practices.

This new, broader, and more ambitious definition of bibliography led to a new definition of the mission of libraries, the institutions devoted to the conservation of texts. At a time when people throughout the world were beginning to rethink the functions and structure of the great national and private libraries, McKenzie's lectures had immediate pertinence, particularly for an audience that must have been preoccupied by the British Library's move to its new quarters.

McKenzie's lectures stress the responsibility of libraries in the collection, classification, conservation, and communication not only of print objects (books, periodicals, journals, maps, prints, etc.) but of the new documents proliferating everywhere in the world today: sound recordings, photographs, films, television programs, videocassettes, computerized information, and more. Even if the preservation of these various categories of "texts" does not necessarily entail their storage in one institution, it is an essential task of libraries today, which are in a unique position to prevent the destruction of objects that are often fragile, subject to the laws of commerce, and neglected by "legitimate" culture. This implies a change in notions traditionally defined in relation to written and printed works: juridical notions (copyright), legal requirements (provision of a copy or copies to a national repository), and biblioeconomic concerns (cataloging). Hence broadening the concept of the "text" leads quite logically to a transformation in the very function of the library.[6]

That notion has a corollary: if forms affect meaning, it is normal and necessary to consult texts in their original material forms. Despite the tendency to replace the circulation of original documents with that of photographic or digital substitutes, we need to remember that presenting a text in a form that is not its original one can seriously impair readers' comprehension. The library latent in McKenzie's pages is thus a library not restricted to books—far from it—but one in which all the texts offered by modern technology have a prominent place. Yet it is also a library in which every text must be available for consultation without the distortion ineluctably brought on by a change in its material support. McKenzie offers a precious lesson for an age when the possibilities opened up by the new electronic technologies make it very tempting to transfer book texts to the monitor screen. This is perhaps a legitimate and useful operation in that it permits (and will continue to permit) better protection and wider circulation of the patrimony of written works. Still, it should not radically separate readers from the form that governed the production, transmission, and interpretation of the texts they read.[7]

Bibliography and the Sociology of Texts is an important book for other reasons as well. In its attempt to find a new basis for bibliography, it maps out a new intellectual space connecting the study of texts, the analysis of their forms, and the history of their uses. This proposition is, first, a way for McKenzie to mark his distance from the various forms of literary criticism in which the production of meaning arises solely from the automatic and impersonal operation of language. Such a position (the one taken by structuralist criticism and by the New Criticism) is based on several postulates: the affirmation that the text is absolute, detached from all specific physical forms and reduced to its verbal structure alone; the disappearance of the author, whose intention has no particular claim to pertinence; the refusal to consider that the way a work was transmitted, received, and interpreted has any importance in establishing its meaning.

In a study that has become a classic, McKenzie took an approach totally different from the view of the text as having no materiality, no author, and no reader (except the literary critic pronouncing on its meaning).[8] His analysis of the changes made by the author and by his publisher, Jacob Tonson, in the 1710 edition of Congreve's plays shows how the status of the work was altered significantly by formal changes with no apparent discursive significance (a shift from a quarto to an octavo volume, the numbering of scenes, the presence or absence of a print ornament between scenes, a note at the beginning of each scene recalling which characters are onstage, marginal indications of who is speaking, mention of entrances and exits). On the one hand, these changes made it possible to read the text in a new way, thanks to a smaller, handier format and a layout that gave a feeling of dramatic movement. This was a clear break with time-honored conventions, respected longer in England than in France, of printing plays with little hint of their theatricality. On the other hand, the typographical devices (borrowed from French editions) used in the 1710 edition of Congreve's works gave those plays a new status, granting them a legitimacy that may have induced their author to refine their style in places to conform better to the dignity of their new form. McKenzie's study teaches a number of lessons: against the abstraction of the text, it shows that the status and interpretation of a work depend on material considerations; against the "death of the author," it stresses the author's role, at the side of the bookseller-printer, in defining the form given to the work; against the absence of the reader, it recalls that the meaning of a text is always produced in a historical setting and depends on the differing and plural readings that assign meaning to it.[9]

If, as McKenzie notes, analytical bibliography and structuralist criticism shared an exclusive interest in the logic and the internal functioning of a system of signs that organizes both the material aspects of a physical object and the meaning of the text, the "sociology of texts" he proposed was in harmony with critical currents that aimed at once more inscribing works into history. Such a method could lead to a sociology of cultural products attentive to the laws and hierarchies of the literary field (or of any other field—artistic, academic, or whatever), to the career strategies they command, and to their translation into the works themselves (in terms of genre, theme, and style).[10] That sort of approach can also lead, as in the "new historicism," to situating the literary work in its relation to the "ordinary"—practical, juridical, political, religious—texts it is built on and that make its intelligibility possible.[11]

Rather than contradicting these approaches, McKenzie's interests lie elsewhere. He strives to reconstruct the process of constructing meaning in all its fundamental historicity. By that token, he defines the history of reading as central to textual criticism and to the history of the book. A text truly comes to life only when readers make it their own. This axiom, in its broadest definition, underlies all the various approaches (hermeneutic, phenomenological, aesthetic, sociological) that have attempted to describe the effects and modalities of reading as an activity. McKenzie agrees with this axiom, but he gives it a fundamentally historical dimension: "New readers of course make new texts, and . . . their new meanings are a function of their new forms." This remark pinpoints the double set of variations (in readers' competence, expectations, and habits; in the forms in which texts are presented for reading) that any history must take into account if it hopes to reconstruct how readers produce meaning as they apprehend a text.

This outline for further work, sketched out in a book whose principal theme lay elsewhere, has already demonstrated its relevance. It has permitted a better understanding of how a text, as it passes from one published form to another, can prompt changes in the social and cultural makeup of its public, in its readers' uses of it, and in its possible interpretations. McKenzie cites as examples the 1710 edition of Congreve's plays, the division of the Bible into verses, and the various editions of James Joyce's *Ulysses*. One might add the particularly exemplary case of the peddlers' books (called chapbooks in England, *pliegos* in Castile, and *plecs* in Catalonia and including the French Bibliothèque bleue), which took texts that had already been published for a more literate audience and gave them a new form in order to reach a broader and humbler public.

The analysis of sociocultural differentiations and the morphological study of specific material devices, far from being mutually exclusive, are thus necessarily linked. On the one hand, the form given to a text is chosen to accord with the supposed competencies and expectations of the public it was destined for. But on the other hand, the devices by which a text is offered (for reading or listening) have a dynamic of their own: they can (or can fail to) create a new public and authorize new appropriations.[12] McKenzie's "sociology of texts" is not a fixed sociology in which crystallized and predetermined social divisions dictate cultural distribution. Quite the contrary, it focuses on the ways texts, thanks to their mobile forms, are open to reuse and reinterpretation by the various publics they reach or invent.

Still, not all uses and interpretations are equal. The control and imposition of meaning are always fundamentally at stake in political and social struggles and are important means of symbolic domination. In an essay that had a special place in his heart because it showed that the scholar's work can also reflect civic commitment, McKenzie demonstrated this point regarding a telling episode in the history of his homeland, New Zealand: the treaty of Waitangi, signed in February 1840, by which forty-six Maori chiefs gave the queen of England sovereignty over their territories.[13] Reconstructing the history of this decisive text entailed reconstructing the history of the imposition of Western customs of writing, literacy, and printing on a totally oral culture. In the twenty years before the Waitangi treaty, the Maori population was subjected to a triple revolution: the indigenous speech was set down as an alphabetical written language; missionaries (of various confessions) carried on literacy campaigns in the vernacular (rather than in English); printing was introduced (in 1830 with the publication of the first work printed in New Zealand—hymns in the native language—and in 1837 with the publication of a Maori New Testament, printed in five thousand copies by William Colenso).

But contrary to what the missionaries thought (or wanted to think), the Maori people's entry into written culture did not signify their understanding or acceptance of the concepts, uses, or meanings associated with the written text in Western civilization. For the Maori, the book, reading, and writing were not invested with the same values the British colonizers saw in them. For the Maori, the book—the Bible in particular—was a ritual object giving power and protection; reading (or listening to reading aloud) was only a precondition for memorizing and reciting texts learned by heart; the written text was secondary to oral conventions. That cultural gap (and one could find many equivalent instances in the rural societies of modern, even contemporary Europe)[14] was invested with greater political significance with the treaty of Waitangi. For the English, the Maori chieftains' signing of the text ceding "to Her Majesty the Queen of England, absolutely and without reservation, all the rights and powers of sovereignty" was an unambiguous recognition of the colonizers' political domination. This was not the case with the Maoris. First, the term translating "sovereignty" in the vernacular version of the treaty *(kawanatanga)* meant only acceptance of British administration, not the abandonment of power over the land; second, the fact of signing the treaty had no particular value for the Maori, since what they considered essential were spoken words and promises made orally.

This superb study is emblematic of all McKenzie's thought on the social uses of writing. Writing is never neutral for him: control of its production, use, and meaning is a potent instrument of political power. Hence the expression and the mark of sovereignty in societies of the ancien régime through a control of "graphic space," particularly in the encouragement of epigraphy through the growing fashion for monuments bearing writing.[15] Hence also the lively competition among all persons (writing masters, notaries, secretaries) who claimed a monopoly on writing expertise[16] and the control over the body encouraged by the techniques of learning how to write.[17] The history of the forms and appropriations of writing is thus not a history without conflicts. They always imply power relations, beginning, as Armando Petrucci put it, with "the power of writing (which belongs to the person who possesses the ability to write and exercises it) and power over writing (held by the authority in place, which delegates it and exercises whatever control over it exists)."[18]

Bibliography and the Sociology of Texts is a book that mixes specializations and blurs canonical frontiers. Its intellectual references are many—philosophical (Plato, Aristotle, Hobbes, Locke), linguistic (Saussure, Peirce), and semiotic (Barthes, Metz, Todorov). In its quotations and allusions, the classics of English literature (Shakespeare, Marlowe, Milton, Spenser, Pope, Sterne) join with the work of contemporary filmmakers and writers (Joseph Mankiewicz, Woody Allen, Tom Stoppard, Umberto Eco). Its analyses range from *Citizen Kane* to *Ulysses,* from the totemic geography

of the Arunta people of Australia to the latest in data-processing technologies. With daring and originality, McKenzie formulates the central
question in both textual criticism and the social sciences today—the question of the production of meaning as it is constructed in the intertwined
relations among forms and interpretations.

SEVEN

The Powers and Limits
of Representation

In 1639 Nicolas Poussin wrote to his friend and client Paul Fréart de Chantelou to advise him that he had sent him a painting titled *La manne*. In commenting on that letter, at a time when the term "reading" was commonly used to designate the deciphering, comprehension, and interpretation of objects or forms that did not fall within the category of written matter (one "read" a landscape, a city, a painting), Louis Marin meant to question the universality of a category that, by implication, referred to reading a written text.[1] "If the term 'reading' is immediately appropriate to the book, is the same true of the painting? If, by the extension of the meaning, one speaks of 'reading' in connection with a painting, the question arises of the validity and the legitimacy of that extension."[2] To respond to that double question and to break with the convenient immediacy of a way of speaking that had been blindly accepted, Marin demanded a rigorous definition of the "theoretical levels and fields of pertinence of the notion of reading as applied to the painting."

Rather than retracing Marin's analysis of Poussin's letter, let us turn to his conclusion. It stressed both the irreducibility and the interrelation of two forms of representation, each of which always exceeds the other—the text and the image, discourse and painting.

The highest meaning operates in the gap between the visible—what is shown, figured, represented, staged—and the legible—what can be said, enunciated, declared; a gap that is both the site of an opposition and the place where an exchange takes place between the two registers, a gap that raises the question of the painting, of this painting of *La manne,* admitting that "manna" (*Mann-hu:* "What is this?") was the question the Hebrews asked about the whitish, sugary, granulated substance, for which they named the thing itself, and by means of which they read the miraculous event. "Manna," the "What is this?"—a thing unknown, unnameable, illegible, out of the picture; the "this is my body" of the eucharistic formula by which an edible word is articulated *legibly* in the mystery.[3]

"Registers," as Marin calls them, intersect, connect, and respond to one another but never merge. The painting has the power to show what words cannot express and what no text can make readable. Inversely, what Marin calls "the failure of the visible in texts" makes the image foreign to the logic of the production of the meaning borne by figures of discourse. Marin reworked this same tension in *Des pouvoirs de l'image,* the last book he read over and corrected before his death. Obviously, the subject matter of that work was a good deal broader, since it posed the more philosophical question of "transcendental conditions—of possibility and legitimacy—of the appearance of the image and of its efficacy," and since, as a response to that question, he reserved the last of his *gloses* (commentaries) for light, which authorizes the image and the gaze: "Light and its inseparable and transcendental inverse, shadow, the invisible of light within light itself. The supreme conditions of seeing and of being seen, light is invisible as such—in its very being."[4] Nonetheless this work, which partakes of the philosophical, the aesthetic, and the theological (as, for example, in the brilliant "vision" before the "secret of transfiguration" in his eighth *glose*), *also* gives the measure, in my opinion, of the importance of Marin's work for the major debates that in recent years have traversed the field of history and, beyond it, all the humane sciences. This is why I shall take it as my point of departure.

Marin's first proposition is this: "The power of the image? Effect/representation in the double sense that we have said, of the presentification of the absent—or the dead—and of autorepresentation instituting and situating the subject of the gaze within the register of affect and meaning, the image is both the instrumentalization of force, the means of strength, and its foundation as a power."[5] A double meaning and a double function are thus assigned to representation: to make an absence present, but also to exhibit its own presence as image, hence to constitute the person who looks at it as the looking subject.

As was his custom, Marin returns to older definitions of the word "representation," using them in a fruitful tension as both the object and the instrument of his analysis. In its 1727 edition, Furetière's *Dictionnaire* identifies two apparently contrary families of meaning: "*Représentation*: image that recalls absent objects to us in idea and in memory, and that paints them for us as they are." In the first part of this definition, representation shows the "absent object" (thing, concept, or person) by substituting for it an "image" capable of representing it adequately. To represent is thus to make things known through the mediation of "the painting of an object," "by words and by gestures," "by some figures, by some marks"—as in enigmas, emblems, fables, and allegories. To represent in the political and juridical sense is also "to take the place of someone, to have his authority in hand." Similarly, the *représentant* is defined in two ways, as "he who, in a public function, represents an absent person who should be there," and as "those who are called to a succession as if being in the place of the person whose right they have." In this acceptation, which is rooted in the older and material meaning of the *représentation* as the effigy that took the place of the dead king on his funeral bier ("When one goes to see dead princes in their processional bed, one sees only their representation, the effigy"), there is a radical distinction between the absent person or thing "represented" and what makes it present or known. Hence a decipherable relation is postulated between the visible sign and what it signifies.

But in Furetière's *Dictionnaire* the term has a second meaning: "*Représentation*: is said at the Palace of the exhibition of something." This led to defining the verb *représenter* as "also means to appear in person and exhibit things." Here representation is the showing of a presence, the public presentation of a thing or a person. In the particular and codified modality of its exhibition, it is the thing or the person that constitutes its own representation. The referent and its image are the same, one body, adhering to one another: "*Représentation*: is sometimes said of living persons. One says, with a grave and majestic countenance, 'There is a person with a fine representation' [Voilà une personne de belle représentation]."

Marin always kept these two definitions together in his reflections on the theory of representation, which ranged from his book on Pascal and on Arnaud and Nicole's *Logique de Port-Royal*[6] through *Le portrait du roi (Portrait of the King)* to *Les pouvoirs de l'image*. Clearly the first definition occupies a more important place in his thought, since it fits neatly into the representational theory of the sign elaborated by the grammarians and logicians of Port-Royal. And if that construction had a particular pertinence for him, it was because it designates and articulates the two operations of representation when it renders present what is absent: "One of the most operational of the models constructed to explore the functioning of modern representation—be it linguistic or visual—is the one that proposes taking into consideration the dual dimension of its mechanism: the 'transitive' or transparent dimension of the statement (every representation *represents* something); the 'reflexive' or opaque dimension (every representation *presents itself* representing something)."[7] This way of understanding how the representational machinery functions was an inspiration for historians who were intent on resisting the formalist seductions of a structural semiotics that lacked historicity and eager to shake off the inertia and the narrow, univocal view of the conventional history of mentalities.

By taking as his point of departure "the construction effected, in the heart of the French seventeenth century, by the logicians of Port-Royal," Marin hoped to avoid "epistemological anachronisms and their retrospective illusions." Stating that "the theory of representation itself had a history,"[8] he read the Port-Royal conceptual elaboration both as an end point in Western thought on representation and as a singular construction that took as the matrix of a theory of the sign the theological model of the Eucharist. It is this model that permits an understanding, in *Portrait of the King,* of how the representation of the monarch operates in a Christian society. Like the Eucharist, the portrait of the king—in painting or in writing—is simultaneously the representation of an absent historical body, the fiction of a symbolic body (in which the kingdom replaces the church), and the real presence of a sacramental body visible in the species that conceals it.[9] In *La parole mangée (Food for Thought),* the same eucharistic model explains the representational theory of the sign as it is stated in part 1, chapter 4, of the *Logic* of Port-Royal, "Of the Ideas of Things and the Ideas of Signs," a section added to the 1683 edition, published twenty years after the first edition of 1662.[10] After recalling the explicit criteria by which that text distinguishes various categories of signs (certainty and probability, continuity and discontinuity, what is natural and what is instituted), Marin shows that the coherence in the series of examples proposed lies, implicitly, in a reference to the theology of the Eucharist. In conclusion, he emphasizes the connections, for the logicians of Port-Royal, between the eucharistic theory of the utterance and the linguistic theology of the Eucharist: "We have seen in what sense the theological body can be said to be the semiotic function itself. Moreover, we have clarified how it was possible in 1683 for the Port-Royal logicians to believe that there existed a perfect adequation between the Catholic dogma of [the real presence] on the one hand and a semiotic theory of meaningful representation on the other."[11]

By connecting the two dimensions—transitive and reflexive—of modern representation to their historicity, Marin shifted scholarly thought in the direction of a study of the techniques and mechanisms by which representations present themselves as representing something. In the introduction to his *L'opacité de la peinture,* he recalls the heuristic effects of displacement that led him from a structuralist semiotics founded on a strict analysis of the linguistic production of meaning to an "insistence particularly focused on exploring the modes and modalities, the means and procedures, of the presentation of representation." Hence a new question, rediscovered and transferred from one book to another:

From that moment on, it was the specific modes particular to the articulation of reflexive opacity and the transitive transparency of representation in the field of the visual arts; it was the figures and configurations—historical and cultural, ideological and political—that this articulation took on, in singular fashion, in a given work, a given command, a given program; it was all these domains of indissolubly historical and theoretical objects that turned out to be the goals of investigation.[12]

Hence also Marin's interest in things that hint at the reflexive function of representation: in a painting, the frame and the ornament, the decor, the architecture represented;[13] for the text, the entire set of discursive and material devices that make up the formal apparatus of the statement.[14] Here Marin's work intersected the work of other scholars who were uncomfortable with an absolute text stripped of its materiality and historicity and who argued for paying greater heed to the way "forms effect meanings" and to "the relation of form to meaning," as D. F. McKenzie put it.

More generally, the concept of representation, as Marin understands it and manipulates it, was a valuable base (and perhaps a more efficacious one than the notion of mentality) for identifying and articulating the many relations that individuals or groups cultivate with the social world. It helped to note, first, the operations of organization and classification that produce the many configurations by which reality is perceived, constructed, and reconstructed; next, the practices and signs that make a social identity recognizable, that exhibit a unique way of existing in the world, and that symbolically signify a status, a rank, or a power; and finally, the institutionalized signs by which the "representers" (single individuals or collective instances) visibly incarnate—"presentify"—the coherence of a community, the force of an individual, or the permanence of a power. Marin's work thus functioned, with the discretion typical of him, to modify (more than is thought) the way historians changed their comprehension of the social world. In fact, it obliged them to rethink the relations between the modalities of the exhibition of the social being or the political power and the mental representations—in Mauss's and Durkheim's sense of collective representations—that grant (or refuse) credence and credit to the visible signs and dramatized forms that help make power, sovereign or social, recognizable as power.

Marin's work thus permits us to understand how confrontations based on brute force or pure violence changed into symbolic struggles—that is, into struggles whose weapons and rewards were representations. The image has this power because it "effects a substitution of the external manifestation in which a force appears, only to annihilate another force in a death struggle, with signs of force, or rather, signals and indications that need only be *seen, noted, shown,* then *narrated* and *reiterated* in order for the force of which they are the effects to be *believed*."[15] This statement returns to the general hypothesis underlying the argument in *Portrait of the King,* which asserts that "the representational framework operates the transformation of force into potential and of force into power, and that twice—on the one hand by *modalizing* the force as potential, and on the other by *valorizing* potential as a legitimate and obligatory state and justifying it."[16]

Pascal is not far off. When Pascal dissects the mechanisms of a "display" (*montre*) that addresses the imagination and produces belief, he contrasts those who need such trappings with those for whom they are totally superfluous. The first group includes judges and physicians:

This mystery has been well known to our magistrates. Their red robes, their ermines in which they wrap themselves like furry cats, the courts where they judge, the *fleurs de lis,* all this august apparel was very necessary, and if physicians did not have their cassocks and slippers and learned doctors their square bonnets and robes that are too large, never would they have duped the world which cannot resist such an authoritative show. If the magistrates had true justice and if the physicians had the true art of healing, they would have no use for square bonnets. . . . But having only imaginary sciences, they must take on these vain instruments that strike the imagination with which they are concerned, and through that, in effect, they attract respect toward themselves.

The only people who had no need to manipulate signs or make use of such machinery for producing respect were the military: "Only men of war have not disguised themselves in this way, because in effect their part is more essential; they establish themselves through force, the others through affectation."[17]

In Marin's reformulation of it, Pascal's opposition has a dual relevance for any history of the societies of the ancien régime. It allows us to situate the forms of symbolic domination (by the image, by display—*la montre*—or by trappings, *attirail,* a word also found in La Bruyère) as a corollary of the monopoly on the legitimate use of force that absolute power intended to reserve to itself. Force has not disappeared with the operation that transforms it into power. Pascal continues his thoughts on imagination: "Therefore our kings seek out no disguise. They do not mask themselves in extraordinary costumes to appear such; but they are accompanied by guards and halberdiers. Those armed and red-faced puppets who have hands and power for them alone, those trumpets and drums which go before them, and those legions round about them, make the stoutest tremble. They have not dress only, they have might." But that force, which is always at the disposition of the sovereign, is as if placed in reserve by the proliferation of devices (portraits, medals, eulogies, narratives, etc.) that represent the power of the king and are calculated to produce obedience and submission without recourse to violence. The instruments of symbolic domination thus guaranteed both "the negation and conservation of the absolute of force: negation, since force is neither exerted nor manifested, since it is at peace in the signs that signify and designate it, and conservation, since force through and in representation will give itself as justice, that is to say as law that obligatorily constrains under pain of death."[18]

The process of eradicating violence, whose manipulation is in theory taken over by the absolute state, makes possible the exercise of a political domination based on the ostentation of symbolic forms and on the representation of the monarchical power, given to be seen and believed even in the absence of the king by signs of his sovereignty. One might add, prolonging this encounter between Marin and Norbert Elias, that it was that same pacification (at least relative pacification) of the social sphere between the Middle Ages and the seventeenth century that transformed open and brutal social clashes into struggles between representations in which the stakes were the ordering of the social world, hence the recognition of the rank of each estate, each body, each individual.

It was, in fact, on the credit granted (or refused) to the representations of itself a political power or a social group put forth that the authority of the first and the prestige of the second depended. Marin makes use of that notion to trace the dual history of modalities for instilling belief and of forms of belief. His works thus combine in a single approach an analysis of the mechanisms—discursive or formal, rhetorical or narrative—that are intended to constrain readers (or spectators), that subjugate or "trap" them, and a study of the possible failure of these mechanisms of persuasion, which are all the more potent for being dissimulated, but all the more inefficacious if they are taken apart. Tension necessarily brings us back to Pascal, who lays bare the workings of the representative machinery and the conditions of its credibility. In the introduction to his *Portrait of the King*, Marin quotes a passage from Pascal that shows how the mechanisms for changing force into power produce respect and terror by reminding spectators of the violence that lies at the origin of power and on which power was founded:

The custom of seeing kings accompanied by guards, drums, officers, and all those things that bend the machine toward respect and terror, causes their face to imprint on their subjects respect and terror even when they appear by themselves, because one does not separate in thought their persons from the retinues with which they are ordinarily seen. And the world, which does not know that the effect comes from this custom, thinks that it comes from a natural force; and from that come these words: "The character of Divinity is imprinted on his face, etc."[19]

The tension between techniques for making people believe and belief itself takes us back to the *Logic* of Port-Royal. In part 2, chapter 14, "On the Propositions in Which One Gives to Signs the Name of Things," the authors identify two conditions necessary in order for the relation of representation to be intelligible: first, the knowledge of the sign as sign, in its difference from the thing signified; second, the existence of shared conventions that regulate the relation of sign to thing. The text notes reasons for a possible deviation and a possible incomprehension of representation. An arbitrary, "extravagant" relation may have been established between the sign and the signified, as when someone takes a fancy to call a stone a horse or an ass the king of Persia. Or the person for whom the communication is destined might lack the "preparation" needed to understand the sign as a sign. This is why one can give "instituted" signs the names of things—as, for example, in parable or prophecy—only when those one speaks to are capable of conceiving that the sign is the thing signified in signification and figure alone. Although Marin has concentrated on the discursive or visual mechanisms aimed at manipulating readers, making them believe what one wants, his work, and the reference to Port-Royal that lies behind it, aids in thinking about the very conditions for the success or failure of that intention. In this his work directly intersects Michel de Certeau's investigation of forms of belief. De Certeau states, "I define 'belief' not as the object of believing (a dogma, a program, etc.) but as the subjects' investment in a proposition, the *act* of saying it and considering it as true—in other words, a 'modality' of the assertion and not its content."[20]

The preconditions for belief refer back, first, to the places and forms of the inculcation of conventions and to the modalities of the "preparation" required for understanding the principles of representation as described by the logicians of Port-Royal. Those preconditions also suppose that reading, deciphering, and interpretation are never either totally controlled or totally constrained by discourses and images. Admittedly, one cannot find in Marin any theory of reception or any history of reading. Still, his painstaking efforts to comprehend "the stratagems, ruses, and machinations"[21] put into play by texts and paintings in order to impose a univocal signification and to enunciate and produce their correct interpretation seem to me to rest on the postulate that the reader or spectator can always rebel. Subjugating readers or spectators to meaning is not an easy task, and the subtlety of the traps laid for them is only as great as their capacity, expert or rudimentary, for making use of their liberty.

As with Michel Foucault, for whom analyzing the apparatus of discipline does not lead to the conclusion that society is necessarily disciplined, for Marin, taking apart the textual machinery that constructs the targeted reader as an effect of the message emitted does not oblige anyone to suppose that real readers behave exactly like the "simulacrum-reader" of discourse. Very clever artifices can be used, and authors can pull off brilliant coups: Marin cites the example of Paul Pellisson-Fontanier, who presented a "Project for the History of Louis XIV" in such a way that its historical narrative would be interpreted as a discourse of praise. Marin remarks, "What is not said at the sending (epithets and eulogies) is—necessarily—said at the reception. That which is not represented in the narrative and by the narrator is so at the narratee's reading in the name of effect of the narrative."[22] Still, such ingenuity turned to producing effects (always thought of as necessary) can never be sure of its readers, whose lack of knowledge or ill will might hinder persuasion. It is that potential liberty, never mentioned but always dreaded, that justifies both Pellisson's discursive machinations and Marin's painstaking exploration of how they work. That same liberty might provide the basis for another investigation, complementary to Marin's, identifying its limits and figures, its regularities and singularities.

In this tension between the effects of meaning that discourses or paintings aim for and their decipherment, relations between the text and the image have always had great importance for Marin. In his last book, *Des pouvoirs de l'image,* his project was not to analyze the procedures for presenting representation (as in the essays in *L'opacité de la peinture*) but rather to study texts that, in a variety of ways, recognize and test the powers of images. He justifies his interest in these terms:

It is in this failure of the visible in the texts—a "visible" that is nonetheless their object—that the texts thus glossed and interglossed derive, by that strange referentiality, a renewed capacity for approaching the image and its powers, as if writing and its specific powers were excited and exalted by an object that, by its semiotic heterogeneity, would necessarily elude their all-powerful grasp; as if the desire for writing (concerning the image) was trying its hand at self-accomplishment in imagination by moving out of language into what in many ways constitutes its inverse or its other, the image.[23]

Défaillance du visible aux textes; hétérogénéite sémiotique between the image and writing: these formulas are a valuable starting place for anyone who refuses to equate all symbolic productions—images, but also rituals or "the practice of everyday life"—with textuality. Against that position, which denies all the basic distinctions of historical work (between text and contextualization, between discourse and image, between practice and writing), we need to posit a radical difference between the logic at work in the production of discourses and other sorts of logic inherent in visualization *(la mise en vision),* rite, and common sense. Marin's work has always been founded on an acute awareness of this heterogeneity, hence of the historicity and the discontinuity of symbolic operations.

This makes Marin's work particularly to the point for anyone who holds, against the more abrupt declarations of the "linguistic turn" or the "semiotic challenge," that the practices constituting the social world and all symbolic forms that do not make use of writing cannot be reduced to the principles that command discourses. Recognizing that past realities are for the most part accessible only through texts intended to organize them, describe them, prescribe or proscribe them does not in itself oblige us to postulate that the lettered, logocentric, hermeneutic logic governing the production of discourses is identical to the practical logic regulating behaviors or the "iconic" logic governing works of art. That practical or iconic logic cannot be reduced to discourse suggests a necessary prudence in the use of the category of "text," a term too often improperly applied to forms or practices whose modes of construction and principles of organization have nothing in common with discursive strategies. Hence the tension that inhabits the texts studied in *Des pouvoirs de l'image,* all of which face the same difficulty, evoked by Marin in the context of Diderot's *Salons:* "How to make an image with words, or . . . how to give to an image constructed in and by words their own power, or inversely, how to transfer to words, to their arrangement and to their figures, the power that the image conceals by its very visuality, the imposition of its presence."[24] Despite all the art of ecphrasis, with this necessary but impossible transposition the varied forces and the powers of the image and of language stand out in their singularity.

The concept of representation, as Marin understands and uses it, is doubly pertinent. First, considered as an essential instrument for comprehending the models of thought and the mechanisms of domination of the society of the French classical age, the concept has obliged historians to banish from their repertory some anachronistic notions applied to realities that were totally foreign to them. The introduction to Marin's *Portrait of the King* describes this process with acuity. He first notes "the prominence that the grammarians and logicians of Port-Royal gave to the notion of representation, as well as the general equivalence they posed or presupposed between it and the notion of sign at whatever level on which they analyzed language (term, proposition, discourse) and in whatever domain that language belonged (verbal, written, iconic)."[25] Next Marin identifies the eucharistic matrix of that theory, then he recognizes the modalities and the effects of the mechanism of representation in the political sphere. The operation of knowing is thus solidly connected to the notional tools that contemporaries themselves used to render their own society less opaque to their understanding.

Beyond this first, historically localized use, the notion of representation took on a broader relevance to designate the set of dramatized and "stylized" forms (Max Weber's term) thanks to which individuals, groups, and powers construct and propose an image of themselves. As Pierre Bourdieu wrote, "The representation which individuals and groups inevitably project through their practices and properties is an integral part of social reality. A class is defined as much by its *being-perceived* as by its *being*, by its consumption—which need not be conspicuous in order to be symbolic—as much as by its position in the relations of production (even if it is true that the latter governs the former)."[26] Understood in these terms, the concept of representation leads to thinking of the social world and the exercise of power according to a relational model. The modalities of presentation of the self are of course commanded by the social properties of the group or by the resources appropriate to a power. They are not, for all that, an immediate, automatic, objective expression of the status of the first or the power of the second. Their efficacy depends on the perception and judgment of those who receive them, on the degree of adherence or distance vis-à-vis the mechanisms of presentation and persuasion put into operation.

In the seventeenth century, that plurality of appreciations was worrisome. Hence the search for necessary relations and stable equivalencies in treatises on civility, between rank and seeming; in political ritual, between the principle of monarchical sovereignty and the forms of its symbolic expression; in the theory of the sign, between the thing that represents and the thing represented. Marin was primarily interested in the conventions that fixed and stabilized social operations and guaranteed full efficacy to symbolic modes of political domination that were all the more powerful because the people they forced into submission knew them and recognized them as legitimate. But between display and imagination, between the proposed representation and the constructed meaning, discordances arose—not only in the less rigidly codified societies after the Revolution, but even during the seventeenth century. Listen to La Bruyère:

You are wrong, Philemon, if with that shiny carriage, that large number of rascals who follow you, and those six animals who drag you along, you think anyone esteems you more highly: one sweeps away all those trappings, which are foreign to you, to penetrate to you yourself, a fatuous nobody. It is not that we must at times pardon someone who, with a large suite, rich clothing, and a magnificent carriage and attendants, thinks himself of higher birth and sharper wit: he reads that in the countenance and in the eyes of all who speak with him.[27]

On the one hand, then, we have a recognition of the strength of representation, which manipulates the receiver, makes him recognize the rank and merit behind the "show," and transforms him into a mirror in which the powerful see and are persuaded of their own power. Yet the text hints at failed deception, artifice unveiled, and a perceptible gap between the signs exhibited—the ostentatious "trappings"—and the reality they cannot hide.

Marin's work has always treated the space between the overwhelming power of representation and its possible denials. By that fact, his works are manna to be dipped into with both hands by all whose operational space is a critical study of the place where works, their circulation, and their meanings and interpretations interconnect. That intersection of questions long considered separately has a fundamental aim: to comprehend how the way an individual reader (or spectator) produces meaning is always enclosed within a series of constraints. These are, first, the effects of meaning aimed at by texts (or images) through their use of enunciative mechanisms and the organization of their utterances; next, the ways the forms that present the work for reading or viewing dictate how they will be deciphered; finally, the interpretive conventions of a time or a community. Just such a program dictated the organization of Marin's last study on the processes and effects of representation in the constitution of the political subject in sixteenth- and seventeenth-century Europe. The summary of his seminar at the Ecole des Hautes Etudes in 1990–91 expresses this aim clearly:

At the center of the problematics of the political realm a question of state power has been posed, focused particularly on how the government put that power into operation and on techniques for creating the consensus necessary to its constitution and its reproduction. How, in that era, did people analyze and construct the various forms of emotional logic that underlay individual or collective behavior, and how were those logics used and developed, for purposes of subjugation, in the manipulation of passions?[28]

Not enough time has gone by to respond to this question, even though in 1991–92, in a seminar that was to be his last, Marin returned to the chiasmus of political power and theatrical representation, crossing the figure of the king as author (James I as author of the *Basilikon Dōron*) with that of the poet as king (Prospero/Shakespeare in *The Tempest*).[29] He did not have time to give us his answer, but by leaving us his questions Marin also suggested a possible approach:

How are we to traverse this text, in its intimacy, without being torn as we leave it? We would have to be just as familiar with the text as someone who habitually takes the rue Traversière (in the twelfth *arrondissement*) *en empruntant* [taking, borrowing], with swift steps, a portion of its course without lingering out of curiosity or pausing out of interest. Simply to move on more quickly to other places or to open up other spaces more easily. This is also the sense of *la traverse:* "a private road notably shorter than the main route or leading to a place to which the high road does not go," perhaps with surprise or astonishment. The shortcut I am taking, surprisingly, leads me elsewhere, where "the high road does not go"; to a different destination that I did not even suspect—discovery. This was not where I wanted to go, yet secretly this place turns out to be that of a true desire; of the desire for truth.[30]

PART 3

Figuration and Habitus:
Norbert Elias

EIGHT

Self-consciousness
and the Social Bond

Die Gesellschaft der Individuen (The Society of Individuals),[1] published in German in 1987 and awarded the Premio Europeo Amalfi as the best work in sociology published that year, is perhaps one of the best possible introductions to the thought and work of Norbert Elias. For one thing, it brings together three texts written by Elias at three different moments in his life. The first, which gives the work its title, was written as part of the lengthy summary that concludes his major work, *Über den Prozess der Zivilisation (The Civilizing Process),* published in Basel in 1939.[2] For reasons he never explained, however, Elias removed this text when his book was in proofs. Sent to a Swedish journal to be published separately, the text instead remained unpublished when the review never saw the light of day. It was not until 1983 that it was revised and reproduced and circulated at the University of Stockholm, and not until 1987 that it became easily accessible. Its importance within Elias's work is nonetheless capital, because it outlines the theoretical bases for his analyses in *The Civilizing Process.*

In 1939, when that work was published, Elias was living in London. He had fled Nazi Germany in April 1933, and with the support of a committee to aid Jewish refugees, it took him only three years to complete that enormous project. The point of departure for *The Civilizing Process* lay in works Elias read in the British Library, where he discovered etiquette manuals almost by chance: "I came across the books on etiquette. I once ordered one of them by chance; I think it was Courtin, and I found it thoroughly exciting. . . . Now I suddenly had material that showed how different standards were in earlier times and allowed reliable statements to be made on how they had changed."[3]

This discovery launched a line of research that rooted the changes in norms of comportment between the Middle Ages and the nineteenth century in transformations in the structure of personality—transformations that had both required such changes and made them possible—and Elias then moved on to seek the conditions for transformations in psychic economy in changes in ways to exert power and exist in society.

The Civilizing Process suffered many tribulations. Elias first sent it to Breslau (now Wrocław) to be printed; a first edition of volume 1 was published at Prague in 1937, with the printing completed later at Breslau. The expenses were paid by Elias's father, who had refused to leave Germany and had obtained permission from the National Socialist administration to draw money out of his bank account to pay the printer. The entire work was eventually published in Basel by Fritz Karger, who had founded a publishing house, the Haus zum Falken, that specialized in works by emigrants from Germany. Once again the going was rough. As Elias later recalled, "When the second volume was ready, I managed to find a publisher in Switzerland who was prepared to publish the book if he was sent the proofs. So my poor father had to go back to the Nazi authorities and ask for an export license for the printer. He achieved all that. Without my father's help I should not have been able to publish the book. I often think that it was only saved by a hair's breadth."[4] The book made little stir in a Europe at war: only ten reviews were published between 1938 and 1942 (among them those of Franz Borkenau in the *Sociological Review* in 1938 and 1939; those of the psychoanalyst S. H. Foulkes in *Internationale Zeitschrift für Psychoanalyse* in 1939 and of Raymond Aron in *Les Annales Sociologiques* in 1941).[5] Thus one of the most important books of the twentieth century long remained unknown and was rescued from oblivion only when it was republished in 1969, and especially with the paperback edition in 1976, which became a best-seller.

The second text in *The Society of Individuals*, "Problems of Self-consciousness and the Image of Man," was written in several stages during the 1940s and 1950s, and its final draft probably dates from the mid-1950s. It lies under the shadow of two historical experiences: on the one hand, World War II and the Shoah (Elias's mother presumably died in Auschwitz in 1941; his father had died the previous year at Breslau); on the other, the Cold War and its confrontation between socialist regimes and capitalist, liberal nations. From 1945 to 1954 Elias held no university post. The book he had published in 1939 had no resonance in Great Britain, and its author had to make a living giving private lessons, teaching adult education courses, and lecturing at the London School of Economics and at Bedford College. One experience during those ten postwar years that left a particular mark on "Problems of Self-consciousness and the Image of Man" was Elias's participation in the Group Analytic Society, founded by several psychiatrists grouped around S. H. Foulkes, who was close to Anna Freud. Elias, who knew Sigmund Freud's work well, was deeply involved in the activities of this small society, which preached group therapy. He himself directed therapeutic groups, and that practice, founded on the relationships created among the individuals who participated in the analysis, is reflected in his theoretical thought of that time.[6] That period of Elias's life ended in 1954, when he accepted a post as lecturer in sociology that had been offered to him, on the initiative of Ilya Neustadt, at the University of Leicester. At age fifty-seven Elias thus had the first stable position in his academic career (from 1930 to 1933 he had been only an assistant at the University of Frankfurt).

The last text in *The Society of Individuals,* "Changes in the 'We-I' Balance," dates from thirty years later and was written during the winter of 1986–87. Elias was by then living in Amsterdam, where he had moved in 1984. Changes in the world at large find an echo in this text: the confrontation between the two superpowers and the risks of nuclear conflict (for instance, Elias alludes to the Chernobyl disaster); the process of supranational integration in Europe; and the tensions created by the presence of immigrant populations, whom Elias divides into the "established" and the "outsiders." He first arrived at that conceptual pairing when he taught sociology at Leicester,[7] and he returned to it as a way to understand the situation of Jews in imperial Germany and the Weimar Republic, who were stigmatized as "outsiders" but saw themselves as "established."[8]

Each one of the three essays that make up *The Society of Individuals* is built on the theoretical and conceptual base that Elias forged during the 1930s, but because he reformulated it at various times and applied it to historical realities that had changed profoundly, that base became richer, more flexible, and more complex. Tracing the trajectory of Elias's thought provides a first reason to read this work.

Another, more fundamental, reason has to do with the book itself. In these three texts Elias takes on the task of challenging an opposition between the individual and society that had been given or thought of as self-evident. He notes the various expressions of that duality. It inhabits ordinary experience, which spontaneously contrasts the "I," seen in positive terms, with society, seen as external and hostile. It underlies the traditional models of comprehending history: on one side, an emphasis on the glorification of the individual, whose free intentions and voluntary actions are supposed to produce historical evolutions; on the other, the dissolution of individualities in an ongoing historical process commanded by necessity. It divides sociological theories into two groups: those that postulate, implicitly, that the individual is anterior to and exterior to society, which is held to be the aggregation or sum of those autonomous individualities; and those that conceive of societies as great machines whose operations are totally independent of individual intentions. It exists in psychology, where the individual psychology uniquely concerned with the single subject opposes a social psychology that knows only groups. Elias set himself the task of displacing or going beyond these dichotomies and, by that means, shattering falsely evident perceptions or conceptions. To do this he had to show that positions that are apparently among the least reducible to one another share a profound solidarity—the very precondition that makes contrasting them possible.

This was far from an easy task. In the first place, it went against the grain of the force of words and of an automatic use of commonly accepted lexical oppositions: individual versus society; consciousness versus the external world; subject versus object, and so on. It also went against deep-seated ideological investments in favor of either the liberty of the individual (in liberal thought) or society's demands (in socialist theories). Finally—and above all—it had to combat the projection as universally valid of a conception, specific to post-seventeenth-century Western European societies, of self-consciousness and a representation of the "I" as separate and autonomous. A different understanding of the relation between the individual and society thus required setting up a distance from present-day schemes of perception and judgment (which the sociologists shared) and in that way objectivizing categories of thought or experience that seem self-explanatory and universal.[9]

This task required specific intellectual instruments, produced either by reusing old notions in unexpected and paradoxical ways (for instance, in the expression "the society *of* individuals") or by proposing new concepts. One of these was "figuration," or configuration, which permits thinking of the social world as a web of relations; another was "social habitus," which Elias defines as the "specific make-up" that "each individual, different as he or she may be from all the others . . . shares with other members of his or her society." The notion of social habitus can be applied on various levels—that of the nation-state, with the formation of distinctive "national characteristics"; that of a particular social form (for instance, the court society); or that of the ethnic group, clan, kinship group, or family.

The basic thrust of the texts that make up *The Society of Individuals* is to historicize the way of thinking that defines the self and the social world as distinct, opposed, and conflictual realities. At what point in the civilizing process did such a conception appear? To what particular social configuration does it correspond? These were the questions Elias set out to resolve.

To follow Elias's thought, we need first to pause over the concept of configuration. In his many books Elias used a variety of images to elucidate this notion, which considers the reciprocal dependencies binding individuals to one another to be the formative matrix of society. In the first study in *The Society of Individuals* he likens configuration to dancing:

Let us imagine as a symbol of society a group of dancers performing court dances, such as the *française* or *quadrille*, or a country round dance. The steps and bows, gestures and movements made by the individual dancer are all entirely meshed and synchronized with those of other dancers. If any of the dancing individuals were contemplated in isolation, the functions of his or her movements could not be understood. The way the individual behaves in this situation is determined by the relations of the dancers to each other. It is similar with the behaviour of individuals in general. Whether they meet as friends or enemies, parents or children, man and wife or knight and bondsman, king and subjects, manager and employees, however individuals behave is determined by past or present relations to other people. Even if they withdraw from all other people as hermits, gestures away from others no less than gestures towards them are gestures in relation to others. Of course, an individual can easily leave a dance if he wishes to, but people do not join up to form a society solely out of a desire for dance and play. What binds them to society is the fundamental disposition of their nature.[10]

Elsewhere Elias uses other figures to explain the "sociological theory of interdependence." In *The Court Society*, a work published only in 1969 but written in 1933 as a habilitation thesis at the University of Frankfurt, he used the image of a chess match:

Nothing better characterizes the problem of human interdependence than the fact that each act of a ruler, while perhaps coming closest to the ideal picture of an individual act based on free decision, makes the ruler dependent on the ruled through being directed at other people who could either oppose it or at least not respond in the expected way. This is exactly what the concept of interdependence expresses. As in a game of chess, each relatively independent act by an individual represents a move on the social chessboard which produces a counter-move by another individual—or frequently, in reality, by many other individuals—which limits the independence of the first and demonstrates his dependence.[11]

In *Was ist Soziologie? (What Is Sociology),*[12] published in 1970, the image Elias picks to clarify configuration (which "serves as a simple conceptual tool to loosen this social constraint to speak and think as if 'the individual' and 'society' were antagonistic as well as different") shifts from a game of chess to a card game:

If four people sit around a table to play cards together, they form a configuration. Their actions are interdependent. . . . The "game" is no more an abstraction than the "players." The same applies to the figuration by the four players sitting around the table. If the term "concrete" means anything at all, we can say that the figuration formed by the players is as concrete as the players themselves. By figuration we mean the changing pattern created by the players as a whole—not only by their intellects but by their whole selves, the totality of their dealings in their relationships with each other. It can be seen that this figuration forms a flexible latticework of tensions. The interdependence of the players, which is a prerequisite of their forming a figuration, may be an interdependence of allies or of opponents.[13]

Elias uses these images to propose a number of fundamental thoughts. For one thing, he points out that the concept of configuration is applied to social formations of highly varied scope, some immediately perceptible as a whole (the examples he gives in *What Is Sociology?* are "teachers and pupils in a class, doctors and patients in a therapeutic group, regular customers at a pub, children at a nursery school") and others (a village, a city, a nation) in which the whole is less obvious. What differentiates them is the varying modality of the chains of interdependence—which may be long or short, simple or complex—linking the individuals who compose them. For another thing, he rejects the substantialist mode of thought that sees reality only in corporeal and material things. For him, networks of relations are quite as "concrete" or "real" as the individuals who make them up. Finally, he suggests that it is reciprocal (which does not mean equal or balanced) dependencies that construct the subjects themselves. Subjects do not exist before or outside the relations that make them what they are at every moment in the social game. At court as on the chessboard, even the king is subject to this law: his capacity for movement is admittedly greater than that of those around him, but his fate nonetheless depends, finally, on the more constrained and more modest moves of those who are linked to him.

In *The Society of Individuals* Elias risks a different image, of another nature, to make the concept of configuration comprehensible and set it apart from spontaneous ways of thinking:

> To get a closer view of this kind of interrelationship one might think of the object from which the concept of the network is derived, a woven net. In such a net there are many individual threads linked together. Yet neither the totality of the net, nor the form taken by each thread in it, can be understood in terms of a single thread alone or even all the threads considered singly; it is understood solely in terms of the way they are linked, their relationship to each other. This linking gives rise to a system of tensions to which each single thread contributes, each in a somewhat different manner according to its place and function in the totality of the net. The form of the individual thread changes if the tension and structure of the whole net change. Yet this net is nothing other than a linking of individual threads; and within the whole each thread still forms a unity in itself; it has a unique position and form within it.[14]

Although it is true that the image of the net, unlike the figure of the group of dancers or chess or card players, suggests by its mere spatial dimension the complexity of the skein of relations that constitute a society, it ignores duration and history: "The individual actually grows . . . from a network of people existing before him into a network he helps to form."

Several assertions result from this way of thinking of the social world as a network of relations. The first has to do with the increasing density and complexity of the interdependencies among individuals, resulting from an increasingly marked differentiation of social functions. This is true for the history of humanity over the very long span, where two fundamental traits combine with it: the monopolizing of the control over violence on the part of a given group, which establishes its power by that means, and the division of tasks, which are doled out in hierarchical fashion among all the groups that make up a society. It is also true on the scale of each particular social formation—the court society, for example, where a closely observed differentiation of functions exercised in relation to the king brings a tight interdependence to those who assume those functions.

A second assertion makes the intensity and modality of the bonds of interdependence determine the structure of personality. By postulating the integrally social nature of mankind, Elias suggests that what is unique to humanity is given by the presence, within each individual, of the structures and the history of the social world to which he or she belongs. The processes that permit this incorporation of the collective into the singular are many, but all share a common matrix in the individual's inscription within a preexisting network of relations: "Without the assimilation of preformed social models . . . the child remains . . . little more than an animal." Thus Elias reformulates in a sociopsychological vein the theme of the "wild child," a topic that was popular throughout the nineteenth century, beginning with the memoirs of Jean-Marc-Gaspard Itard, a physician who wrote about Victor, the wild boy from the Aveyron, and that was prefigured in eighteenth-century fiction—for example, by Marivaux in *La dispute*, a play produced in 1744.

Finally, it is the balance of tensions proper to each configuration that permits a definition of the scope of the exercise of "liberty" or "power." Elias replaces the aporias of philosophical dissertations on liberty and determinism with a view that measures individuals' field of possibilities (therefore their "liberty") by their greater or lesser capacity to act on the network of interdependencies within which they operate. By that token, Elias suggests a negative definition of power, understood as a lesser submission to obligatory social constraints, and he shifts the old question of the role of the "great man" in history. If one man is "greater" than another (that is, freer), he owes it to a position within the structure of dependency relations that grants him a degree of initiative and capacity to act that other individuals lack. The classic example of such a position is the absolute king in the court society, since he is both an integral part of the court machinery, as are his courtier subjects, and endowed with a unique power to manipulate the network of relations and the balance of tensions that are the foundation of his domination.[15]

The central idea in *The Society of Individuals* is that the concept of the self—the separate, autonomous "I"—that poses the social world as external, even hostile, to it was born at a particular stage in the civilizing process, when a greater severity in "command over individual behavior" was necessary, as was rigorous self-control in public behavior.

This notion goes back to the basic thesis of Elias's masterly *Civilizing Process* of 1939, where he notes that between the Middle Ages and the nineteenth century, and for greater and greater segments of the population of the West, the necessary control of impulses was transferred from an exterior prohibition, imposed if need be by force, to a stable mechanism of self-restraint. For Elias, the essential transformation of the structure of personality resides in this shift in the mode of containing affect, henceforth consigned to an internalized mechanism for censorship rather than to an authority situated outside the individual.

Such a change could take place only under certain conditions: a marked differentiation of social functions and state monopoly of the exercise of violence.

As the social fabric grows more intricate, the sociogenetic apparatus of individual self-control also becomes more differentiated, more all-round and more stable. But the advancing differentiation of social functions is only the first, most general of the social transformations which we observe in enquiring into the change in psychological make-up [*psychische Habitus*] known as "civilization." Hand in hand with this advancing division of functions goes a total reorganization of the social fabric. It was shown in detail earlier why, when the division of functions is low, the central organs of societies of a certain size are relatively unstable and liable to disintegration. It has been shown how, through specific figurational pressures, centrifugal tendencies, the mechanisms of feudalization, are slowly neutralized and how, step by step, a more stable central organization, a firmer monopolization of physical force, are established. The peculiar stability of the apparatus of mental self-restraint which emerges as a decisive trait built into the habits of every "civilized" human being, stands in the closest relationship to the monopolization of physical force and the growing stability of the central organs of society. Only with the formation of this kind of relatively stable monopolies do societies acquire those characteristics as a result of which the individuals forming them get attuned, from infancy, to a highly regulated and differentiated pattern of self-restraint; only in conjunction with these monopolies does this kind of self-restraint [*Selbskontrollapparatur*] require a higher degree of automaticity, does it become, as it were, "second nature."[16]

This development established a decisive link between the process of construction of the modern state, in the absolutist form it took in Western societies, and the fashioning of a new psychic economy that permitted individuals to adjust their behavior to the new norms inculcated in them.

Such was the evolution that makes possible and thinkable the representation of the separate "I"—the autonomous *homo clausus* exterior to and anterior to the social world. On the one hand, the constitution of a private sphere of existence, free from the rules that govern public behavior, becomes a refuge for intimacy, and by that token a privileged place for the singularity of the subject. The affirmation of the irreducible originality of the "I," the primacy given to internal values, and the idea that a person's essence is expressed in private behaviors are all figures— thought and lived—of the dissociation of the individual from society. On the other hand, the internalizing of mechanisms for the regulation and censorship of affect, impulse, and emotion sets up a mechanism or device for control within individuals that is designated "conscience" or "reason." A basic duality is thus established between the subject and the world, conceived as two separate "realities."

The form of self-consciousness that characterizes both a social habitus in which the " 'we-I' balance" gives primacy to the "I" and a fundamental dualism that opposes, term by term, the interiority of consciousness and the reality of the external world—the subject and the object, the spirit and the body—is thus a particular and historically datable form of the way individuals conceive of their relation to the world. Hence Elias's philosophical iconoclasm, which sees the classical theory of cognition, as it developed from Descartes's *cogito,* as dependent on transformations in the structure of personality engendered by the construction of the modern state and the "civilizing process." However it is expressed, that theory contains two essential traits: it postulates the existence of a priori and universal forms of understanding; and it represents the subject as independent of other subjects and the world.

Elias borrows from Condillac to offer a fine parable of "thinking statues" to help his reader understand the vision of man he is challenging:

On the bank of a broad river, or on the steep slope of a high mountain, stands a row of statues. They cannot move their limbs. But they have eyes and can see. Perhaps ears as well, that can hear. And they can think. They have "understanding" [Verstand]. We can assume that they do not see each other, even though they well know that others exist. Each stands in isolation. Each statue in isolation perceives that something is happening on the other side of the river, or the valley. Each forms ideas of what is happening, and broods on the question [of] how far these ideas correspond to what is happening. Some think that such ideas simply mirror the happenings on the other side. Others think that much is contributed by their own understanding; in the end one cannot know what is going on over there. Each statue forms its own opinion. Everything it knows comes from its own experience. It has always been as it is now. It does not change. It sees. It observes. Something is happening on the other side. It thinks about it. But whether what it thinks corresponds to what is going on over there remains unresolved. It has no way of convincing itself. It is immobile. And alone. The abyss is too deep. The gap is unbridgeable.[17]

This parable enables Elias to mark his distance from classical philosophy, opposing to the immobility of the thinking statues the historicity of the categories of thought and experience, and to their isolation the insertion of every thinking subject within a network of relations that limits what it is possible to think. A critique of the classical philosophical tradition is one of the major constants in Elias's thought. It is rooted in his student years, when he studied philosophy (and medicine) at the University of Breslau, the city where he was born. In the autobiographical notes he published in 1990 Elias relates the friction between him and Richard Hönigswald, the neo-Kantian professor who was his thesis director. Tense relations became conflict in 1922, when Elias submitted a work titled "Idee und Individuum: Eine kritische Untersuchung zum Begriff der Geschichte." Elias tells us:

In the course of my work on my doctoral dissertation I had gradually—in painful arguments with myself—arrived at the conviction that the whole idea of a priori truth did not hold water. I could no longer ignore the fact that all that Kant regarded as timeless and as given prior to all experience, whether it be the idea of the causal connections or of time or of natural and moral laws, together with the words that went with them, had to be learned from other people in order to be present in the consciousness of the individual human being. As acquired knowledge they therefore formed a part of a person's store of experiences. And as this now seemed to me irrefutable, I wrote as much in my doctoral dissertation. Hönigswald pronounced it downright wrong. Without giving any reasons that I found convincing, he instructed me to change my argument. He could not accept it as it was. We both stood by our opinions—as I have done up to this day—until I had to admit that his power potential was greater than mine. I deleted the most explicit passages, toned down a few others, sent him the diminished product, which he accepted without comment, and I was thus made a D. Phil. of Breslau University.[18]

He defended his dissertation on 30 January 1924, and a short extract from it was printed.[19]

After 1925, when he settled in Heidelberg to write his habilitation thesis, Elias abandoned philosophy for sociology. But this initial formation left a lasting imprint on his thought. It gave him a culture that appears in the references (which are not abundant, however) in the three texts that make up *The Society of Individuals*. Out of the thirty or so authors Elias mentions, ten fit within the canon of classical philosophy (Plato and Aristotle, of course, but also Descartes, Spinoza, Berkeley, Locke, Hume, Kant, Hegel, and Husserl). Elias also mentions the masters of sociology—Comte, Marx, Weber, and Durkheim—Freud, the philosophers of history Spengler and Toynbee, three classic authors of German literature, Goethe, Rilke, and Thomas Mann, plus Sartre *(La nausée)* and Camus *(L'étranger)*. But the aporias encountered in his philosophical preparation encouraged Elias to reject the classical conception of the relation of humankind to the world. At least this was his view in a retrospective presentation of the intellectual itinerary that began with his 1924 dissertation: "Even in my dissertation, which, in view of the circumstances, was still written in a wholly philosophical style, with a consequent tendency to see human history as if it were the mental product of individual people, I had stated unambiguously that the traditional concept of the 'individual' needed to be developed further."[20] But that intellectual itinerary arrived at a new way of thinking only with Elias's conversion to sociology: he speaks of his "fight against the still dominant image of the person as *homo clausus*," but he states, "It took a great deal of time for me to move away from the dominant image of the human being sealed from the outside world, and to find my way to the opposite image of the individual fundamentally attuned to a world, to that which he or she is not, to other things and especially other people—a process closely linked to my decision to abandon the study of philosophy."[21]

Until the last years of his life, Elias held firm to his critical attitude toward classical philosophy, which he saw as guilty both of isolating the individual and of dissolving the historicity of categories of thought. In an interview given in 1985 he stated:

I think, based on an examination of the facts and not on simple opinion, that nothing exists like what Kant conceptualized speculatively with a priori or transcendental categories—that is, by postulating the existence of inborn forms of thought. I have indicated on several occasions that if Kant could consider reason to be given to us by nature, it was because in his times biology was not sufficiently developed to give the term "nature" a purely biological meaning. It seems to me absurd to think that concepts such as "cause," "substance," "nature," "natural laws," and others are given to human beings innately. Thus it is not I but the facts that show that the "a prioris" or the transcendental limits of knowledge do not exist.[22]

Against the Kantian concepts, Elias proposed another way of thinking that established the historical variability of forms of thought and of self-consciousness. The transformations of self-consciousness are governed by a paradoxical law: the thicker the reciprocal ties of dependence among individuals, the stronger their awareness of their autonomy. Thus one can understand why the representation of an "I" separate from the external world and independent of it was emphasized in nineteenth- and twentieth-century societies. In the second text in *The Society of Individuals,* Elias places this process of the reinforcement of individualization within the divorce that all democratic societies set up between the social "aspirations" of individuals, encouraged by the many possible destinies they might contemplate, and the limitations that hedge in their objective "chances for success" according to their position in society. The apparently open possibilities in a society that no longer puts differences of estate into a hierarchy engender competitions that are all the more painful for being based in the individual's ability to stand out in a world that denies the legitimacy of differentiation. The foiled ambition of all who fail to obtain the positions they aspire to changes into a frustration that imputes individual disappointments to the injustice of the social world. The tension between the wounded "I" and the cruel world outside makes the awareness of a radical separation between the person and society even more acute. The rivalries and bitterness of the democratic age thus transform the dichotomies constructed by the classical theory of knowledge into a widely shared experience.

The Society of Individuals is not just a book devoted to the historical conditions that led to the emergence of the modern concept of the individual, closed within the self and separated from society. The work also helps us understand the nature of the civilizing process, which Elias carefully distinguishes from biological processes. For him the very long-term changes that have profoundly modified the structure of the personality in Western Europe have three principal characteristics: they were irregular, with alternating spurts forward and stagnant moments; they were marked by gaps and discontinuities; they even saw regressions. Concerning the first of these, Elias stresses the advance of "civilization," made possible by a domestication of natural forces that in turn depended on the scientific revolution of the seventeenth century. Because it permits a greater differentiation of social functions, hence a greater interdependence, and because it supposes a mastery of immediate impulses, that domination, based on the conquests of modern physics, brings accelerated changes in psychic economy: "Control of nature, social control and self-control form a kind of chain ring; they form a triangle of interconnected functions which can serve as a basic pattern for the observation of human affairs. One side cannot develop without the others; the extent and form of one depend on those of the others; and if one of them collapses, sooner or later the others follow."[23]

The second trait of the evolution of the structure of personality lies in the potential discontinuities between the development of ties of interdependence among individuals and the form of their social habitus. Situations of that sort appear when, in a given configuration, there is a gap between the degree of social integration and the degree of fixity in the identity of the "we."[24] Elias is talking about discordances of this kind when he speaks of the "fossilization of the social habitus." He gives several examples. The first comes from contemporary African societies—societies of which he had firsthand knowledge from the two years he spent (1962 to 1964) as a professor at the University of Accra in Ghana. He stresses continued reliance on equating the "we" with the level of the ethnic or kinship group (which controls the distribution of public offices) within the process of construction of a national state that raises reciprocal dependence to a higher level. A second example points out the contrasts in the perpetuation of fixed collective identities on the level of national states in a world unified by interdependence on a planetary scale—as attested by the notion of the rights of man, which limits the systems of law particular to the various states in the name of each individual's membership in all of humanity, and given the risk of nuclear destruction, by the extension of the "survival unit" of humanity to the entire planet. Elias uses an excellent image to describe such instances of hysteresis (effects that lag behind their causes): "In relation to their own group identity and, more widely, their own social habitus, people have no free choice. These things cannot be simply changed like clothes."[25]

Finally, Elias does not exclude the possibility of regression during the course of the civilizing process:

The cumulative experience of many hundreds of generations was needed before foresight, and the ability to restrain and control internal and external natural forces, grew continuously. And because the development in this direction was not a biological one, was not, as often seems to be believed, rooted in human nature, it can also be reversed. The long chains of actions with their division of functions can shrink again. The social and psychological control of behaviour can be reduced—not just here and there, as happens constantly at all times, but over the whole of humanity. And the specific kind of behaviour referred to by words like "civilized" or "individualized" can give way to forms of behaviour and experience driven by short-term animal impulses.

But this text, haunted by the memory of Nazi brutality, the war, and the Shoah, ends with the assertion that the evolution of societies does not seem to permit a total reversal of direction:

Movements in both directions can always be observed in history, even if in the last millennia a particular movement has been predominant for long periods: the social and mental transformation of relatively small groups acting in a relatively short-term manner, with simple needs and uncertain fulfillment of these needs, into larger, more populous groups with a sharper division of functions, stronger control of behaviour, more complex and diverse needs and a more highly developed apparatus of co-ordination or government.[26]

This reflection, within a text written toward the end of the 1940s or in the early 1950s, seems to anticipate the objections that were raised when Elias's 1939 *Civilizing Process* gained a broader circulation. At that time, two major objections were raised concerning the ineluctable nature of that process.[27] The first of these started off by noting that constraints regulating behavior in contemporary societies are much relaxed. Some saw this "informalization" of social behavior—unaccompanied by any reduction in the density or the intensity of interdependencies—as an inversion of the course of increased severity in the control of affect since the Middle Ages.[28] This criticism itself raises some doubts, however, given that the process of "informalization" begun at the end of the nineteenth century and accentuated during the 1960s in no way involves a move backward toward substituting external constraints for the mechanisms of self-control. To the contrary, with less rigidity in the conventions that restrain spontaneous acts, the internalized control of impulses and emotions becomes even more necessary and more demanding. Elias presents sports, in active practice or as spectacle, as an exemplary figure of the "highly controlled decontrolling of emotional controls"—the strict constraint that limits the liberties taken in the repression of emotion.[29] Far from contradicting the civilizing process, the relaxation—temporary or lasting—of norms of behavior is an indication of an advance in its discipline.

The second major objection raised to Elias's *Civilizing Process* was founded in the fact—a reality he found sickening—of the return to barbarity in the middle of the century and in the land of high culture that was his homeland. Here too the contradiction is perhaps only apparent. Nazi violence can be seen as an extreme form of the state's monopolizing of the use of force—a force that in this case was turned against a portion of its own population. The Shoah, which relied on a painstaking differentiation of functions and tasks and occurred within a "pacified" society, is witness to a terrible connection between the most radical sort of state violence and the strict control of emotions demanded of those who carried out the "final solution."[30] In this case as in others (for example, the Terror), even if state violence creates occasions for the liberation of cruel impulses, it is only within the fabric of the process of "civilization," which reserves force to the state and disciplines individuals, that it can be established. For the worse.

The Society of Individuals casts light on yet another question raised by Elias's views—that of the modalities for the incorporation, within each of the individuals who make up a social formation, of the collective habitus proper to that configuration. Elias lays down two lines of investigation for comprehending the mechanisms that guarantee "social modeling," understood as fashioning a structure of personality common to the members of a given society. One focuses on "instinctive relations"—the first experiences of early childhood and the immediacy of relations with close family. The other stresses the role of the social institutions (the court is one example) charged with inculcating norms of behavior and rules of conduct. In both cases but in different ways, it is the individual's inscription within a network of relations that gives humankind its specific nature: "Man is to a special degree a social being, dependent on the society of other people."[31]

Norbert Elias died in Amsterdam on 1 August 1990, at age ninety-three. His long life merges with the history of our century at its most somber. Little by little, thanks to the publication of many previously unpublished pieces, to translations, and to monographs about him,

Elias's lifework appears for what it is: one of the most fundamental contributions of our times. *The Society of Individuals* gives us a better comprehension of the theoretical bases of his works—bases that were in opposition to the idealist philosophical tradition and were organized around the two central notions of process and configuration. But this book also shows Elias's interest in the transformations of the world in which he wrote. For him sociological analysis must always be both theoretical and empirical. In the study he wrote immediately after the war as in the essay written in the winter of 1986, he offers an original reading of the realities of our times that draws on his very long-range perspective. At every turn his perception is keen, rooting contemporary events in long-term evolution and proposing models of interpretation with a strong conceptual framework. Elias's sharp critique of the sociologists' "retreat into the present" after World War II should not be interpreted as a lack of interest in the present.[32] Quite the contrary. A difficult detour by way of history—which for Elias is not the event-crammed history of the historians—is the precondition for elaborating the true intelligibility of the contemporary world. In an age easily satisfied by summary judgments and fond of shortcuts, this is a lesson to ponder.

The Double Bind
and Detachment

In what tense are we to understand Norbert Elias's *Engagement und Distanzierung (Involvement and Detachment)*?[1] Does the history of the past decade oblige us to read the book in the past tense? The world has changed since Elias wrote the essays that make up this work. There is no longer the confrontation between two superpowers, the United States and the Soviet Union, that he analyzes here as the paroxysmal figure for an interdependence that neither partner could control or break. And with its disappearance, everything that expressed the inexorable rivalry between the two blocs has also gone: the Cold War and the clash of ideologies, the arms race, the atomic balance of terror. The collapse of one of the rivals has permitted a significant reduction of the nuclear arsenal and a search (as yet hesitant) for a form of international arbitration that might be capable of preventing, or at least limiting, the use of violence among nations. Our world today seems to have little in common with the world of the late 1970s in which Elias wrote or rewrote these texts.

Moreover, for Elias what is essential lies in what he calls "unplanned social processes" working within the necessary dynamics of configurations that impose their laws on social actors. Dramatic changes in the world situation seem to have thrust back into the limelight individual decisions, voluntary actions, and the unexpected, unpredictable initiatory event. By that token one might well wonder what pertinence there is in a thought whose central concepts, as they appear in this book (configuration, functional interdependence, the double bind, unplanned process, balance of tensions, and more), stress objective determinations that individuals may be unaware of but that hold their thoughts and actions strictly in check.

A "past tense" reading of *Involvement and Detachment,* though faithful to the spirit of our time, seems to me to miss what makes Elias's work perpetually relevant. The book is still important, first, because it is wholly germane to the debates that have invaded all the social sciences in recent years, history in particular, and that continue to do so today. The basic question in those debates is whether the models forged for the exact sciences can be used to make social processes intelligible. Criticizing the application of the "Galilean paradigm" (the expression is Carlo Ginzburg's)[2] to the study of human societies, Elias insists that an analytical approach, which proceeds by dismantling the component parts in order to know the whole, is inadequate to account for complex organizations and configurations. Configurations, he states, are defined by the system of relations interconnecting their elements, not by a simple juxtaposition of those elements. Hence the need for (and the legitimacy of) an approach that breaks with representations of the autonomous subject that were set up in the seventeenth century and takes as its prime object the interdependencies, close or remote, perceived or invisible, within which individuals are "chained."

In the two fragments on contemporary biology and astronomy that end the book, Elias goes one step further to stress that models proper to the physical and chemical sciences are inadequate to a grasp of "integrated structures" of a "higher level of integration" (137) that result from biological or cosmological processes. The same sort of remark applies to the natural sciences, where it marks both the limits of a method that operates by separating and classifying elements and the need for a diametrically different approach: a model can be found by studying the most complex organizations, whose instrument is "synthesis," for constructing "models"—a "model of models" (127). This leads Elias to a close critique of the notions and representations that hinder comprehension of evolution taking place on a higher level of integration: examples are the difficulties involved in imagining processes that have no beginning, the temptation to apply to all organizations the commanding structure of physical and chemical phenomena, and the definition and isolation of bodies of scientific knowledge according to objects supposed to be proper to that domain. One can easily find in Elias's pages on the natural sciences and cosmology—whose validity is a matter for specialists to decide—themes that he developed further in the context of human societies in his *Die Gesellschaft der Individuen (The Society of Individuals)*. In particular, we find the essential idea that social configurations, organized into a hierarchy according to their level of integration, cannot be understood based on the atomistic representation of the isolated "I"—the independent individual.[3]

The concept of configuration, as Elias constructs it, was immediately useful to the thoughts and discussions that emerged when interactionist approaches were applied to the study of history. Historians (in particular those who practice "microhistory" in the Italian *microstoria* tradition) rejected the concentration on structures and positions—hence on social groups, understood as abstract entities in a hierarchy—that had long been the rule in favor of small-scale observation of the networks and situations in which individuals are the actors.[4] This shift is legitimate and fruitful, on condition (Elias reminds us) that we remember not to limit the ties of dependency between individuals to ones they may have experienced or been aware of. Situations for interaction and networks of relations are always connected to remote and invisible determinations that both make them possible and give them structure. As is often the case, Elias's thought here is an invitation to leave behind false oppositions (between relations and structures, between experienced situations and a system of positions) and to consider that individuals are just as apt to be ignorant of the ties that make them what they are as to be aware of them.

The second reason for the timeliness of Elias's *Involvement and Detachment* is its discussion of the ties of dependency linking the knowledge produced by the social sciences and the interests, judgments, and engagements of the people who produce them. Here two things are needed. First, if we want to verify the effects of such specific determinations, we must learn about them precisely in the places and institutions where knowledge is elaborated. It is only by objectivizing their own positions that investigators can detach themselves from the dependencies that constrain them without their knowledge and can practice the "emotional disenchantment" (67) that separates "scientific" knowledge from unmediated representations and spontaneous prejudices. Next Elias defines it as the special task of the sociology of knowledge to note how various individuals' memberships in groups, positions, and interests work to organize not only their declared ideological positions but also—and more interesting—their most neutral scientific practices and most technical decisions: how they choose and group objects, how they constitute and treat data, what forms of demonstration they use, and so on. Elias's reflections suggest an outline for research aimed at noting the way particular mechanisms (theoretical, analytical, or discursive) translate into the language that is specific to the production of knowledge the determinations of all sorts (institutional, social, national, etc.) governing the relations of scientists or scholars to the objects they study. "Involvement," as Elias conceives it, is not always obvious; it lurks camouflaged within procedures intended to present the results of the research as purely objective. One example of this is the transfer of models of intelligibility borrowed from the physical sciences, a transfer that in many cases creates a facade of detachment behind which a clearly involved position is concealed.

Many historians and not a few sociologists find it difficult to understand that societies, which are, after all, nothing but networks of functionally interdependent human beings, can have a structure of their own, or—what is saying much the same—that human beings as individuals or groups are bound to each other in specific figurations whose dynamics have a constraining and compelling influence on those who form them. (79)

Even more than historians and sociologists, the individuals who are caught up in these chains of reciprocal dependence perceive them emotionally and by means of their imaginations. They impute the unavoidable effects of social ties to hostile intentions or consider them unpredictable threats, thus reinforcing their own vulnerability to aggression: "The ever-present danger nurtures a high affectivity of thought and action, a low ability to constrain strong feelings which, in turn, makes for the perpetuation of a high danger level, for an inability to bring those dangers under control" (108). To designate the circularity of a dependency that is both the effect and the cause of this danger, Elias borrows the psychiatric notion of the "double bind" that Gregory Bateson uses to describe the family background common in schizophrenia and the pathogenesis of the psychotic syndromes that underlie it.[5] Constant Piqueray gives this definition of "the theory of the double bind":

[It] establishes that an individual may well present symptoms that will qualify him as insane if he is frequently subjected, by someone close to him, to a message made up of an injunction plus a second injunction bearing on the first and contradictory to it. Bateson stresses that in order for there to be a double bind, these paradoxical messages must be inscribed in a context where the individual who receives them can neither escape them nor denounce this situation as a metacommunicant.[6]

Elias uses this notion, detaching it from all reference to schizophrenia, as one of the central concepts of "sociological theories of unplanned processes" (99) that "bind" individuals, first by their own dynamics, in which individual, voluntary action plays no part, and then by the anxious understanding of them that individuals subjected to them develop through affect and imagination.

At the same time that it produces new configurations of the "double bind," the expansion of the civilizing process, understood as a growing control over emotional and anxiety-ridden representations of phenomena, offers ways to loosen that bind. This hard-won detachment nonetheless has its discontinuities and contradictions. The first is the gap between the mastery over natural forces, stripped of their magic by technological and scientific knowledge, and a continuing insecurity in social life. The second is the contrast between the gradual containment of violence among men, made possible by the state's monopolizing of violence, and the perpetual threat of recourse to force in relations among nation-states that lack a central entity strong enough to impose rules and prohibitions on potential belligerents. This means that in the contemporary world, relations among states are organized according to the model of interdependence that ruled relations among individuals *before* the modern state (first in its absolutist form) established the constraints—which then became self-restraints—that gradually pacified the social sphere:

In people's social life with each other, and particularly at the inter-state level, the force of the double-bind is still almost unbroken. Here, the reciprocal reinforcement and perpetuation of a relatively low capacity for controlling the dangerous processes on which the survival and well-being of humans depends—or, in other words, the capacity for more reality-oriented practice, and a low capacity for a relatively detached mode of thinking, for curbing affects and fantasies, for restraining immediate wishes and fears and preventing them from dominating action and thought—are still operative and still largely beyond human control. (101).

The strength of Elias's approach is the close connection he makes between the conquest of detachment and the various stages of the civilizing process. The reference to Edgar Allan Poe's "A Descent into the Maelström" (1841), which lends its title to the second study in *Involvement and Detachment,* makes this connection metaphorically. Only when individuals have enough control over their own impulses can they limit the investment of affect and imagination and turn to comprehending natural phenomena, social processes, or relations among states. Conversely, if there is a gap between the "relatively high level of self-control" and "high capacity for producing more reality-oriented knowledge" that has been "attained in people's relationship with nature" and "their ability to control the dangers inherent in their coexistence within the framework of states" (111), it is because the reinforcement of self-restraint does not destroy the emotional involvement that openly characterized the earlier stage in the fashioning of psychic economy but rather buries it in the structure of personality. As is frequently true in Elias's work, here he converges with Freud, but without accepting either Freud's concepts or his definitions. Remarking that in evolved societies the forms of social differentiation and of the organization of power have led individuals to internalize a high degree of control over their emotions, Elias notes that "in later-stage societies" of a "comparatively high level of emotional detachment, of reality-orientation as distinct from fantasy-orientation," the latter, "even in private life, becomes more controlled." Elias continues: "Receiving less support from the public fund of knowledge and its powerful guardians, the primary code of human experience, without losing its force, becomes, while people grow up, a more or less submerged layer of the personality-structure. Freud discovered it there and called it—with a not wholly appropriate term—the 'unconscious.'" But to mark his difference from Freud, Elias adds, "not wholly appropriate, for it refers to experience which although stored in memory, as a result of some blockage cannot normally be remembered at will, even though it continues indirectly to participate in steering people's conduct" (62).

Can "figurational sociology," a powerful instrument for understanding evolution in the very long term, help us decipher our present or warn us of what is in store in the near future? Our sudden and unpredictable entry into a world no longer dominated by the conflict between two ideologically antagonistic superpowers seems to remove all pertinence—now that one is triumphant and the other disbanded—from an analysis that uses the theory of the "double bind" and reciprocal dependence to describe competition between the United States and the Soviet Union. Let us read more closely:

But inter-state conflict itself does not, as is often believed, derive its whole dynamic force from intra-state conflicts between workers and managers and from the social beliefs which identify and legitimize the two sides. . . . The relationships between states and the conflicts they generate have a dynamics of their own. [The] antagonism [of both sides] and the dynamics [of intrastate conflict] in no way differ structurally from the hegemonial struggles into which, as far back in the past as we can see, the power units that have emerged as strongest from a long drawn-out elimination contest have almost invariably been drawn. . . . Only what is at stake this time is hegemony over the whole of humanity. (91–92)

Elias adds somewhat later, "Inherently, the drift towards empire-building of the two greatest hegemonial powers of the late twentieth century has little to do with the social ideals of either communism or capitalism. As I have already said, inter-state relations have a dynamics of their own" (92).

This statement sounds a warning not to be too quick to equate the end of the confrontation between two antagonistic social ideologies (Elias calls them the social religions of our time) with the end of the rivalry between powers engaged in an automatic and obligatory competition to occupy a position of planetwide hegemony—a rivalry in which the "mechanism of monopolization" of the contemporary age differs radically from older forms always limited to one particular geographical area.[7] That one of the former adversaries seems for the moment so weakened that it is no longer a dangerous rival, thus apparently eliminating all competition, tells us little about the situation in the future. Nor does it guarantee there will be no return to a balance of forces based on fierce rivalry between the most powerful states: "Both try to increase their security; and every move made by one of them in order to gain greater security is likely to heighten the insecurity of the other side. Each side tries to increase its potential for destruction. That, too, has a spiralling effect" (89).

In order to understand, control, and lessen the dangers inherent in the mechanisms at work in unplanned social processes, those processes need to be seen from a distance. Although Elias's sociology concentrates on discovering connections rather than on an all-powerful human intention, it is by no means a submission to necessity or a theory of powerlessness and fatality. Its efficacy supposes one precondition, however—the "unlearning" of the most habitual categories and the most traditional ways of ordering reality. In a challenge to intellectual laziness, the "figurational sociology" brings together objects usually dispersed among different specialized disciplines and treats as evolutions over the very long term realities that traditional disciplines consider only synchronously. The theory of the "double bind" (one of the few conceptual instruments that Elias added in later years to the body of notions he elaborated in the 1930s) gives an adequate representation of processes and interdependencies: "As a theoretical model, double-binds, with their inescapable circularity, their eventual loosening, and their possible break-up, can serve as an example of the advance in reality-orientation which becomes possible if one overcomes the tendency towards departmental isolation and process-reduction in the formation of concepts" (114). The only possible safeguard against dangers that present a more lasting threat than we might suppose from the state of the world today is the "detour by detachment" given by knowledge. Social phenomena, governed by laws and dynamics of their own, are and will remain—at least until a certain stage in their development—modifiable by human action. "There is no reason to assume that we have yet reached the point of no return in the maelstrom in which we are drifting" (246–47).

TEN

Sports, or The Controlled Decontrolling of Emotions

Quest for Excitement, by Norbert Elias and Eric Dunning, was published in 1986,[1] but the book's history begins thirty years earlier. Elias was fifty-seven years old in 1954. He fled Nazi Germany in April 1933, and after a few months in Paris he moved to London. With the support of a committee to assist Jewish refugees and thanks to the collections of the British Library, it took him only three years to complete an immense work published in Basel in 1939, *Über den Prozess der Zivilisation: Soziogenetische und psychogenetische Untersuchungen. (The Civilizing Process).*[2] The book went practically unnoticed in a Europe at war, and it was totally unknown in England. In London, both during and after the war, Elias held only temporary positions. For some time he was a research assistant at the London School of Economics, then he made his living teaching adult extension courses at the University of London and giving group therapy sessions under the auspices of the Group Analytic Society, an association founded by several psychiatrists gathered around S. H. Foulkes, whom Elias had known in Frankfurt before 1933 and who, like him, had fled Germany.

There were difficult years, but in 1954 Elias's life changed:

I received two offers of lectureships in sociology; one from Leicester and another from Leeds. Characteristically, both came from people [Ilya Neustadt and Eugene Grebenik] who were themselves refugees, but younger than I was, so that they had been educated at English universities. I decided in favour of Leicester, where

Neustadt, who came from Odessa, had a chair. [Elias had met Neustadt when the latter, who was twenty years younger than he, was librarian at the London School of Economics.] It was one of the new sociology departments that were being set up in England at that time. . . . Leicester was a pretty, clean, medium-sized city, and had the additional advantage that one could travel to London and back in a day.[3]

Thus Elias received his first permanent university position at age fifty-seven, first as a lecturer in sociology at the University College of Leicester, then as reader in the newly established (1957) department of sociology of the University of Leicester.

The sociology department at Leicester was expanding rapidly—it had only two members in 1954 (Neustadt and Elias), three in 1957, six in 1959, and twenty in 1962—and its reputation was growing. Elias gave a two-part introductory course in sociology for freshmen, "Comparative Studies of Contemporary Societies at Different Stages of Development" and "Selected Theories of Social Development." He enjoyed teaching, but his writings remained largely unknown and underestimated, and he was turned down for the chair in sociology created at the university in 1960. As Richard Brown, a junior lecturer at Leicester at the time, explained,

Über den Prozess der Zivilisation was unavailable in English [the book was translated in 1978 and 1982] and difficult to get hold of in German; and two articles in the British Journal of Sociology [in 1950 and 1956], on the genesis of the naval profession and on involvement and detachment, although important contributions, could not fill the gap. When he did publish during his time in Leicester it was as likely to be in German as in English, as in the case of his paper on public opinion in England (Elias 1959).[4]

In 1962, when he reached retirement age, Elias left England for Ghana, where for two years he was professor of sociology at the University of Accra. During the eight years he spent in Leicester Elias had published very little: only one article in the British Journal of Sociology and a study in German that had little resonance. Much later, in 1984, he recalled his experience in that British university with a regret tinged with bitterness:

I also took great care to ensure that only really gifted people became lecturers, which had the very curious result that, after London, Leicester was the leading supplier of professors of sociology in England. Many of the people who were lecturers with us now have chairs. However, I do find it sad that practically none of them took my approach further. Most of them regarded my way of thinking in long-term processes as lying outside the mainstream. And they were not mistaken, for it might have cost them their careers had they followed that approach. It was not at all fashionable in sociology to think in long-range processes.[5]

These recollections long after the fact are not totally accurate. At least two people who had been students at Leicester adopted Elias's ideas and coauthored publications with him after his return to England from Ghana. The first of these was *The Established and the Outsiders,* a book that developed out of John L. Scotson's master of arts thesis.[6] In that work Elias used a monographic study of a community in the suburbs of Leicester as the basis for a theory of the relations between "established groups" and "marginal groups." The same theory later proved useful for understanding the outbreaks of violence that occur in contemporary society and the situation of the Jews in the German empire and the Weimar Republic, where they were stigmatized as "outsiders" but saw themselves as being among the "established."[7]

The second former student who pursued Elias's interests was Eric Dunning, with whom Elias published first articles and then books. A student at Leicester who played cricket and football (soccer), Dunning read *The Civilizing Process* when Ilya Neustadt lent him the German edition. He proposed to Elias that they work together on sports and leisure activities, a subject that did not immediately spring to mind in the 1950s, when it would not have been considered a legitimate topic for sociological research. At the beginning of the introduction to *Quest for Excitement,* Elias recalled that "when we started on this work, the sociology of sports was still in its infancy. I well remember Eric Dunning discussing with me the question of whether sport, and particularly football, would be considered by the authorities to be a respectable subject of research in the social sciences and, in particular, for an MA thesis. I think we helped a little to make it that."[8] It was only some years after his return from Ghana, however, that Elias began to publish on sports, alone or more often with Eric Dunning.

Quest for Excitement, which was published in 1986, clearly shows the three stages of Elias's interest in this topic. Five of the six studies in this work (one signed by Elias alone, four written with Dunning) were published elsewhere between 1966 and 1971.[9] Elias drifted away from the subject, but after Eric Dunning had written *Barbarians, Gentlemen, and Players* with Kenneth Sheard (published in 1979), he became internationally recognized as a specialist on the topic, as attested by the four articles or lectures written from 1979 to 1983 and reprinted in *Quest for Excitement.*[10] Finally, in addition to a piece on sports and violence, Elias wrote a long introduction to the English-language edition of *Quest for Excitement* (a collection of some of the same pieces had been published earlier in German),[11] situating sports in the long term of the civilizing process and studying them from the viewpoints of national differences (between England and France in particular) and changes through time.

With these works, Elias and Dunning invented a genuinely new topic of study. Their first task was to describe it. Despite a continuity of vocabulary and a similarity in the actions involved, modern sports and traditional games had more differences than they had traits in common. Elias and Dunning took the accepted notion that "sports" were universal, existing in all cultures, ancient and contemporary, European and non-European, and opposed to it a discontinuity, defining sports according to characteristics that distinguish them from other forms of leisure activity and competition existing before or concurrently with them. The texts that make up *Quest for Excitement* thus stress what is specific to modern sports: a diminution in the violence permitted when bodies are placed in a game situation; the existence of written and uniform rules to codify practices; making sports play (and sports spectacles) autonomous from war or ritual combat.

When they stress the differences between modern wrestling or boxing and the pancratium of classical antiquity (chapter 3), or between "folk football" and modern football or rugby (chapter 5), Elias and Dunning break with three notions that underlay—and often still underlie—studies of sports and games. These were placing all contemporary sports in a long-term genealogy of more or less direct descent from ancestor sports; supposing that all societies are like our own in devoting a portion of their activities and their time to "sports"; explaining such practices, held to be comparable through time and across space, by the universal psychological dispositions of a *homo ludens* who needed games and entertainments once the tasks necessary to the survival of the species and the individual had been attended to.[12] From the Greeks to the Aztecs, from the Middle Ages to the twentieth century, one category—"sports"—had been used to designate a supposedly unvarying reality in competitive physical exercise.

This was the concept of sports that Elias and Dunning were combating when they stressed the difference, even when the two shared certain acts and activities, between sports and traditional games. Folk football, called *soule* in French, provides an example. In the traditional view, these sometimes rather rough competitions between two rival teams were con-

sidered the ancestor of the modern sports of football and rugby that supposedly derived from them. Elias and Dunning show that this is far from
true. "Folk football" fielded two teams whose makeup reflected a prees-
tablished social identity: residence in the same village community or the
same seignorial domain; the exercise of the same craft or profession;
membership in the group of the "young" men (bachelors of all ages) or
the married men. The game thus reproduced cleavages both anterior and
external to it—the very same differences by which festive rituals were organized.

Hence the dual temporality of collective games: at times they were
part of the calendar of religious and folk celebrations; at other times they
occurred on dates with no special significance, negotiated between the
competing groups. Even when they did not take place on holidays, however, games had a connection with the Christian calendar, since the
matches were held on Sundays, either after mass or after vespers. If folk
football had no special time dedicated to it, the same was true of its space:
matches were played in the ordinary places of daily life, borrowed for the
occasion. Any community space might be used, at one time or another,
for a game that not only had no fixed, marked place of its own but also
had no uniform rules. The conventions that enabled teams to play one another remained rudimentary, local, and based in custom. From one region
to another, one village to another, even one match to another, all the elements of the game might differ: the number of players, the duration of
play, the rules the teams accepted, the ball and other paraphernalia used,
the criteria for winning.

Modern sports arose in opposition to these characteristics. In a first
and fundamental difference, modern sports, as a matter of principle, have
no ritual function or festive purpose; by that token they are aimed at eliminating rather than reproducing the differences that permeate and organize the social world. Modern sports suppose a neutralizing of the participants' social attributes, minimizing them in the interest of equalizing
the chances for winning of players or competitors classed and set apart
by their physical performance alone. Just as suffrage postulates a formal
equality among voters of all social conditions, modern sports are based
on an equality among individuals stripped, for the duration of a competition, of the characteristics of their social being. This process of abstraction obviously does not mean that sports are not also an expression
or a transposition of a number of rivalries (national, racial, social, religious, and more). Even if they reject explicit reference to expressions of

opposition in society, modern sports cannot avoid determinations that inject the social properties of the competitors and their supporters into their practice. But the precondition of this return of the social (or of the national) is the autonomy that differentiates sports from ritual and communitarian forms of competition.

When they became autonomous, modern sports created their own spaces and times. The stadium (but also the gymnasium, the bicycle track, the skating rink) is a specific place to contain the performance and the spectacle of sports within a site reserved to them. Unlike the traditional games, which were played in the ordinary spaces of daily activities, sports require a space that is adequate, set off, and reproducible elsewhere. In like fashion, they replace the festive time of the traditional games with a schedule that is deliberately constructed and specific to them. The long and indeterminate duration of the communitarian clashes gives way to regulated schedules, confined within precise limits, divided into ordered sequences, and timed to the minute. Sports replace the old religious and folk calendar of collective rituals with their own calendar of competitions whose timing follows the annual rhythm of each sport. That does not mean that the place and time for sports events are insensitive to the demands of the social world. The location and architecture of the stadium are closely connected to considerations of crowd management and commercial expectations. The length of the match and the schedule of games are subject to time constraints dictated by the media, by the normal work schedule, and by leisure habits. But here too that the practice of sports is vulnerable to external constraints modifying the conditions of its exercise supposes its autonomy.

That autonomy is most explicit in the rules drawn up for the various sports. The multiple, temporary, and ill-defined conventions that bound participants in the traditional games give way, in modern sports, to fixed rules that permit a uniform and potentially universal practice of the sport. As shown in Elias and Dunning's study of football and rugby, the history of every sport is basically the history of the formulation of an increasingly detailed and precise body of rules that impose a single code of ways to play and compete, whereas formerly rules had been strictly local or regional. Although it was radically different from the folk football of the Middle Ages and the Renaissance, the football played in British public schools in the early nineteenth century was nonetheless marked by extreme diversity. The size and shape of the field differed from school to school, as did the rules of the game, the moves permitted, and so on. The legendary innovative act of W. W. Ellis, who, one fine day in 1823, grasped the ball in his hands and ran forward with it on the playing field of the Rugby Public School, in no way changes the basic principle: the thirty-seven rules drawn up in 1845 for the game that he transformed did indeed guarantee it a coherence unknown in the traditional games, but for a long time they were respected only within the school community of Rugby.

The spread of football in the schools and universities and the formation of a number of municipal football clubs made consistent rules an urgent need if one team was to play another without confusion and conflict. Still, even after rugby football, which recognized hand carries as legitimate, had split off from the football association, which refused to admit hand carrying the ball as an option, a number of problems remained. Schools and clubs differed regarding moves that were permitted or forbidden (one such was "hacking," the right to kick an opponent below the knee), the number of players on a side, the shape and weight of the ball, the way the score should be kept, and the presence and duties of referees. Every match had to be preceded by a conference between the two teams to define and agree on, by contract, the rules to be followed, which were generally those of the home team. The creation of the Rugby Football Union in 1871, covering the principal clubs in and around London, then of the International Rugby Football Board in 1890, which defined the four British "nations," only slowly brought unity to the rules of the game, with the result that the outcome of the first matches between England and Scotland in 1871 and 1884 was contested long and bitterly for lack of a clear statement of how goals were to be scored.

Football, like boxing, shows that sports rules, like all other juridical codifications, imply the existence of a body of legislators responsible for drawing them up, changing them, and seeing to it that they are respected. Modern sports thus differ from the traditional games in two ways: not only did uniform rules gradually replace local customs, but specialists were charged with instituting and promulgating a specific code of laws, separate from the common law, to govern sports. Not that sports fall outside the law; sports-related contentions can be brought before the law courts. Still, it is based on their own code of rules that two of the most fundamental characteristics of sports should be understood—the reduction of the level of violence found tolerable in physical confrontations, and the development of an ethic of loyalty that does not separate the desire to win from respect for the rules or from taking pleasure in the game, win or lose.

These two characteristics lead to the essential question in *Quest for*

Excitement. How are we to situate, within the long history of the civilizing process, the transformations in the structure of personality that made it possible to relax controls over emotions without at the same time giving free rein to spontaneous (and dangerous) surges of impulse and affect? For Elias, the key concept that lets us account for the appearance of sports (as discontinuous from the older competitions) is the "controlled decontrolling of emotions." The pleasure derived from playing a sport or watching a match comes from an excitement produced by an unconstrained interaction among bodies that nonetheless remains respectful of life, and from the vicissitudes of a struggle that may seem severe but is only a simulacrum of the violent clashes of war. That tension, which Elias expresses in a number of ways (as "a controlled, a well-tempered excitement"; as "a controlled but enjoyable emotional excitement"; as "a controlled battle in an imaginary setting"), supposes two conditions. The first, investigated in the theory of leisure proposed in the first two studies in *Quest for Excitement,* lies in the rise and diffusion of recreation whose mimetic nature permits a relaxation of the control ordinarily exercised over the emotions, either in the sphere of work and public life or in many activities in the private domain. Here Elias and Dunning replace an oversimplified opposition between work and leisure with a more complex typology of free-time pursuits that situates the practice or the spectacle of sports among leisure activities that are mimetic or play directed. Such pastimes, which are not all sports related, permit their participants to feel and express emotions that ordinarily must be held in check or repressed.

The second condition for a "controlled decontrolling of emotions" has to do with the development of the civilizing process. A temporary, localized relaxation of control over impulse and affect is possible only when the mechanisms of self-constraint are sufficiently widespread and strongly enough internalized. Emotions can be liberated in specific pursuits without threatening society with a savage return to aggression and violence only when such mechanisms of self-control govern all behaviors consistently and uniformly.

Thus Elias's work on sports is inseparable from his ongoing reflections, from the 1930s on, in which he saw the history of the West between the Middle Ages and the twentieth century in terms of a gradual but profound transformation of emotional economy. The leading element in that transformation is a change in the balance between externally imposed constraints on the individual's impulses and constraints that spring from a constant and rigorous self-control. The violence whose only meaningful limit had long remained counterviolence came to be prohibited, suppressed, and repressed. The pacification (at least the partial and potential pacification) of social space brought on by the monopoly on the legitimate use of force that absolutist states reserved to themselves had as its first corollary a transfer to within the individual of conflicts and tensions that formerly had often been expressed in open and bloody confrontation with others. The essential change affecting the structure of personality lay in that displacement of the way affect was subjected to tension—by the internal mechanism of self-censure and no longer (or not solely) by an external authority that constrains the individual.

In a letter written in 1976 to the Dutch sociologist Cas Wouters, Elias warns against a simplistic interpretation of his thesis and against describing the process of civilization merely as an increasingly severe reinforcement of self-restraint:

I have always considered the idea that the principle characterizing a process of civilization is the growth of "self-control" to be a fundamental misunderstanding. One reason for this is that you often find in relatively simple societies a very strong demand for "self-control." . . . Thus, if anyone says that for Elias a process of civilization is characterized by an ever-higher level of self-constraint, it is simply wrong.

Three characteristics define an advanced stage in the civilizing process: first, the generalization of self-control, no longer confined to certain specific practices; next, "the equality of constraints in all sorts of relations, with weak differences of level between those required in private and those demanded in public"; finally, a moderation of self-restraint. Here Elias states, "My theory is and has always been that it is the integration of a temperate 'self-control' (neither too weak nor excessive) that is the criterion for identifying the highest levels attained by a process of civilization."[13] The rise of sports, understood as a strict control of the violence inherent in physical clashes, is possible only when those three traits, which characterize the advance of any process of civilization, play a major role in shaping the social habitus of Western men and women.

After describing the differences between sports and traditional games and identifying the psychic mutations that make the change possible, *Quest for Excitement* turns to situating the particular historical context of the first appearance of physical confrontations that were clearly subjected to rules intended to avoid putting either bodies or lives in danger. Elias and Dunning see in England during the eighteenth century the earliest emergence of a social configuration that liberated affect and impulse through physical exertion while rejecting dangerous violence and insisting on self-control and a respect for constraining prohibitions. Foxhunting—where the pleasure consists in hunting the fox to the exclusion of all other game, in hunting without arms and with no intention of eating the prey, and in delegating to the dog pack the violence done to the animal—and boxing, with its many rules, were the most spectacular and the most highly regarded of the "sports," practiced or watched, that brought strict conventions to bear on the pursuit or the spectacle of brutality. Elias calls "sportization" the evolving process of transforming the traditional pastimes and confrontations, which had no fixed rules and no stringent restrictions on violence, into "civilized" leisure activities.

This shift, in which the specific forms of modern sports are part of an unplanned long-range process, is based on two preconditions. The first is the establishment of an ethic, at first exclusive to the dominant classes—the aristocracy and the gentry—that admits and enjoys competition, confrontation, and challenge but euphemizes and limits the violence they can engender. This paradoxical "controlled decontrolling of emotions" demands a particular form of the internalization of constraints that was characteristic of the eighteenth-century English elite classes. The second precondition is linked to the model of social and political competition that obtained in England after Walpole. There, as elsewhere, that model included a state monopoly on legitimate violence, but only in England was there also a peaceful (or pacified) political struggle between two parties, the Whigs and the Tories, who expressed the rival interests of different segments of the landowning class but also reflected their solidarity. The "sportization" of traditional pastimes was thus inseparable from the establishment of the parliamentary regime. Both postulated the legitimacy of competition, even rough competition, and the exclusion of destructive violence directed at the adversary. Both were based on a "horizontal" model of confrontation that led to euphemized but direct clashes carried on according to commonly accepted rules and in an autonomous space, in which the stakes were victory, on the hustings or on the field. The same habitus was displayed and shaped in different and heterogeneous fields of practice.

Thus Elias and Dunning note connections among political forms, modes of interdependence among groups, and an economy of affectivity within a specific social configuration. Their approach suggests several remarks. First, it allowed them to think historically about psychic and emotional categories, with all their gaps and displacements, and to inscribe the changes in the practice of physical activities within a more fundamental change in the mechanisms for regulating and controlling confrontational impulses. The ways psychic economy is structured are not unvarying, universal natural dispositions. Hence sports cannot be described according to a single, unique function (magical, religious, ritual, or other), identical everywhere and in all cases. Sports can be described only by relating specific rules to the particular—and historically specific—structure of personality that makes possible their formulation, their acceptance, and their respect.[14]

That structure is directly dependent on the forms taken by struggles for power. "Sportization" is possible only in a society in which political tensions take a regulated and pacific form, in which the groups that participate in power struggles admit they have an equal chance as political actors and obey commonly accepted rules. At first contained within an aristocratic parliamentary society (as in eighteenth-century England), that sociopolitical configuration spread in the age of democratic states, bearing with it a universal expansion of sports, whose rules transposed and represented, in another sphere, the rules governing a political practice founded in nearly universal suffrage. The spread of sports throughout the world does not imply, however, that the same conditions that led to their emergence in eighteenth-century England were reproduced in each national situation. It does suppose the generalizing of a mode for the exercise of power and of a model for confrontation and a balance of tensions that oblige individuals to maintain great control over their emotions—which is precisely what makes the emotional excitement prompted by the practice and the spectacle of sports possible, agreeable, and free of excessive risk.

Finally, Elias and Dunning's study of sports allows us to follow the gaps and discontinuities that marked the civilizing process in the West. Violence in sports—player violence and, even more, violence among fans (especially the ones the British call "hooligans")—should be understood as a lesser capacity for and a lower value accorded to self-imposed restraint of impulses by a portion of the population, people who, through exclusion or marginalization, have not reached the same stage in the process of civilization as the greater part of their society. There is thus a basic connection linking brutal, prohibited, and reprehensible behavior, a social habitus that, far from having internalized the necessary control over aggression, recognizes violence as a positive value, and the presence of "outsiders" in the social world, people remote from the institutional or social mechanisms that instill mechanisms of self-control in individuals.

The importance of Elias and Dunning's book can be measured by the pertinence of the questions it raised. Is it fair to set up a break between modern sports and traditional games as clean as the one it proposes? Is it certain that the conditions that led to the appearance and diffusion of sports in eighteenth-century England also obtained in other times and places? Are we not oversimplifying the multiple meanings invested in sports in contemporary societies when we define sports, basically, by the psychological mechanism—the controlled decontrolling of emotions—that makes them possible? And when we insist on that shared characteristic, do we not do away with diversity in the ways of practicing and consuming sports chosen by groups and individuals in accordance with very different ethical dispositions, lifestyles, and relations to one's own body—habits that have been profoundly transformed by the rise of professionalism? Recent years have seen an increasing number of studies investigating all these questions. Such studies have at times taken notably different positions on how one should conceive of the significance of sports, often testing Elias's and Dunning's hypotheses in historical or sociological case studies.[15]

The studies gathered in *Quest for Excitement* have held and still hold a central place in these debates. The first reason is that they offer a comparative approach without anachronism because they treat modern sports and the Greek and medieval games without postulating that they belong to the same category. As Pierre Bourdieu has written, comparison in Elias, far from being in the service of an illusory quest for origins, "aims . . . to grasp the specificity of sporting practice, or, more precisely, to determine how certain pre-existing physical exercises, or others which may have received a radically new meaning and function . . . become sports, defined with respect to their rewards, their rules, and also the social identity of their participants—players or spectators—by the specific logic of the 'sporting field.'"[16] The second reason is that these texts, which take sports as a separate and fully legitimate object of scientific study, never confine that study by a narrow spirit of specialization. By inscribing them within evolving forms of competition for political power, controls exerted on violence, and the very structure of personality, Elias and Dunning make sports a privileged place from which to observe long-term changes in Western society.

Epilogue

Friendship with History

Philippe Ariès

Of all the books written by Philippe Ariès, *Le temps de l'histoire* is perhaps the least known. Never reprinted after its publication in 1954, it has long been out of print, accessible only in libraries except to the small number of readers who bought it for six hundred francs in the edition with the image of a Greek goddess on its cover published by Editions du Rocher, 28, rue Comte-Félix-Gastaldi in Monaco. If the work is unknown to the considerable public that has loyally followed the work of Ariès from one book to the next, *Le temps de l'histoire* has also long been ignored by the academic world. During the fifteen years preceding its republication in 1986,[1] the work was cited in French or foreign social science reviews on only two occasions. The first was an article by Fernand Braudel, "Histoire et sciences sociales: La longue durée," that appeared in the *Annales* in 1958. Braudel mentions the book in a note, adding, "Philippe Ariès has insisted on the importance of *dépaysement* [a sense of strangeness], of surprise in historical explanation: you run into something odd in the sixteenth century—odd for you, a man of the twentieth century. Why this difference? The problem is posed."

The second mention was in an article by Micheline Johnson published in the *Revue d'Histoire de l'Amérique Française*. She cites the work but fails to find in it a satisfactory definition of historical time: "Philippe Ariès, in his fine book *Le temps de l'histoire,* describes the evolution of

the historical sense through the ages after first analyzing the historical sense of the men of his own generation, of the right (royalists in France) and of the left (Marxists or historians of Marxist tendencies). But for him the historical sense is a given, a sort of 'adherence to time.' . . . He does not analyze that attitude: he simply states it through the many objects that nurture it."[2] Even the growing interest in the history of history in recent years has not managed to draw the book out of oblivion, and it is rarely mentioned in works on the Middle Ages and the seventeenth century, the topic of its two central chapters. The references to the book by Gabrielle Spiegel, Orest Ranum, and Erica Harth are still exceptions.[3] The work was quoted at length, however, in William Keylor's biography of Jacques Bainville, which relies on Ariès's interpretation to explain the success of Bainville's *Histoire de France,* published in 1924.[4]

A forgotten book, but a book that needs to be rediscovered now. When it appeared in 1954, Philippe Ariès was forty years old. He was director of the Centre de Documentation of the Institut de Recherches sur les Fruits et Agrumes Tropicaux, an institution he had joined in 1943. He had already published two texts. In 1943 his *Les traditions sociales dans les pays de France* had a proud place among the first of the series Cahiers de la restauration française put out by Editions de la Nouvelle France.[5] The information card inserted in review copies described the author as "a young man, a geographer and a philosopher who will make his mark in his generation" and his work as a study "of the origin and the force of the various religious, political, economic, social, and literary customs that, as they accumulated, gave some of the major regions of France a character of their own and gave France its structure and its aspect." This summary of the guiding idea of the book is itself in tune with the spirit of the times and with the *francisque* (battle-ax; emblem of the Vichy government) with which the publishers thought it proper to decorate the series. They state on the back cover, "By the antiquity and the solidity of its customs, France possesses a power of stability [and] a capacity for perseverance that constitute, for its children, a powerful reason for confidence. Free of all regard for timeliness, this book nonetheless contains a great lesson of national hope."

In 1948, after the war, Ariès published his first real book, *Histoire des populations françaises et de leurs attitudes devant la vie depuis le XVIIIe siècle.* This book, begun in 1943 and finished in 1946, was rejected by Librairie Plon and published by a new publishing house, Editions Self. The historical journals ignored it, but the book nonetheless had a certain resonance: André Latreille analyzed it in one of his columns on history in *Le*

Monde. Above all, the demographers noted it, and Ariès, who had remained on the fringes of the university world after two unsuccessful attempts to obtain his *agrégation* (the second time in the 1941 competition), received his first invitation to contribute to a scientific review, *Population,* in which he published an article (in 1949) titled "Attitudes devant la vie et la mort du XVIIᵉ au XIXᵉ siècle: Quelques aspects de leur variations" (463–70), and in 1953 another short article, "Sur les origines de la contraception en France" (465–72).

The following year *Le temps de l'histoire* was ready. Once again Plon refused the manuscript, even though Ariès had close connections with the house both as a reader (in particular, of the many narratives and memoirs written after the war) and as editor of the series Civilisations d'hier et d'aujourd'hui in which he had already published *La société militaire* by Raoul Girardet, a friend from his Sorbonne years, and *Toulouse au XIXᵉ siècle* by Jean Fourcassié. Ariès's book was published by a small house, Editions du Rocher, founded by Plon's literary editor Charles Orengo when he struck out on his own, whose catalog, as listed on the back cover of Ariès's book, included autobiographical texts giving witness to the times (among others the *Mémoires d'un monarchiste espagnol, 1931–1952* by Juan Antonio Ansaldo, the *Journal d'un expatrié catalan, 1936–1945* by Juan Antonio Güell y Lopez del Piélago, and Jean Giraudoux's posthumous *Armistice à Bordeaux*), books on history in a classical vein (Louis d'Illier, *Deux prélats d'ancien régime: Les Jarente*); and monographs regarding the contemporary world (Raymond Ronze, *Le commonwealth britannique et le monde anglo-saxon,* with a preface by André Siegfried). Although he had connections with one of the larger Paris publishing houses, Ariès had to publish his first two works with small houses, enterprises that were highly representative of the postwar scene, when a fashion for "I was there" narratives brought spectacular (but not always lasting) success to some new publishing houses. For example, in 1948, the same year that *Histoire des populations* was published, Editions Self put out Victor Kravchenko's *J'ai choisi la liberté (I Chose Freedom).* Long misunderstood by the *maîtres* of the university, Ariès's brand of history also failed to appeal to the established publishing houses, hence it was doubly thrust aside.

Le temps de l'histoire is a collection of eight texts written over a period of five years, printed one after the other with no introduction or conclusion, as if their coherence and continuity sufficed to express the purport of the work. The oldest, and the first in order in the book, was written in 1946. In *Un historien du dimanche* Ariès explains: "I began with an autobiographical chapter, the idea for which came to me after my brother's death, as a way to prove to myself the determining role that my childhood had played in my vocation and my choices."[6] The severe blow (not mentioned in *Le temps de l'histoire*) to Ariès of the death of his brother Jacques Ariès, second lieutenant in De Lattre's army and killed in combat on 23 April 1945, provides a key to the piece. The upheavals of the new times riddled with grief and marked by a "monstrous invasion of man by History" made it obligatory to situate oneself within that collective history and in relation to one's own past. This explains the attempt at autobiography, somewhat unusual in a man who was only thirty-two but wanted to clarify the reasons for his attitude toward history. It was an effort at self-comprehension, then, but also at self-expression. This first chapter, in fact, had a first reader, Primerose Ariès (they were married in 1947): "I remember, I had sent it to Toulouse to my fiancée like a confession of my state of mind at the moment."[7]

After his marriage Ariès wrote the other texts that were to make up *Le temps de l'histoire:* first, during that same year, the essay "L'histoire marxiste et l'histoire conservatrice"; in 1948, "L'engagement dans l'histoire" (which reflects his experience as a reader for Plon); in 1949, the three final essays in the book; in 1950, the chapter on the Middle Ages; the following year, the chapter on the seventeenth century. The work was constructed gradually, starting with the narration of a personal itinerary, then moving through various ways of understanding, speaking, or writing history—those of family tradition, of the university historians, of the historians of rightist and nationalist Action Française, and of the *Annales*—toward a study of two historical relationships with history, that of the Middle Ages and that of the age of French classicism. Ariès recalled twenty-five years later: "What happened to me then was what always happens to me: the topic relating to the current scene that had me in its grip became the point of departure for retrospective reflection; it sent me back toward other times."[8]

The first way to read *Le temps de l'histoire* is thus as the progress of a historian through the various conceptions of history that coexisted in his age. What lies at its heart is the distance that a family man, a man of tradition and royalist opinions, brought up with the legends of the lost monarchy, an impassioned reader of Bainville and a man loyal to Maurras and to Action Française, set between himself and the attachments of his childhood and youth. This explains the surprising comparison Ariès draws—which doubtless scandalized his own milieu—between historical materialism and what he calls "conservative historicism," or history written by the historians of "the Capetian school of the twentieth century," brought together by their common ideology and by their publisher, Fayard, and its series Grandes études historiques. These two ways of considering history had antagonistic points of departure—a nostalgia for the past for the "Capetian school," a hope of a radical break for the Marxists—but their fundamental principles were the same. Both rejected histories of particular communities in a collective becoming (of the national state or of all humanity); both aimed at establishing laws governing the repetition of identical situations; both dissolved the singular facets of concrete existence either in the abstraction of institutions or in the anonymity of class. To bring together Marx and Bainville in this manner (worse, criticizing both) was not without audacity. In any event, it repudiated the philosophy of history proclaimed by the very persons to whom Ariès was closest by family, emotional, and political ties.

It was Ariès's reflection on "the great lacerations of 1940–45" and his discovery of new ways of thinking about history that brought about that rupture. A systematic survey of the authors and works mentioned in the book (setting aside the strictly scholarly chapters on medieval and seventeenth-century history) demonstrates this clearly. It shows, first, the three-part base of Ariès's historical culture in academic history, university history, and the history of Action Française. He enumerates the academic historians from Barante (whom his grandfather read) to Madelin; he describes their public, a "cultivated and serious bourgeoisie: magistrates, men of the law, men with an independent income . . . men with great leisure, at a time when monetary stability and secure investments permitted living on one's revenues" (210); he depicts the most prominent traits of their strictly political and totally conservative history. History as practiced in the universities left him just as dissatisfied. It was admittedly learned, impartial, and erudite, but it had retreated into itself, cut off from the present and from readers of history, confined within a simplistic conception of the historical event and of historical causality. In his student days at Grenoble and then at the Sorbonne, Philippe Ariès had known that history firsthand: it was dry, gray, written by professors for other professors or for future professors. He describes it sociologically, linking the closed nature of university history to the constitution of a "new social category," a tight and densely packed "republic of professors" that was lay and leftist and recruited outside the traditional elites, who were put off by the university. He also describes it epistemologically, by a critique of the theory of history in which history is a science of facts to be exhumed, tied together, and explicated, as exemplified by Louis Halphen's *Introduction à l'histoire,* published in 1946. Ariès recalls some (actually, few) of his university professors: at Grenoble, he tells us, no outstandingly brilliant professor drew students to history (202); the only professor at the Sorbonne he refers to (but does not mention by name) is Georges Lefebvre, who gave a lecture that Ariès attended in 1946 (61). He mentions only a few titles by university historians, and always critically: Joseph Calmette's *La société féodale* (1923) and his *Charles V* (1945); the first volume of Emile Bréhier's *Le monde byzantin (The Life and Death of Byzantium)* (1947); and Halphen's *Introduction à l'histoire.*

The author Ariès cites by far the most is Jacques Bainville, whose name appears some fifteen times and whose mentioned works include *L'histoire de deux peuples: La France et l'empire allemand* (1915), *L'histoire de France* (1924), and *Napoléon* (1931). It is in fact with Bainville that he launches his essential dialogue, because Bainville's *Histoire de France* was the "breviary" of Ariès's adolescence; because his way of writing history dominated all historical popularization in the 1930s, surpassing even that of the authors of Action Française; because his works were best-sellers;[9] and because after the war he remained a household word for all conservative-minded families. To move away from Bainville and call his history "a mechanistic physics" or a "mechanics of facts" was equivalent to blasphemy in Ariès's milieu. This is perhaps why, in responding to the questions of *Aspects de la France* in an interview published on 23 April 1954, Ariès speaks somewhat euphemistically about the opinion of Bainville and his "continuers" that he had expressed in the book:

Bainville had a great talent. His *Histoire de la IIIᵉ République,* for example, has an admirable purity of line. And then, what lucidity in the analysis of events! Look at the luminous works that were put together after his death by setting his newspaper articles one after the other. I might add that he was too great a master not to have been sensitive to both the particular and the general, to differences as well as resemblances. But I think that a certain danger might come from Bainville's continuers, who tend to apply his method of interpretation inflexibly and to make history a repeating mechanism that gives us, always and everywhere, pre-prepared lessons. To hear them, France may soon cease to be a living reality and become an abstraction subjected to mathematical laws alone.

In spite of the prudence of a response couched to avoid a frontal clash with the readers of the monarchist journal, it is clear that when he wrote

"L'histoire marxiste et l'histoire conservatrice" in 1947, Ariès intended to break with the intellectual habits of his political family, just as, some years earlier, during the war, he had moved away from Maurras and Action Française: "I was emancipated from my former teachers and determined not to take on others. The umbilical cord was cut!"[10]

Books helped Ariès to cut that cord, historically speaking. During the war and in the postwar period he read both out of passion and out of professional obligation, and *Le temps de l'histoire* enables us to reconstitute the new acquisitions in his library. Marxism was an early interest. At the time it seemed to attract the entire intellectual world and to furnish a few simple ideas to "men abandoned naked in history," ideas that Ariès summarizes as "surpassing political conflicts, weight of the masses, sense of a determinate movement of history" (53). The Marxism he knew was thus above all a twentieth-century ideology, on its way to becoming dominant, more than the corpus of ideas of Marx himself, none of whose specific works Ariès cites. The interview given to *Aspects de la France* clarifies what Ariès meant by that definition, just as it clarifies his participation, at that time, in the review *Paroles Françaises,* which he directed with Pierre Boutang, and which published the first dossier on the Soviet massacre at Katyn Forest. Ariès states:

I am absolutely persuaded that history is not oriented in one direction or in another. Nothing is more false than the idea of a continual progress, of a perpetual evolution. History with an arrow does not exist. . . . The more one studies the concrete conditions of existence, throughout the centuries, the better one sees what is artificial in the Marxist explanation that many Christians adopt today. The history attentive to all the forms of lived experience inclines, to the contrary, to a traditionalist conception.

Ariès had read one of the few books of Marxist history in the more narrow and more "professional" sense of the term, Daniel Guérin's *La lutte des classes sous la Première République: Bourgeois et "bras nus" (1793–1797)* (1946) and found in it, once again, a law of historical repetition that related historical materialism to conservative historicism despite their vastly different premises.

Two sorts of reading matter contributed to upsetting Ariès's old certitudes. The first was the proliferating literature of witness to recent events and the autobiographical narratives that he read for Plon (which, incidentally, published none of the texts he mentions). These persuaded him that a new consciousness of history had appeared in which individuals perceive their personal existence as merged and identified with collective becoming. Ariès doubtless found reflected in these relations of life stories the experience that he himself had so painfully undergone at the death of his brother. Through first-person accounts of experiences at the limits of endurance—stories of combat like Hugh Dormer's, reports of Nazi death camps like David Rousset's, or accounts of Stalinist terror as described by Kravchenko and Jan Valtin—there emerged a collective, shared sense of general upheaval that meant that no individual existence could still be sheltered from the events of greater history. Hence the abolition of the old frontier between the private and the public: "From now on one can state that there is no private life indifferent to questions of conscience involving public morality." This became one of the major themes of all Ariès's later books, from *L'enfant et la vie familiale sous l'ancien régime (Centuries of Childhood)* to the project for *Histoire de la vie privée (A History of Private Life)*. Hence also a new perception, imposed on everyone, that dissolved individual histories and histories of family lineages, territorial communities, or social groups into a consciousness of the common destiny that has everyone in its grip.

History, as historians write it, should not duplicate or reinforce that immediate and spontaneous perception—which is what historical materialism and conservative historicism do, each in its own way. Quite the contrary, the task of history is to restore to individuals a sense of single histories, irreducible to one another, and an awareness of the differences that make societies, territories, and groups unique. This was what made Ariès's discovery of the *Annales* during the war years so important to him. More than the review itself, which he cites only once, it was the major works of Marc Bloch and Lucien Febvre that permitted Ariès to think in unaccustomed ways and to detach himself from the history of his adolescence. He commented on Marc Bloch's *Les caractères originaux de l'histoire rurale française* (1931) and his *La société féodale* (1939) *(Feudal Society)* and on Lucien Febvre's *Le problème de l'incroyance au XVIᵉ siècle: Le religion de Rabelais* (1942) *(The Problem of Unbelief in the Sixteenth Century: The Religion of Rabelais)* and his *Autour de l'Heptaméron: Amour sacré, amour profane* (1944), and he mentioned in a note the recent publication (in 1953) of Febvre's collection of articles in *Combats pour l'histoire*. When he gathered together the fundamental ideas of the "new historiography" (225) in his chapter "L'histoire existentielle," Philippe Ariès produced a text that today might seem banal, both because the principles he states have now been accepted by all French historical schools, well beyond the *Annales* group, and because recent years have seen a large number of works explaining what that "new history" was. This was far from true in 1954, and we need to read *Le temps de l'histoire* with the eyes of those years.

Defining history as a "science of structures" rather than as "objective knowledge of facts"; speaking of his plan to write a total history that organizes all historical data and economic and social phenomena as well as political or military events; affirming that the historian must "psychoanalyze" the documents to find the "mental structures" of each sensibility; positing that the only possible history was in a comparison between "total, self-contained structures irreducible to one another"—all these were not obvious propositions in 1954. Ariès's very vocabulary ("historical psychoanalysis," "structural history," "mental structures") was enough to make his friends and the proponents of Bainvillean history shudder. It also raised doubts in the university milieu, which was still unwilling to grant full acceptance—despite its respect for Marc Bloch's works—to a way of thinking of and writing history so far from the traditional credos of works like Halphen's *Introduction à l'histoire*. For that reason *Le temps de l'histoire* was perhaps the first book written by a historian who did not belong to that "school" to show quite such an acute comprehension of the rupture effected by the *Annales* and by the work of Bloch and Febvre—that is, Ariès not only recognized the quality of their books but grasped that after them history could never again be what it had been before. Where historians had been thinking in terms of continuity and repetition, they had to learn to recognize gaps and discontinuities; where they had concentrated exclusively on facts and events linked by causal relations, they had to come to recognize structures; where they had seen only clear ideas and explicit intentions, they had to learn to decipher the unknown determinations of spontaneous behaviors.

There were perhaps two reasons for Philippe Ariès's enthusiastic and intelligent rallying to the *Annales* sort of history. First, it was capable of reforging the lost link between scholarly research and the reading public. As a history of differences and of civilizations, the history of Bloch and Febvre could bring men and women of the twentieth century what they lacked—a comprehension of both the radical originality of their own times and the survivals still present in their society. In that manner, the old societies and mentalities could be grasped in their singularity, with no anachronistic backward projection of the ways of thinking and acting of our own times; history, in return, could help everyone understand why the present is what it is. Philippe Ariès was to remain faithful to that dual idea from book to book, always rooting his quest for historical difference in an interrogation concerning contemporary society, its conceptions of the family, or its attitudes toward death.

Ariès may perhaps have found something more in the history of the *Annales*—a way to reconcile his loyalties, family and political, with his scholarly interests. Indeed, the new vocabulary of the history of discontinuous structures permitted a return to the particular histories of simple communities—which are neither classes nor the state—still surviving despite "technocratic standardization" within a "great, total, and massive History." This may explain Ariès's somewhat surprising call for an alliance between the newest of scholarly histories, the product of the republican and progressive university, and one of the traditions of Action Française—not Jacobin royalism but the more provincial tradition of the local sociabilities and communities of kinship or place of groups outside the state. At first sight this might seem a paradoxical mix, but listen to Ariès's response to the *Aspects de la France* interviewer:

[Interviewer:] According to you, the true historian—who would also be a true Maurrassian—should set about doing the history of the real country, with its communities, its families. . . .

[Ariès:] Exactly. History is for me the sentiment of a living tradition. Michelet, in spite of his errors, and Fustel, so perspicacious, were well aware of this. Today that history is even more necessary. Marc Bloch showed the way, and Gaxotte, in his *Histoire des Français,* saluted him as an initiator. . . . Given that many traditions have disappeared (especially after the 1880 break that Péguy spoke of), that history permits us to become fully conscious of what was once experienced spontaneously and, in fine, unconsciously.

"History seen from the bottom up," absorbed by the study of specific mentalities and unconscious determinations, thus merged with a political (even more, an existential) attachment to the perpetuation of singularity and the maintenance of difference.

What resonance did Ariès's works have? In *Un historien du dimanche* he says, speaking of *L'histoire des populations françaises* and *Le temps de l'histoire:* "Those two books had a rather clandestine *succès d'estime.*"[11] The press clippings for the second of these works add a slight corrective to his memory.[12] Admittedly, neither the major newspapers nor the historical journals reviewed the book; in particular, the *Annales* said nothing about the work, even though it presented a lucid statement of its own program. Nonetheless, twenty periodicals mentioned, analyzed, or reviewed *Le temps de l'histoire*. The book was interpreted very differently from one review to another: as an account of an intellectual itinerary ("This presence of the personality of the author as he shares with us the debates within his conscience gives this work a particularly appealing character"; *Action Populaire*, September–October 1955); as a reflection on the present (which often led to citing the last sentence in the book, "History must give back its lost sense of particularities to a civilization that eliminates differences"); or as an investigation of the various conceptions of history that have succeeded one another in recent years. If we heed these notices, Philippe Ariès was not universally well known. If some reviewers seem to have known perfectly well who Philippe Ariès was and what he had written (Frédéric Mauro, writing in the *Bulletin de l'Université de Toulouse*, calls him a "demographer/historian," and the book column in *Oran Républicain* gives the titles of his two previous books and mentions that he was "editor of the series Civilisations d'hier et d'aujourd'hui and historical chronicler for the *Revue de la Table Ronde*"), others thought him a professional historian, as *Dimanche-Matin* stated, or, according to *Flandre Libérale*, "engaged in teaching." I might add that the book received one of the prizes awarded in 1954 by the Académie des Sciences Morales et Politiques, the Chaix d'Est-Ange prize "for a work of history," which Ariès shared with Roland Mousnier for his *Histoire générale des civilisations* (Presses Universitaires de France) on the sixteenth and seventeenth centuries.

The most interesting of these reviews are obviously the ones that saw the originality of the book's proposal to join an attachment to tradition with an adherence, in ideas and in acts, to a history that was neither that of the university nor that of Ariès's political clan. As Romain Sauvat wrote in *L'Indépendant*: "Here is a work that is sure to cause a stir in the Landerneau ['small world'] of the professional historians, and that will oblige some amateur historians (myself among them) to revise their ideas. . . . I am inclined to think that it is going to astonish and scandalize certain of the author's friends." Although the promised stir hardly materialized in the university milieu, the astonishment of the author's friends was genuine. We find a trace of it in a review in the *Journal de l'Amateur d'Art* signed "P. C."—certainly Pierre du Colombier, a contributor to *Paroles Françaises* and a friend of Ariès's, who wrote Ariès a long letter about *Le temps de l'histoire* in which he developed the same criticisms made in the *Journal de l'Amateur d'Art* :

On history in general and on what is called, in an expression that will soon disappear, our *engagement dans l'histoire* [involvement in history], one will find in this book extremely brilliant and special [specious?] insights with which I frankly declare I do not agree. I find in it the ravages made in all disciplines by a certain philosophy. I admit that I do not understand either what is "existential" history or why we are more "involved" in history than the generations that went before us.

Robert Kemp, writing in *Les Nouvelles Littéraires,* expressed his reservations less directly and with a pinch of irony:

Starting off from the doctrines of Action Française but respectfully detaching himself from them, he [Ariès] notes the role of Jacques Bainville and of his three great works, notably his *Histoire de France,* in that metamorphosis. Now he turns up as *[le voilà]* a disciple of Marc Bloch and Lucien Febvre. The old school attacked Bainville mercilessly. It guessed that he was dangerous. It is true that the new school often manifests itself in works of popularization.

In *Le Bulletin de Paris* a columnist, Michel Montel, concluded his long article titled "Notre temps peut-il se contenter d'une histoire 'existentielle'?" (Can our times be content with an "existential" history?) with these words:

The history that studies this shifting diversity, "existential" history, surely corresponds to the curiosities and the needs of our times. I do not believe that it exhausts the taste of the "honest man" for the vast perspectives in which reason is pleased to discover the relation between effects and causes. It is perhaps appropriate to join the teachings of Marc Bloch to the example of Bainville. But hasn't this already been done? See the admirable *Histoire des Français* of Pierre Gaxotte.

Gaxotte, incidentally, is mentioned only once in *Le temps de l'histoire.* When faced with a mode of thought they found difficult to understand, the authors who were ideologically the closest to Ariès expressed their discomfort through explicit rejection or a negation of differences.

Pierre Debray returned to the book in February 1955 in an article in *Aspects de la France*. His criticism is unambiguous:

Ariès speaks with a certain resentment of history "à la Bainville," which can be explained by the painful conflict he had to overcome between a monarchist family tradition and the university traditions. How can he fail to comprehend that all Bainville wanted to do was to grasp the national particularity of France through her *political* continuity?

Debray, a royalist, adds: "Existential history can render services only to the degree to which one recognizes its limitations—which are great." Debray then surveys those limitations. First, he borrows Henri-Irénée Marrou's criticism of Lucien Febvre in *De la connaissance historique;* next, and somewhat less predictably, he contrasts Febvre with "his friend Marc Bloch—the same Marc Bloch whose last lectures I had the inestimable fortune to attend. Can I admit that rereading the thick tome on 'the thaumaturgic kings' of that Jewish historian, a republican and a good democrat, enabled me to take the decisive step toward monarchy?" Debray continues with a reading of Bloch that is not precisely Ariès's: "So strong is the hold of prejudices on people's minds—even the most rigorous of them—that Marc Bloch imagined himself poles apart from Maurras. Nonetheless, he was doing organizer's empiricism just as [Molière's] bourgeois gentleman was writing prose—without knowing it." This Bloch in a Maurras vein, this historian of national continuity (Pierre Debray quotes, admiringly but inaccurately, the title, *Caractères originaux de l'histoire rurale en France [française]*), is obviously not the Bloch of *Le temps de l'histoire,* a historian of structural differences. Behind the common reference we can read Debray's inability to admit Ariès's originality.

It is nonetheless striking to see this respectful presence of Marc Bloch—in a variety of readings—in milieus that might seem poles apart, by culture and opinions, from those of the *Annales.* The role of that journal was of course recognized by Ariès's closest friends, who shared his overall approach but at times showed some irritation with it, as in the article on Ariès's book that Raoul Girardet wrote for *La Table Ronde* (a review to which Ariès regularly contributed) in February 1955. Although Girardet expresses his basic agreement with a way of considering history aimed at combining a "sense of diversity" and a "sense of heritage" with "lucidity and fidelity," he nonetheless adds:

Philippe Ariès risks falsifying the picture of contemporary historical thought by insisting somewhat too exclusively on the role of the review *Annales* and on the group of historians it brings together. Doubtless they were trainers; we are less sure they were innovators. It would perhaps be fairer to show the activities of the

Annales group as one of the aspects—often the most brilliant but at times the most contestable as well—of the work of an entire generation.

Here Girardet tempers his zeal for their common cause of redefining the task of the historian with a certain reticence about showing too much enthusiasm for the *Annales* group and a reluctance to support the tendency of that school or "group" to present itself as the sole champion of innovation.

How about the university? How was Ariès's book received in that milieu? In the absence of reviews in the "professional" historical journals, we have to rely on letters addressed to Philippe Ariès by some of the professors prominent at that time. Three of these are of particular interest; they all are generous with praise, but they hint at reservations regarding some of Ariès's formulations. Philippe Renouard, professor of medieval history at the University of Bordeaux, stressed concern for the role of the individual, who risked obliteration in a history of structures:

Historiography changes like everything else, but it is because our predecessors did what they did that we can do something else, which I think preferable, as you do. I just find that history is total only if, along with the study of currents of thought, mental structures, social groups, prevailing economic conditions *[la conjoncture]*, and disease, it reserves a place for the individuals who were in a position to orient events. You have not taken a clear position on that point. (Letter of 18 April 1954)

Charles-Henri Pouthas, professor at the Sorbonne, may have been expressing his distrust of new ideas when he communicated his regret that the book did not say more about scholarship and neglected François Guizot:

I would have given more space and rendered more justice to the movement of scholarly work that has always—since the sixteenth century—accompanied, but modestly and obscurely, the literary and superficial work that occupied the middle of the stage. I would have insisted much more on the eminent value and the lesson for the profession represented by my old Guizot. (Letter of 28 March 1954)

Victor-Lucien Tapié, also a professor at the Sorbonne, spoke in a fine letter written in a confidential tone of his debt to the founders of the *Annales* and of his fundamental agreement with the approach Ariès had adopted, following their lead. But like Pouthas, Tapié stressed erudition and the demands of university teaching, which differed from the instruction offered at the Sixth Section of the Ecole Pratique des Hautes Etudes (founded in 1947), the teaching institution of the *Annales* "group." This comment can be read as a discreet expression of reservations and a warning about hasty uses of a program for total and structural history.

These letters and articles clearly show that Philippe Ariès was somewhat out of phase from the beginning of his career as a historian. Too enthusiastic an adept of Bloch and Febvre for the *maîtres* of the university, too detached from Bainville's brand of history for his Action Française milieu, probably too much the amateur for the historians of the *Annales,* he found himself intellectually closer to people who ignored him and ideologically loyal to people who only half understood his definition of history. The misunderstandings created by these multiple but incongruent allegiances were not easily dissipated, and they put Philippe Ariès the author in a category of his own, long led the university to look at him askance, and induced the *Annales* to ignore his works—one exception was André Armengaud's critique of one chapter of *Histoire des populations françaises*[13]—until the review, as late as 1964, of *L'enfant et la vie familiale (Centuries of Childhood).*[14] They also made him suspect in the eyes of conservatives, who were bothered by Ariès's detachment from an established order founded on the immediate family, the all-powerful state, and the society of consumption. The misunderstandings and rejections that Ariès often laughed at later (but suffered from at the time) began with the publication of *Le temps de l'histoire.*

We need to read Ariès's book by putting it back in its time, one still marked by fresh memories of a war fertile in unexpected combinations and paradoxical stands. But we also need to read it in relation to the way history is written today. Indeed, the book's two central chapters on attitudes toward the history of the Middle Ages and the seventeenth century show that Ariès was one of the first to draw up an outline for a history of history. After those two studies, written in 1950 and 1951, that discipline took off, as attested by the proliferation of general titles (by definition excluding the works of one author) listed under the heading, "Historiographie" in the *Bibliographie Annuelle de l'Histoire de France* (eight titles in 1953–54, fifty-three in 1982, and forty-seven in 1983), the publication of bibliographies devoted to historiography alone,[15] and the existence of an International Commission on Historiography for historians specializing in the genre. Although the procedure is often hard on pioneers, we can thus compare what Ariès was writing more than thirty years ago with what accumulated research in the history of history has taught us since.

Philippe Ariès notes three traits essential to defining the Middle Ages: first, the church's preservation of a sense of time measurement (needed to fix the date of Easter and bring individual chronologies into concordance with biblical chronology); second, a division, until the thirteenth century, between history, which was the monopoly of the monasteries and the church, and the epic, which narrated seignorial and royal traditions; third, the establishment of a history that was both dynastic and national, was divided into reigns, and was made visible and intelligible in the statues and the stained-glass windows of Reims, the tombs of Saint-Denis, and the *Grandes chroniques de France,* a work that was both a "romance of the kings" and the "first history of France." These traits are the same ones that historians of the history of the Middle Ages today—Bernard Guenée in particular—now consider essential. In the abbeys, liturgical concerns are recognized as having been of primary importance in the interest in chronology that lent monastic chronicles their form and meaning. Guenée states: "For centuries the science of ecclesiastical computation and a concern for time, spurred on by the passion of the liturgy, profoundly marked monastic culture."[16] In the secular courts, on the other hand, history was the province of jongleurs and minstrels; it was written in the vernacular, first in verse and then in prose, and was founded on topics from the oral tradition and from the chansons de geste: "Thus, by the nature of its sources, by the literary culture of its authors, by the tastes of the publics to which it was addressed, that history was irresistibly drawn toward the epic. It breathed the same air as the epic; it cared little for chronology; it had no scruples about mixing truth and poetry."[17] This basic opposition, which Philippe Ariès had clearly perceived, provided an organization to the writing of history until the rise of the modern states gave it other aims in the celebration of dynastic continuity and the exaltation of a national identity. This development brought a new role for the historian: "History was no longer the servant of theology and of law; it became very officially the auxiliary of power. The official historian certainly had no intention of renouncing truth, but he knew himself, and he chose to be first a servant of the state." Hence a new function for history of reinforcing the feeling of belonging to a nation identified by its past.[18]

In treating the seventeenth century, Philippe Ariès constructed his description of the history written in the age of French classicism on a clearly defined opposition: to one side there was a well-established genre—the history of France—the domain of compilers and continuers who, title after title, simply offered variations on a theme that had been given once and for all; to the other side there was erudition based on the study, collection, and publication of manuscripts or iconographic documents. This made a sharp contrast between a narrative history innocent of all historical criticism and differing from one author to another not by the advancement of knowledge but thanks to shifting ideas and sensibilities and a historical erudition born of the curiosity of collectors, carried out in the milieus of the *bourgeoisie d'offices* (the juridical and administrative bourgeoisie), and crowned by the collective work of the Benedictines of Saint-Maur.

Ariès blazed a number of new paths in this essay on the seventeenth century: first, by his comparison of relations of the same episodes (the stories of Childeric and of Joan of Arc) in the various histories of France published between the sixteenth century and the early nineteenth; next, by noting the treatment and the function of history in a decidedly nonhistorical genre, the novel; and finally, by giving prime importance to iconographic documents (from portrait galleries and *cabinets d'histoire*). Such documents arose out of an interest in preserving historical curiosity, "as if history, expelled from literature, had taken refuge in iconography and, scorned by the writers, had taken shelter with the collectors"; later they contributed to the constitution of an erudition based on a quest for ancient monuments and a passion for collecting them. For perhaps the first time on a similar scale, Ariès discovered the image and its importance for the historian—a discovery that sealed forever his connivance with his wife, Primerose, who had studied art and had taught him to look, and that launched their collaboration on historical projects. In *Un historien du dimanche* Ariès recalls the genesis of one of the most original passages in his study of seventeenth-century history:

During our bicycle jaunts along the banks of the Loire, we visited a gallery of historical portraits in the château de Beauregard that deeply impressed me. The idea came to me that they were a form of representation of the times that was comparable to that of the chroniclers but more concrete and more familiar. It was the first time an artistic document furnished me with a novel theme for reflection. One thing followed another, and I passed from portrait galleries to seventeenth-century picture collectors, and that took us, my wife and I, to the Cabinet des Estampes [Print Collection] of the Bibliothèque Nationale to study Gaignères's collections. . . . The die was cast. We were soon to install our headquarters in the Cabinet des Estampes, where we gathered part of the documentation for my next book, *L'enfant et la vie familiale sous l'ancien régime*.[19]

Ariès's analysis of seventeenth-century histories still seems valid, reread in the light of work done during the past fifteen years, but it calls for one or two remarks. The first concerns Ariès's evaluation of the role of milieus of "the robe"—magistrates and officials—in the development of a genuinely historical curiosity turned to a search for and interpretation of documents. Thanks to the books of George Huppert and Donald Kelley, we now have a better appreciation of the importance of the history written by such men of law. Its high point was not in the early seventeenth century but before, in the last third of the sixteenth, between 1560, the year of the publication of Etienne Pasquier's *Recherches de la France,* and 1599, the year La Popelinière's *Idée de l'histoire accomplie* appeared, or perhaps 1604, the date of the latter's *Histoire des histoires.* With such men, as with others Ariès does not mention (Jean Bodin, Louis Le Roy, Nicolas Vignier), a new practice of history resulted from a novel merging of the antiquarians' demand for an erudition based on the collection of archives and on philological knowledge; the establishment of a close connection between law and history, both understood from the perspective of a fundamental historicism; and the project for a "new," "perfect," and "accomplished" history aiming, for each people under consideration, at a rational comprehension of all human activities—what La Popelinière called "the representation of everything."[20]

From this perspective, then, the erudition of men of "the robe" in the early seventeenth century was not the starting point of a renewal of historical knowledge but, to the contrary, the trace of an alliance, by then dissolved, that once linked the rigors of the critical method and the design for a universal history capable of explaining societies in their entirety and in their becoming. Admittedly, Duchesne, Godefroy, Peiresc, and later Du Cange and the Benedictines of Saint-Maur went back to the erudite tradition, but they turned it to the publication of texts, to monumental collections, and to dictionaries rather than to history itself, which was left to compilers and men of letters. The contrast Ariès recognizes between narrative history and historical erudition thus existed in the seventeenth century, but it should be understood as the result of a dissociation of elements put together during the last third of the sixteenth century by historians formed in the municipal *collèges* and the newly revived law faculties, all of them lawyers or officeholders, men of the law interested in viewing together the history of humanity and the history of the nation.

A second remark concerning Philippe Ariès's evaluations relates to the opposition he sets up between erudition and the history of France in the classical age. It is clear that the authors of general histories of France were not unaware of the works of erudition, citing and making use of collections of ancient and medieval texts, chronicles and old memoirs, and the research of antiquarian scholars from Etienne Pasquier to Théodore Godefroy. After 1650 the repertory of references opens to include new titles: the new collections of documents of such scholars as Duchesne, Dom d'Achery, and Baluze; the studies of the libertine scholars of the first half of the century (Pierre Dupuy, Gabriel Naudé, Pierre Petau); and the works of the Saint-Maur group under the leadership of Mabillon.[21] Moreover, the project of some of the historians who wrote a history of France in the seventeenth century is not all that far from the intentions of the champions of the "new" history of the sixteenth. Mézeray, for example, devotes a portion of each of his chapters to the mores and customs of the peoples and times he treats.[22] Even when it was organized by reigns and totally guided by the destiny of the monarchy, general history did not completely forget the preoccupations of the antiquarians and the "erudites." After all, the same Mézeray, who was no stranger to the learned discussions that took place in the library of the Dupuy brothers, wrote a *Dictionnaire historique, géographique, étymologique, particulièrement pour l'histoire de France et pour la langue française,* unpublished during his lifetime. Thus it is perhaps wiser not to overemphasize the cleavage between the two forms of history that Philippe Ariès identifies, which are less foreign to one another than might be thought, given that the more literary variety was well aware of the more erudite.

A grasp of why the distance between the two nonetheless seems so great leads us to a point Ariès underestimates—the enrollment of history in the service of monarchic glory and the exaltation of the prince. His interest in liberating the history he wanted to write from the weight of the state and the primacy of the political led him to downplay the effects of royal patronage and the direction of letters on the history produced during the seventeenth century. The division between "erudites" and historians did not reside only in a difference of manner and method but referred to two functions that were very differently recognized by the monarch: whereas the first, even when they benefited from royal gratifications, remained outside the enterprise of celebration of the king and the dynasty, the second, whether or not they held the posts of historiographers of the king or historiographers of France, participated very directly in fashioning the glory of the reigning sovereign by writing the history of the reigns of his predecessors and relating his own history.[23] Hence—and necessarily—the central position of the king, who was ultimately the unique object of a discourse always calculated to persuade the spectator of the grandeur of the prince and the absolute power of sovereigns. "The history of a Kingdom or a Nation has as its object the Prince and the State; there is, so to speak, the center to which everything must tend and relate." This statement of Father Gabriel Daniel, given in the preface of his *Histoire de France* (1713), echoes a remark that Pellisson had made forty years earlier: "The King must be praised everywhere, but, so to speak, without praise."[24] All the histories of France of the seventeenth century responded to that program, each in its own way, whether or not they were directly commissioned or sponsored by the state; by that token, they conformed to the demands of the sovereign power.

Friendship with history. Philippe Ariès says somewhere in *Le temps de l'histoire* that by rejecting that friendship, the conservative societies of the twentieth century closed themselves within their own values, denied other traditions, and eventually dried up because of their inability to grasp the diversity of their world. It is because he was curious about differences and eager to understand what was outside his own culture—that of his times and that of his milieu—that Philippe Ariès was able to escape that futile retreat into timeworn certitudes. This is perhaps the most forceful lesson of this book that says there is no identity without confrontation, no living tradition without experiencing today, no intelligence of the present without comprehension of the discontinuities of history. Philippe Ariès's entire life and his lifework were dominated by the small number of ideas he formulated in a slim collection published in Monaco in 1954, the ideas of a man who truly felt a great friendship with history.

Notes

Introduction

1. Michel de Certeau, "Microtechniques et discours panoptique: Un quiproquo," in de Certeau, *Histoire et psychanalyse entre science et fiction* (Paris: Gallimard, 1987), available in English as "Micro-techniques and Panoptic Discourse: A Quid pro Quo," *Humanities in Society* 5, 3–4 (1982): 257–65, and in de Certeau, *Heterologies: Discourse on the Other,* trans. Brian Massumi, foreword by Wlad Godzich, Theory and History of Literature 17 (Minneapolis: University of Minnesota Press, 1986), 185–92.

2. Roger Chartier, *The Cultural Uses of Print in Early Modern France,* trans. Lydia G. Cochrane (Princeton: Princeton University Press, 1987); Chartier, *The Cultural Origins of the French Revolution,* trans. Lydia G. Cochrane (Durham, N.C.: Duke University Press, 1991); Chartier, *The Order of Books: Readers, Authors, and Libraries in Europe between the Fourteenth and Eighteenth Centuries,* trans. Lydia G. Cochrane (Cambridge: Polity Press; Stanford: Stanford University Press, 1994); Chartier, *Forms and Meanings: Texts, Performances, and Audiences from Codex to Computer* (Philadelphia: University of Pennsylvania Press, 1995).

3. In France, three publications describe the state of affairs in the discipline of history: *Histoire sociale, histoire globale?* Actes du colloque des 27–28 janvier 1989, ed. Christophe Charle (Paris: Editions de la Maison des Sciences de l'Homme, 1993); *Passés recomposés: Champs et chantiers de l'histoire,* ed. Jean Boutier and Dominique Julia (Paris: Editions Autrement, 1994); and *L'histoire et le métier d'historien en France 1945–1995,* ed. François Bédarida with the collaboration of Maurice Aymard, Yves-Marie Bercé, and Jean-François Sirinelli, preface by Jacques Le Goff and Nicolas Roussellier (Paris: Editions de la Maison des Sciences de l'Homme, 1995). For the United States, see Joyce Appleby, Lynn Hunt, and Margaret Jacob, *Telling the Truth about History* (New York: W. W. Norton, 1994).

4. Jacques Rancière, *Les mots de l'histoire: Essai de poétique du savoir* (Paris: Editions du Seuil, 1992), 45, available in English as *The Names of History: On the Poetics of Knowledge,* trans. Hassan Melehy, foreword by Hayden White (Minneapolis: University of Minnesota Press, 1994), quotation 45.

5. Maurice Agulhon, Pierre Chaunu, Georges Duby, Raoul Girardet, Jacques Le Goff, Michelle Perrot, and René Rémond, *Essais d'ego-histoire,* ed. Pierre Nora (Paris: Gallimard, 1987). For a South American example, see *Pensar la Argentina: Los historiadores hablan de historia y política,* ed. Roy Hora and Javier Trimboli (Buenos Aires: Ediciones El Cielo por Asalto, 1994).

6. Arlette Farge, *Le cours ordinaire des choses dans la cité du XVIIIᵉ siècle* (Paris: Editions du Seuil, 1994). See also Farge, *Le goût de l'archive* (Paris: Editions du Seuil, 1989); Michel Foucault, "La vie des hommes infâmes," *Les Cahiers du Chemin* 29 (1977): 12–29, reprinted in Foucault, *Dits et écrits, 1954–1988,* ed. Daniel Defert and François Ewald with the collaboration of Jacques Lagrange, 4 vols. (Paris: Gallimard, 1994), 3:237–53.

7. Alain Desrosières, *La politique des grands nombres: Histoire de la raison statistique* (Paris: Editions de la Découverte, 1993).

8. Pierre Bourdieu, *La distinction: Critique sociale du jugement* (Paris: Editions de Minuit, 1979), available in English as *Distinction: A Social Critique of the Judgment of Taste,* trans. Richard Nice (Cambridge: Harvard University Press, 1984).

9. Richard Rorty, "The Historiography of Philosophy: Four Genres," in *Philosophy in History: Essays on the Historiography of Philosophy,* ed. Richard Rorty, J. B. Schneewind, and Quentin Skinner (Cambridge: Cambridge University Press, 1984), 49–75.

10. Alasdair McIntyre, "The Relationship of Philosophy to Its Past," in Rorty, Schneewind, and Skinner, *Philosophy in History,* 31–48.

11. Armando Petrucci, *La scrittura: Ideologia e rappresentazione,* Piccola Biblioteca Einaudi 473 (Turin: Einaudi, 1986), available in English as *Public Lettering: Script, Power, and Culture,* trans. Linda Lappin (Chicago: University of Chicago Press, 1993); Petrucci, *Le scritture ultime: Ideologia della morte e strategie dello scrivere nella tradizione occidentale* (Turin: Einaudi, 1995).

12. For one attempt to tie together within one history a work, its forms and "performances," its publics, and its meanings, see Roger Chartier, "George Dandin, ou le social en représentation," *Annales: Histoires, Sciences Sociales* 2 (1994): 277–309, available in English as "From Court Festivity to City Spectators," trans. Lydia G. Cochrane, in Chartier, *Forms and Meanings,* 43–82.

13. Michel de Certeau, *L'écriture de l'histoire* (1975), 3d ed. (Paris: Gallimard, 1984), available in English as *The Writing of History,* trans. Tom Conley (New York: Columbia University Press, 1988); Paul Ricoeur, *Temps et récit,* 3 vols. (Paris: Editions du Seuil, 1983–85), available in English as *Time and Narrative,* trans. Kathleen McLaughlin and David Pellauer, 3 vols. (Chicago: University of Chicago Press, 1984–85).

14. François Hartog, "L'art du récit historique," in Boutier and Julia, *Passés recomposés,* 184–93.

15. Ricoeur, *Temps et récit,* 3:203–5; *Time and Narrative,* 3:142–4.

16. Eric W. Hobsbawm, "The Historian between the Quest for the Universal and the Quest for Identity," special issue, "The Social Responsibility of the Historian," *Diogenes* 168 (1994): 51–64, quotation 59. Eric Hobsbawm refers here to Benedict Anderson, *Imagined Communities: Reflections on the Origin and Spread of Nationalism* (1983), rev. ed. (London: Verso, 1991).

17. Appleby, Hunt, and Jacob, *Telling the Truth about History,* 259, 283.

18. Paul Ricoeur, "History and Rhetoric," trans. Thomas Epstein, special issue, "The Social Responsibility of the Historian," *Diogenes* 168 (1994): 7–24, quotations 22–23.

Chapter 1. History between Narrative and Knowledge

1. "Histoire et sciences sociales: Un tournant critique?" *Annales ESC* 43 (1988): 291–93, quotation 291–92.

2. David Harlan, "Intellectual History and the Return of Literature," *American Historical Review* 94 (1989): 879–907, quotation 881.

3. Carlo Ginzburg, "Spie: Radici di un paradigma indiziario," in Ginzburg, *Miti, emblemi, spie: Morfologia e storia* (Turin: Einaudi, 1986), 158–209, available in English as "Clues: Roots of an Evidential Paradigm," in Ginzburg, *Clues, Myths, and the Historical Method,* trans. John Tedeschi and Anne Tedeschi (Baltimore: Johns Hopkins University Press, 1989), 96–125, in French translation as "Traces: Racines d'un paradigme indiciaire," in Ginzburg, *Mythes, emblèmes, traces: Morphologie et histoire* (Paris, Flammarion, 1989), 139–80.

4. Giovanni Levi, *L'eredità immateriale: Carriera di un esorcista nel Piemonte del Seicento* (Turin: Einaudi, 1989), available in English as *Inheriting Power: The Story of an Exorcist,* trans. Lydia G. Cochrane (Chicago: University of Chicago Press, 1988); Jaime Contreras, *Sotos contra Riquelmes: Regidores, inquisidores y criptojudíos* (Madrid: Anaya/Mario Muchnik, 1992).

5. Giovanni Levi, "Les usages de la biographie," *Annales ESC* 44 (1989): 1325–36, quotation 1333–34.

6. Contreras, *Sotos contra Riquelmes,* 30.

7. Michel de Certeau, *L'écriture de l'histoire* (1975), 3d ed. (Paris: Gallimard, 1984), available in English as *The Writing of History,* trans. Tom Conley (New York: Columbia University Press, 1988); and Paul Ricoeur, *Temps et récit,* 3 vols. (Paris: Editions du Seuil, 1983–85), available in English as *Time and Narrative,* trans. Kathleen McLaughlin and David Pellauer, 3 vols. (Chicago: University of Chicago Press, 1984–85).

8. Jacques Rancière, *Les mots de l'histoire: Essai de poétique du savoir* (Paris: Editions du Seuil, 1992), 21, quoted from Rancière, *The Names of History: On the Poetics of Knowledge,* trans. Hassan Melehy, foreword by Hayden White (Minneapolis: University of Minnesota Press, 1994), 8.

9. Hayden White, *Metahistory: The Historical Imagination in Nineteenth-Century Europe* (Baltimore: Johns Hopkins University Press, 1973); White, *Tropics of Discourse: Essays in Cultural Criticism* (Baltimore: Johns Hopkins University Press, 1978); White, *The Content of the Form: Narrative Discourse and Historical Representation* (Baltimore: Johns Hopkins University Press, 1987).

10. Reinhart Koselleck, "Erfahrungswandel und Methodenwechsel: Eine historisch-anthropologische Skizze," in *Historische Methode,* ed. Christian Meier and Jörn Rüsen (Munich: Deutscher Taschenbuch, 1988), 13–61.

11. Philippe Carrard, *Poetics of the New History: French Historical Discourse from Braudel to Chartier* (Baltimore: Johns Hopkins University Press, 1992).

12. John E. Toews, "Intellectual History after the Linguistic Turn: The Autonomy of Meaning and the Irreducibility of Experience," *American Historical Review* 92 (1987): 879–907, quotations 882.

13. Keith Michael Baker, *Inventing the French Revolution: Essays on French Political Culture in the Eighteenth Century* (Cambridge: Cambridge University Press, 1990), 9, 5.

14. Marcel Gauchet, "Changement de paradigme en sciences sociales?" *Le Débat* 50 (1988): 165–70, quotation 169.

15. Gabrielle M. Spiegel, "History, Historicism, and the Social Logic of the Text in the Middle Ages," *Speculum: A Journal of Medieval Studies* 65, 1 (1990): 59–86, quotation 60.

16. Pierre Bourdieu, *Choses dites* (Paris: Editions de Minuit, 1987), 76.

17. Stephen Greenblatt, "Towards a Poetics of Culture," in *The New Historicism,* ed. H. Aram Veeser (New York: Routledge, 1989), 1–14, quotation 12.

18. On the works of Norbert Elias, see *Materialen zu Norbert Elias' Zivilisationstheorie,* ed. Peter R. Gleichmann, Johan Goudsblom, and Hermann Korte, 2 vols. (Frankfurt am Main: Suhrkamp, 1979, 1982); Hermann Korte, *Über Norbert Elias: Das Werden eines Menschenwissenschaftlers* (Frankfurt am Main: Suhrkamp, 1988); Stephen Mennell, *Norbert Elias: Civilization and the Human Self-Image* (Oxford: Basil Blackwell, 1989); Roger Chartier, "Formation sociale et économie psychique: La société de cour dans le procès de civilisation," preface to Norbert Elias, *La société de cour* (Paris: Flammarion, 1985), i–xxviii, available in English as "Social Figuration and Habitus: Reading Elias," in Chartier, *Cultural History: Between Practices and Representations,* trans. Lydia G. Cochrane (Cambridge: Polity Press; Ithaca: Cornell University Press, 1988), 71–94; Chartier, "Conscience de soi et lien social," foreword to Norbert Elias, *La société des individus* (Paris: Fayard, 1991), 7–29, translated below, chapter 8.

19. Louis Marin, *Le portrait du roi* (Paris: Editions de Minuit, 1981), available in English as *Portrait of the King,* trans. Martha Houle (Minneapolis: University of Minnesota Press, 1988); Marin, *Des pouvoirs de l'image: Gloses* (Paris: Editions du Seuil, 1993); Bronislaw Geremek, *Inutiles au monde: Truands et misérables dans l'Europe moderne (1350–1600)* (Paris: Gallimard/Julliard, 1980), Geremek, *La potence ou la pitié: L'Europe et les pauvres du Moyen Age à nos jours* (Paris: Gallimard, 1987); Carlo Ginzburg, *I Benandanti: Stregoneria e culti agrari tra Cinquecento e Seicento* (Turin: Einaudi, 1966), available in English as *The Night Battles: Witchcraft and Agrarian Cults in the Sixteenth and Seventeenth Centuries,* trans. John Tedeschi and Anne Tedeschi (Baltimore: Johns Hopkins University Press, 1983; New York: Penguin, 1985).

20. Pierre Bourdieu, *La noblesse d'état: Grandes écoles et esprit de corps* (Paris: Editions de Minuit, 1989), 10.

21. Arlette Farge and Michelle Perrot, "Au-delà du regard des hommes," *Le Monde des Débats* 2 (1992): 20–21.

22. Thomas Laqueur, *Making Sex: Body and Gender from the Greeks to Freud* (Cambridge: Harvard University Press, 1990), 5–6.

23. White, *Tropics of Discourse,* 82.

24. White, *Content of the Form,* 192–93.

25. Pierre Vidal-Naquet, *Les assassins de la mémoire: Un "Eichmann de papier" et autres essais sur le révisionnisme* (Paris: La Découverte, 1987), 148–49, quoted from Vidal-Naquet, *Assassins of Memory: Essays on the Denial of the Holocaust,* trans. Jeffrey Mehlman (New York: Columbia University Press, 1992), 110–11.

26. Anthony Grafton, *Forgers and Critics: Creativity and Duplicity in Western*

Scholarship (Princeton: Princeton University Press, 1990); Julio Caro Baroja, *Las falsificaciones de la historia (en relación con la de España)* (Barcelona: Seix Barral, 1992).

27. Carlo Ginzburg, foreword to Lorenzo Valla, *La Donation de Constantin (Sur la Donation de Constantin, à lui faussement attribuée et mensongère)*, text translated, with commentary, by Jean-Baptiste Giard (Paris: Les Belles Lettres, 1993), ix–xxi, quotation xi.

28. Michel de Certeau, "L'opération historiographique," in de Certeau, *L'écriture de l'histoire*, 63–120, quoted from de Certeau, "The Historiographical Operation," in de Certeau, *Writing of History*, 56–113, quotation 103 n. 5.

Chapter 2. Four Questions for Hayden White

1. Hayden White has replied to my questions in "A Response to Professor Chartier's Four Questions," published in Spanish as "Respuesta a las cuatro preguntas del profesor Chartier," *Historia y Grafía* 4 (1995): 317–29. The original English text will be published in *Storia della Storiografia*. The works of Hayden White cited in this chapter are *Metahistory: The Historical Imagination in Nineteenth-Century Europe* (Baltimore: Johns Hopkins University Press, 1973); *Tropics of Discourse: Essays in Cultural Criticism* (Baltimore: Johns Hopkins University Press, 1978); and *The Content of the Form: Narrative Discourse and Historical Representation* (Baltimore: Johns Hopkins University Press, 1987).

2. Paul Veyne, *Comment on écrit l'histoire: Essai d'épistémologie* (Paris: Editions du Seuil, 1971, 1978), available in English as *Writing History: Essay on Epistemology*, trans. Mina Moore-Rinvolucri (Middletown, Conn.: Wesleyan University Press, 1984); Michel de Certeau, "L'opération historique," in *Faire de l'histoire*, vol. 1, *Nouveaux problèmes*, ed. Jacques Le Goff and Pierre Nora (Paris: Gallimard, 1974), 3–41.

3. François Furet, "L'histoire quantitative et la construction du fait historique," *Annales ESC* 26 (1971): 63–75, reprinted in Le Goff and Nora, *Faire de l'histoire*, 1:42–61, and available in English as "Quantitative Methods in History," in *Constructing the Past: Essays in Historical Methodology*, ed. Jacques Le Goff and Pierre Nora, intro. by Colin Lucas (Paris: Editions de la Maison des Sciences de l'Homme; Cambridge: Cambridge University Press, 1985), 12–27.

4. Veyne, *Comment on écrit l'histoire*, 111; *Writing History*, 87.

5. Michel de Certeau, "Une épistémologie de transition: Paul Veyne," *Annales ESC* 27 (1972): 1317–27; Michel de Certeau, "L'opération historiographique," in de Certeau, *L'écriture de l'histoire* (1975), 3d ed. (Paris: Gallimard, 1984), 63–120, available in English as "The Historiographical Operation," in de Certeau, *The Writing of History*, trans. Tom Conley (New York: Columbia University Press, 1988), 56–113.

6. Gabrielle M. Spiegel, "History, Historicism, and the Social Logic of the Text in the Middle Ages," *Speculum: A Journal of Medieval Studies* 65 (1990): 59–86, quotation 64; David Harlan, "Intellectual History and the Return of Literature," *American Historical Review* 94 (1989): 581–609, quotation 593 n. 48.

7. Hans Kellner, "A Bedrock of Order: Hayden White's Linguistic Humanism," suppl. 19, "*Metahistory*: Six Critiques," *History and Theory* (1980): 1–29, quotation 23.

8. Harlan, "Intellectual History and the Return of Literature," 593.

9. Hayden White, " 'Figuring the Nature of the Times Deceased': Literary Theory and Historical Writing," in *The Future of Literary Theory,* ed. Ralph Cohen (New York: Routledge, 1990), quotation 28.

10. Arnaldo Momigliano, "The Rhetoric of History and the History of Rhetoric: On Hayden White's Tropes," in Momigliano, *Settimo contributo alla storia degli studi classici del mondo antico* (Rome: Edizioni di Storia e Letteratura, 1984), 49–59; Carlo Ginzburg, "Just One Witness," in *Probing the Limits of Representation: Nazism and the "Final Solution,"* ed. Saul Friedlander (Cambridge: Harvard University Press, 1992), 82–96; Spiegel, "History, Historicism, and the Social Logic of the Text in the Middle Ages," 64, 69, 75; Russell Jacoby, "A New Intellectual History," *American Historical Review* 97 (1992): 405–24; on Hayden White, see 407–13.

11. White, " 'Figuring the Nature of the Times Deceased,' " 39.

12. For a refutation of the opposition between rhetoric and proof, see Carlo Ginzburg, foreword to Lorenzo Valla, *La Donation de Constantin (Sur la Donation de Constantin, à lui faussement attribuée et mensongère),* trans. and ed. Jean-Baptiste Giard (Paris: Belles Lettres, 1993), ix–xxi.

13. De Certeau, "L'opération historiographique," 64, quoted from "Historiographical Operation," 103.

14. White, " 'Figuring the Nature of the Times Deceased,' " 29.

15. Gene H. Bell-Villada, "Criticism and the State (Political and Otherwise) of the Americas," in *Criticism in the University,* ed. Gerald Graff and Reginald Gibbons, TriQuarterly Series on Criticism and Culture 1 (Evanston, Ill.: Northwestern University Press, 1985), 124–44, quotation 143; White, " 'Figuring the Nature of the Times Deceased,' " 31.

16. Pierre Vidal-Naquet, *Les assassins de la mémoire: Un "Eichmann de papier" et autres essais sur le révisionnisme* (Paris: Découverte, 1987), available in English as *Assassins of Memory: Essays on the Denial of the Holocaust,* trans. Jeffrey Mehlman (New York: Columbia University Press, 1992).

17. Hayden White, "Historical Emplotment and the Problems of Truth," in Friedlander, *Probing the Limits of Representation,* 37–53, quotation 38.

18. See, in this connection, Jonathan Spence, *The Question of Hu* (New York: Knopf, 1988), and Simon Schama, *Dead Certainties (Unwarranted Speculations)* (New York: Knopf, 1991), works that play, each in its own manner, with the frontier between history and fiction. See also Bruce Mazlish, "The Question of *The Question of Hu,*" and Cushing Strout, "Border Crossings: History, Fictions, and *Dead Certainties,*" *History and Theory* 31 (1992): 143–52 and 152–62, respectively.

Chapter 3. Michel de Certeau

1. Michel de Certeau, *La prise de la parole* (Paris: Desclée De Brouwer, 1968), 22.

2. Michel de Certeau, *Le mémorial de Pierre Favre* (Paris: Desclée De Brouwer, 1960); de Certeau, *Guide spirituel de Jean-Joseph Surin* (Paris: Desclée De Brouwer, 1963); de Certeau, *Correspondence de Jean-Joseph Surin* (Paris: Desclée De Brouwer, 1966); de Certeau, *La fable mystique, XVIe–XVIIe siècle* (Paris: Gallimard, 1982), available in English as *The Mystic Fable,* vol. 1, *The Sixteenth and Seventeenth Centuries,* trans. Michael B. Smith (Chicago: University

of Chicago Press, 1992); de Certeau, *La possession de Loudun* (1970), 2d ed. (Paris: Gallimard Archives, 1980; Gallimard/Julliard, 1990).

3. De Certeau, *La possession de Loudun,* 10–13.

4. Michel de Certeau, "Un langage altéré: La parole de la possédée," in de Certeau, *L'écriture de l'histoire* (1975), 3d ed. (Paris: Gallimard, 1984) 249–73, available in English as "Language Altered: The Sorcerer's Speech," in de Certeau, *The Writing of History,* trans. Tom Conley (New York: Columbia University Press, 1988), 244–68.

5. Michel de Certeau, "Ethno-graphie: L'oralité, ou L'espace de l'autre: Léry," in de Certeau *L'écriture de l'histoire,* 215–48, available in English as "Ethno-Graphy: Speech, or the Space of the Other: Jean de Léry," in de Certeau, *Writing of History,* 209–43; Michel de Certeau, Dominique Julia, and Jacques Revel, *Une politique de la langue: La Révolution française et les patois. L'enquête de Grégoire* (Paris: Gallimard, 1975).

6. Michel de Certeau, "L'opération historique," in *Faire de l'histoire,* vol. 1, *Nouveaux problèmes,* ed. Jacques Le Goff and Pierre Nora (Paris: Gallimard, 1974), 3–41; de Certeau, "L'opération historiographique," in de Certeau, *L'écriture de l'histoire,* 63–120, available in English as "The Historiographical Operation" in de Certeau, *Writing of History,* 56–113.

7. De Certeau, "L'opération historiographique," 64 n. 5; quoted from "Historiographical Operation," 103.

8. Paul Veyne, *Comment on écrit l'histoire: Essai d'épistémologie* (Paris: Editions du Seuil, 1971), available in English as *Writing History: Essay on Epistemology,* trans. Mina Moore-Rinvolucri (Middletown, Conn.: Wesleyan University Press, 1984).

9. Michel de Certeau, "Une épistémologie de transition: Paul Veyne," *Annales ESC* 27 (1972): 1317–27.

10. François Furet, "L'histoire quantitative et la construction du fait en histoire," *Annales ESC* 26 (1971): 63–75, reprinted in Le Goff and Nora, *Faire de l'histoire,* 1:42–61, quoted from Furet, "Quantitative Methods in History," in *Constructing the Past: Essays in Historical Methodology,* ed. Jacques Le Goff and Pierre Nora, introduction by Colin Lucas (Paris: Editions de la Maison des Sciences de l'Homme; Cambridge: Cambridge University Press, 1985), 12–27, quotation 20–21.

11. Emmanuel Le Roy Ladurie, *Le territoire de l'historien* (Paris: Gallimard, 1973), 14, quoted from Le Roy Ladurie, *The Territory of the Historian,* trans. Ben Reynolds and Siân Reynolds (Chicago: University of Chicago Press, 1979), 6.

12. Michel Foucault, "Sur l'archéologie des sciences: Réponse au Cercle d'épistémologie," *Cahiers pour l'Analyse* 9 (1968): 9–40, reprinted in Foucault, *Dits et écrits, 1954–1988,* ed. Daniel Defert and François Ewald with the collaboration of Jacques Lagrange, 4 vols. (Paris: Gallimard, 1994), 1:696–731; Foucault, introduction to *L'archéologie du savoir* (Paris: Gallimard, 1969), 9–28, available in English as Foucault, *The Archaeology of Knowledge and The Discourse on Language,* trans. A. M. Sheridan Smith (New York: Pantheon, 1972); Foucault, *L'ordre du discours* (Paris: Gallimard, 1969), available in English as "Orders of Discourse" in appendix to *Archaeology of Knowledge.*

13. De Certeau, "L'opération historiographique," 99; "Historiographical Operation," 84.

14. Paul Ricoeur, *Temps et récit,* 3 vols. (Paris: Editions du Seuil, 1983–85), available in English as *Time and Narrative,* trans. Kathleen McLaughlin and David Pellauer, 3 vols. (Chicago: University of Chicago Press, 1984–85).

15. Lawrence Stone, "The Revival of Narrative: Reflections on a New Old History," *Past and Present* 85 (1979): 3–24.

16. De Certeau, "L'opération historiographique," 110; "Historiographical Operation," 93.

17. Hayden White, *Metahistory: The Historical Imagination in Nineteenth-Century Europe* (Baltimore: Johns Hopkins University Press, 1973).

18. De Certeau, "Une épistémologie de transition," 1324.

19. Michel de Certeau, interview in *Le Nouvel Observateur,* 25 September 1982, 118–21.

20. Michel de Certeau, *L'invention du quotidien,* vol. 1 of *Arts de faire* (1980), new ed., ed. Luce Giard (Paris: Gallimard, 1990), available in English as *The Practice of Everyday Life,* trans. Steven F. Rendall (Berkeley: University of California Press, 1984).

21. Michel de Certeau, "Le rire de Michel Foucault," *Revue de la Bibliothèque Nationale* 14 (1984): 10–16, reprinted in de Certeau, *Histoire et psychanalyse entre science et fiction* (Paris: Gallimard, 1987), 51–65, available in English as "The Laugh of Michel Foucault," in de Certeau, *Heterologies: Discourse on the Other,* trans. Brian Massumi, foreword by Wlad Godzich, Theory and History of Literature 17 (Minneapolis: University of Minnesota Press, 1986), 193–98.

Chapter 4. The Chimera of the Origin

1. Michel Foucault, "Qu'est-ce qu'un auteur?" *Bulletin de la Société Française de Philosophie,* 1969, 73–104, reprinted in *Littoral* 9 (1983): 3–23, and in Foucault, *Dits et écrits, 1954–1988,* ed. Daniel Defert and François Ewald with the collaboration of Jacques Lagrange, 4 vols. (Paris: Gallimard, 1994), 1:789–821, and available in English (without the debate that followed the lecture) as "What Is an Author?" in Foucault, *Language, Counter-Memory, Practice: Selected Essays and Interviews,* ed. Donald F. Bouchard, trans. Donald F. Bouchard and Sherry Simon (Ithaca: Cornell University Press, 1977), 113–38; Foucault, *L'ordre du discours: Leçon inaugurale au Collège de France prononcée le 2 décembre 1970* (Paris: Gallimard, 1971), available in English as "The Discourse on Language" in appendix to *The Archaeology of Knowledge and The Discourse on Language,* trans. A. M. Sheridan Smith (New York: Pantheon, 1972).

2. Foucault, *L'ordre du discours,* 31, quoted from "Discourse on Language," 222.

3. Michel de Certeau, "Le rire de Michel Foucault," *Revue de la Bibliothèque Nationale* 14 (1984): 10–16; reprinted, in modified form, in de Certeau, *Histoire et psychanalyse entre science et fiction* (Paris: Gallimard, 1987), 51–64, and available in English as "The Laugh of Michel Foucault" in de Certeau, *Heterologies: Discourse on the Other,* trans. Brian Massumi, foreword by Wlad Godzich, Theory and History of Literature 17 (Minneapolis: University of Minnesota Press, 1986), 193–98.

4. Michel Foucault, "Nietzsche, la généalogie, l'histoire," in Foucault, *Hommage à Jean Hyppolite* (Paris: Presses Universitaires de France, 1971), 145–72, reprinted in Foucault, *Dits et écrits,* 2:136–56, and available in English as "Nietzsche, Gene-

alogy, History," in Foucault, *Language, Counter-Memory, Practice.* The quotations from this article in the following paragraphs can be found on pp. 160–61 of *Hommage à Jean Hyppolite* and 153–55 of the English version.

5. Michel Foucault, "Sur l'archéologie des sciences: Réponse au Cercle d'épistémologie," *Cahiers pour l'Analyse* 9 (1968): 9–40, quotation 11–12; reprinted in Foucault, *Dits et écrits,* 1:696–731. For a similar statement, see *Archaeology of Knowledge,* 12.

6. Foucault, *L'ordre du discours,* 58; "Discourse on Language," 230.

7. Foucault, *L'ordre du discours,* 59; "Discourse on Language," 230.

8. Michel Foucault, *L'archéologie du savoir* (Paris: Gallimard, 1969), 86; *Archaeology of Knowledge,* 31–39.

9. Foucault, "Réponse au Cercle d'épistémologie," 29.

10. Foucault, *L'archéologie du savoir,* 86; *Archaeology of Knowledge,* 65.

11. Foucault, *Archéologie du savoir,* 212; *Archaeology of Knowledge,* 164, 162.

12. Keith Michael Baker, *Inventing the French Revolution: Essays on French Political Culture in the Eighteenth Century* (Cambridge: Cambridge University Press, 1990), 5.

13. Michel Foucault, "La poussière et le nuage," in Foucault, *L'impossible prison: Recherches sur le système pénitentiaire au XIXe siècle,* ed. Michelle Perrot (Paris: Editions du Seuil, 1980), 34–35, reprinted in Foucault, *Dits et écrits,* 4:10–19.

14. Michel Foucault, "Table ronde du 20 mai 1978," in *L'impossible prison,* ed. Perrot, 49, reprinted in Foucault, *Dits et écrits,* 4:20–34.

15. Foucault, "La poussière et le nuage," 35.

16. Ibid., 36.

17. Foucault, "Postface," in *L'impossible prison,* ed. Perrot, 317–18, reprinted in Foucault, *Dits et écrits,* 4:35–37.

18. Foucault, *L'archéologie du savoir,* 288, 231; *Archaeology of Knowledge,* 175, 177.

19. Baker, *Inventing the French Revolution,* 7.

20. Michel Foucault, *Surveiller et punir: Naissance de la prison* (Paris: Gallimard, 1975), 134, quoted from Foucault, *Discipline and Punish: The Birth of the Prison,* trans. Alan Sheridan (New York: Pantheon, 1977), 131.

21. Foucault, *Surveiller et punir,* 223–24; quoted from *Discipline and Punish,* 222.

22. See "L'oeil du pouvoir: Entretien avec Michel Foucault," in Jeremy Bentham, *Le panoptique* (Paris: Pierre Belfond, 1977), 20, reprinted in Foucault, *Dits et écrits,* 3:190–207, available in English as "The Eye of Power," in Foucault, *Power/Knowledge: Selected Interviews and Other Writings, 1972–1977,* ed. Colin Gordon (New York: Pantheon, 1980).

23. Alphonse Dupront, *Les lettres, les sciences, la religion et les arts dans la société française de la deuxième moitié du XVIIIe siècle* (Paris: Centre de Documentation Universitaire, 1963), 21.

24. Ibid., 11.

25. Michel Foucault, "Un cours inédit," *Le Magazine Littéraire* 207 (May 1984): 35–39, reprinted in Foucault, *Dits et écrits,* 4:679–88. For a very different version of this text published in English, see "What Is Enlightenment?" in *The Foucault Reader,* ed. Paul Rabinow, trans. Catherine Porter (New York: Pantheon, 1984), 32–50.

26. Immanuel Kant, *Der Streit der Facultäten in drey Abschnitten* (Königsberg: F. Nicolovius, 1798), consulted in French as *Le conflit des facultés en trois sections: 1798*, trans. Jean Gibelin (Paris: Vrin, 1988), quotations 100–108, and quoted here from Kant, *The Conflict of the Faculties*, trans. and intro. Mary J. Gregor (New York: Abaris, 1979), 152–71.

27. Foucault, "Un cours inédit," 35.

28. Michel Foucault, *Naissance de la clinique* (Paris: Presses Universitaires de France, 1963; reprint 1990), 212, quoted from Foucault, *The Birth of the Clinic: An Archaeology of Medical Perception* (New York: Pantheon, 1973), 199.

29. Foucault, "La poussière et le nuage," 35.

30. Foucault, "L'oeil du pouvoir," 29, 30, quoted from "Eye of Power," 163–64.

31. Foucault, *Surveiller et punir*, 315; *Discipline and Punish*, 308. The next-to-last sentence in this work reads in full, "In this central and centralized humanity, the effect and instrument of complex power relations, bodies and forces subjected by multiple mechanisms of 'incarceration,' objects for discourses that in themselves elements for this strategy, we must hear the distant roar of battle."

32. Foucault, "La poussière et le nuage," 37.

33. Roger Chartier, "Figures de l'auteur," chapter 2 of Chartier, *L'ordre des livres: Lecteurs, auteurs, bibliothèques en Europe entre XIVe et XVIIIe siècle* (Aix-en-Provence: Alinea, 1992), 35–67, available in English as "Figures of the Author," in Chartier, *The Order of Books: Readers, Authors, and Libraries in Europe between the Fourteenth and Eighteenth Centuries*, trans. Lydia G. Cochrane (Cambridge: Polity Press, 1994).

34. Michel Foucault, discussion following "Qu'est-ce qu'un auteur?" *Littoral* 9 (1983): 28–29.

35. Michel de Certeau, "Microtechniques et discours panoptique: Un quiproquo," in de Certeau, *Histoire et psychanalyse entre science et fiction*, 37–50, available in English as "Micro-techniques and Panoptic Discourse: A Quid pro Quo," *Humanities in Society* 5, 3–4 (1982): 257–65, and in de Certeau, *Heterologies*, 185–92.

36. See a series of articles published in the *American Historical Review (AHR)*: John E. Toews, "Intellectual History after the Linguistic Turn: The Autonomy of Meaning and the Irreducibility of Experience," *AHR* 92 (1987): 879–907; David Harlan, "Intellectual History and the Return of Literature," *AHR* 94 (1989): 581–609; David A. Hollinger, "The Return of the Prodigal: The Persistence of Historical Knowing," *AHR* 94 (1989): 610–21; Joyce Appleby, "One Good Turn Deserves Another: Moving Beyond the Linguistic; A Response to David Harlan," *AHR* 94 (1989): 1326–32.

37. This rejection is expressed, for example, in the discussion following Foucault's lecture, "Qu'est-ce qu'un auteur?" 28, and in "Discourse on Language," 234.

38. Marcel Gauchet, "Changement de paradigme en sciences sociales?" *Le Débat* 50 (May-August 1988): 165–70.

39. Paul Veyne, "Foucault révolutionne l'histoire," in Veyne, *Comment on écrit l'histoire suivi de Foucault révolutionne l'histoire* (Paris: Editions du Seuil, 1978), 236.

40. Ibid., 217, 231–32.

41. De Certeau, "Microtechniques et discours panoptique," 44; "Microtechniques and Panoptic Discourse," in de Certeau, *Heterologies*, 189.

42. De Certeau, "Microtechniques et discours panoptique," 49; "Microtechniques and Panoptic Discourse," 192.

43. Michel Foucault, *Histoire de la sexualité,* vol. 2, *L' usage des plaisirs,* 19 (Paris: Gallimard, 1984), quoted from *The History of Sexuality,* vol. 2, *The Use of Pleasure,* trans. Robert Hurley (New York: Vintage/Random House, 1980), 13.

Chapter 5. Discourses and Practices

1. Roger Chartier, *Les origines culturelles de la Révolution française* (Paris: Editions du Seuil, 1990), available in English as *The Cultural Origins of the French Revolution,* trans. Lydia G. Cochrane (Durham, N. C.: Duke University Press, 1991).

2. François Hartog, "Liberté des anciens, liberté des modernes: la Révolution française et l'antiquité," in *Les Grecs, les Romains et nous: L'antiquité est-elle moderne?* ed. Roger-Pol Droit (Paris: Le Monde Editions, 1991), 119–38.

3. Robert Darnton, *Edition et sédition: L'univers de la littérature clandestine au XVIIIe siècle* (Paris: Gallimard, 1991), 214–15. In his book *The Forbidden Bestsellers of Pre-Revolutionary France* (New York: W. W. Norton, 1995), complemented by *The Corpus of Clandestine Literature in France, 1769–1789* (New York: W. W. Norton, 1995), Robert Darnton replies to some of the arguments I have developed in this essay and in *Cultural Origins of the French Revolution.*

4. Jacques Revel, "Marie-Antoinette in Her Fictions: The Staging of the Hatred," in *Fictions of the French Revolution,* ed. Bernadette Fort (Evanston, Ill.: Northwestern University Press, 1991), 11–129.

5. Darnton, *Edition et sédition,* 178.

6. Arlette Farge, *Dire et mal dire: L'opinion publique au XVIIIe siècle* (Paris: Editions du Seuil, 1992), 61–62, quoted from Farge, *Subversive Words: Public Opinion in Eighteenth-Century France,* trans. Rosemary Morns (University Park: Pennsylvania State University Press, 1995), 35.

7. Farge, *Dire et mal dire,* 257; *Subversive Words,* 174.

8. Fred E. Schrader, *Augustin Cochin et la République française,* trans. Marie-Claude Auger (Paris: Editions du Seuil, 1992).

9. Margaret C. Jacob, *Living the Enlightenment: Freemasonry and Politics in Eighteenth-Century Europe* (Oxford: Oxford University Press, 1991), quotation 18.

10. Keith Michael Baker, *Inventing the French Revolution: Essays on French Political Culture in the Eighteenth Century* (Cambridge: Cambridge University Press, 1990), 9, 5.

11. Pierre Bourdieu, "Lecture, lecteurs, lettrés, littérature," in Bourdieu, *Choses dites* (Paris: Editions de Minuit, 1987), 132–43, available in English as "Reading, Readers, the Literate, Literature" in Bourdieu, *In Other Words: Essays toward a Reflexive Sociology,* trans. Matthew Adamson (Stanford: Stanford University Press, 1990), 94–105.

12. Baker, *Inventing the French Revolution,* 305, 3–4.

13. Isser Woloch, "On the Latent Illiberalism of the French Revolution," *American Historical Review* 95 (1990): 1425–70.

14. Denis Richet, *La France moderne: L'esprit des institutions* (Paris: Flammarion, 1973, 1980), 57.

15. Reinhart Koselleck, *Kritik und Krise: Eine Studie zur Pathogenese der bür-*

gerlichen Welt (Fribourg: Karl Albert, 1959; Frankfurt am Main: Suhrkamp, 1976), consulted in French as *Le règne de la critique* (Paris: Editions de Minuit, 1979), and available in English as Koselleck, *Critique and Crisis: Enlightenment and the Pathogenesis of Modern Society* (Cambridge: MIT Press, 1988).

16. Baker, *Inventing the French Revolution*, 3–4.

17. Jürgen Habermas, *Die Strukturwandel der Öffentlichkeit: Untersuchungen zu einer Kategorie der bürgerlichen Gesellschaft* (Neuwied: Hermann Luchterhand, 1962), consulted in French as *L'espace publique: Archéologie de la publicité comme dimension constitutive de la société bourgeoise* (Paris: Payot, 1978), and available in English as *The Structural Transformation of the Public Sphere: An Inquiry into a Category of Bourgeois Society,* trans. Thomas Burger and Frederick Lawrence (Cambridge: Polity Press; Cambridge: MIT Press, 1989).

18. Michel Foucault, "Un cours inédit," *Le Magazine Littéraire* 207 (May 1984): 35–37, reprinted in Foucault, *Dits et écrits, 1954–1988,* ed. Daniel Defert and François Ewald with the collaboration of Jacques Lagrange, 4 vols. (Paris: Gallimard, 1994), 4:679–88.

Chapter 6. Texts, Forms, and Interpretations

1. Some champions of bibliographic tradition expressed varying degrees of hostility to McKenzie's ideas in their reviews of this work: Hugh Amory in *Book Collector* 36 (1987): 411–18; T. N. Howard-Hill in *Library,* 6th ser., 10 (1988): 151–58; G. Thomas Tanselle, "Textual Criticism and Literary Sociology," *Studies in Bibliography* 42 (1991): 83–143 (esp. 87–99). In contrast, literary critics tended to review the work favorably: for example, Jerome J. McGann in *London Review of Books,* 18 February 1988, 20–21.

2. For example, Ronald B. McKerrow, *An Introduction to Bibliography for Literary Students* (Oxford: Clarendon Press, 1927; New Castle, Del.: Oak Knoll Press, 1994); Fredson Bowers, *Bibliography and Textual Criticism* (Oxford: Clarendon Press, 1964), and Bowers, *Essays in Bibliography: Text and Editing* (Charlottesville: University Press of Virginia, 1974); Philip Gaskell, *A New Introduction to Bibliography* (Oxford: Clarendon Press; New York: Oxford University Press, 1972). French works include Roger Laufer, *Introduction à la textologie: Vérification, établissement, édition des textes* (Paris: Larousse, 1972); Giles Barber et al., *La bibliographie matérielle,* table ronde organized for the CNRS by Jacques Petit (Paris: Editions du CNRS, 1983).

3. The major work illustrating this approach is Charlton Hinman, *The Printing and Proof-Reading of the First Folio of Shakespeare* (Oxford: Clarendon Press, 1963). For a summary of bibliographic scholarship on Shakespeare editions, see Fredson Bowers, "A Search for Authority: The Investigation of Shakespeare's Printed Texts," in *Print and Culture in the Renaissance: Essays on the Advent of Printing in Europe,* ed. Gerald P. Tyson and Sylvia S. Wagonheim (Newark: University of Delaware Press; London: Associated University Presses, 1986), 17–44.

4. See, for example, D. F. McKenzie, "Compositor B's Role in *The Merchant of Venice* Q2 (1619)," *Studies in Bibliography* 12 (1959): 75–89; McKenzie, "Eight Quarto Proof Sheets of 1594 Set by Formes: *A Fruitfull Commentarie,*" *Library,* 5th ser., 28 (1973): 1–13; McKenzie, "Stretching a Point, or, The Case of the Spaced-out Comps," *Studies in Bibliography* 37 (1984): 106–21.

5. D. F. McKenzie's major works, which run through his entire intellectual career, are D. F. McKenzie, *The Cambridge University Press, 1696–1712: A Bibliographical Study* (Cambridge: Cambridge University Press, 1966); McKenzie, "Printers of the Mind: Some Notes on Bibliographical Theories and Printing-House Practices," *Studies in Bibliography* 22 (1969): 1–75; McKenzie, *The London Book Trade in the Later Seventeenth Century,* Sandars Lectures, Cambridge, 1976, typescript (a summary by David Gerard is available in *Library,* 5th ser., 33 [1978]: 242–46). For other treatments of the connection between analytical bibliography and the history of book production, see G. Thomas Tanselle, "Analytical Bibliography and Renaissance Printing History," *Printing History* 3, 1 (1981): 24–33; Jeanne Veyrin-Forrer, *La lettre et le texte: Trente années de recherches sur l'histoire du livre,* Collection de l'Ecole Normale Supérieure de Jeunes Filles 34 (Paris, 1987), especially "Troisième partie: De la fabrication des livres à la bibliographie matérielle," 271–366.

6. Geoffrey Nunberg, "The Place of Books in the Age of Electronic Reproduction," *Representations* 42 (1993): 13–37.

7. Roger Chartier, "Representations of the Written Word," in Chartier, *Forms and Meanings: Texts, Performances, and Audiences from Codex to Computer* (Philadelphia: University of Pennsylvania Press, 1995), 6–24.

8. D. F. McKenzie, "When Congreve Made a Scene," *Transactions of the Cambridge Bibliographical Society* 7, 2 (1979): 338–42, and especially, McKenzie, "Typography and Meaning: The Case of William Congreve," in *Buch und Buchhandel in Europa im achtzehnten Jahrhundert/The Book and the Book Trade in Eighteenth-Century Europe,* ed. Giles Barber and Bernhard Fabian, Proceedings of the fifth Wolfenbüttler Symposium, 1–3 November 1977 (Hamburg: Ernst Hauswedell, 1981), 81–126.

9. For one study written in the same spirit as McKenzie's study of Congreve, see Francisco Rico, "La *princeps* del *Lazarillo:* Título, capitulación y epigrafes de un texto apócrifo," in *Homenaje a Eugenio Asensio* (Madrid: Editorial Gredos, 1988), 417–46, reprinted in Rico, *Problemas del Lazarillo* (Madrid: Cátedra, 1988), 133–51.

10. See, for example, Alain Viala, *Naissance de l'écrivain: Sociologie de la littérature à l'âge classique* (Paris: Editions de Minuit, 1985). Pierre Bourdieu provided a theoretical base for this approach, particularly in two early articles: Pierre Bourdieu, "Champ intellectuel et projet créateur," *Les Temps Modernes* 246 (1966): 865–906; Bourdieu, "Structuralism and Theory of Sociological Knowledge," *Social Research* 25, 4 (1968): 681–706; and more recently, in Bourdieu, "Le champ littéraire," *Actes de la Recherche en Sciences Sociales* 89 (1991): 3–46.

11. See, for example, Stephen Greenblatt, *Shakespearean Negotiations: The Circulation of Social Energy in Renaissance England* (Berkeley: University of California Press, 1988). For an overall view, see H. Aram Veeser, ed., *The New Historicism Reader* (New York: Routledge, 1989).

12. For an illustration of this perspective regarding a totally different intellectual tradition, see Lawrence W. Levine, "William Shakespeare and the American People: A Study in Cultural Transformation," *American Historical Review* 89 (1984): 34–66; Levine, *Highbrow/Lowbrow: The Emergence of Cultural Hierarchy in America* (Cambridge: Harvard University Press, 1988).

13. D. F. McKenzie, *Oral Culture: Literacy and Print in Early New Zealand,*

the Treaty of Waitangi (Wellington: Victoria University Press with the Alexander Turnbull Library Endowment Trust, 1985). A first version of this essay was published as "The Sociology of a Text: Orality, Literacy and Print in Early New Zealand," *Library,* 6th ser., 6 (1984): 333–65, reprinted in *The Social History of Language,* ed. Peter Burke and Roy Porter (Cambridge: Cambridge University Press, 1987), 161–97.

14. For examples in two different contexts (Lutheran Germany of the seventeenth and eighteenth centuries and the Pyrenees in the eighteenth and nineteenth centuries), see Etienne François, "Les protestants allemands et la Bible: Diffusion et pratiques," in *Le siècle des lumières et la Bible,* gen. ed. Yvon Belaval and Dominique Bourel, Bible de tous les temps 7 (Paris: Beauchesne, 1986), 46–58; Daniel Fabre, "Le livre et sa magie," in *Pratiques de la lecture,* gen. ed. Roger Chartier (Marseilles: Rivages, 1985), 181–206.

15. Armando Petrucci, *La scrittura: Ideologia e rappresentazione,* Piccola Biblioteca Einaudi 473 (Turin: Einaudi, 1986), available in English as *Public Lettering: Script, Power, and Culture,* trans. Linda Lappin (Chicago: University of Chicago Press, 1993).

16. Christine Métayer, "De l'école au Palais de Justice: L'itinéraire singulier des maîtres écrivains de Paris (XVIe–XVIIIe siècles)," *Annales ESC* 45 (1990): 1217–37; Laura Antonucci, "La scrittura giudicata: Perizie grafiche in processi romani del primo Seicento," *Scrittura e Civiltà* 13 (1983): 489–534.

17. Michel Foucault, *Surveiller et punir: Naissance de la prison* (Paris: Gallimard, 1975), 151–58, available in English as *Discipline and Punish: The Birth of the Prison,* trans. Alan Sheridan (New York: Pantheon, 1977); Jonathan Goldberg, *Writing Matter: From the Hands of the English Renaissance* (Stanford: Stanford University Press, 1990).

18. Armando Petrucci, "Pouvoir de l'écriture, pouvoir sur l'écriture dans la Renaissance italienne," *Annales ESC* 43 (1988): 823–47, quotation 823–24.

Chapter 7. The Powers and Limits of Representation

1. Louis Marin, "Lire un tableau: Une lettre de Poussin en 1639," in *Pratiques de la lecture,* gen. ed. Roger Chartier (Marseilles: Rivages, 1985), 102–24; new ed., Petite Bibliothèque Payot (Paris: Editions Payot et Rivages, 1993), 129–57, reprinted in Marin, *Sublime Poussin* (Paris: Editions du Seuil, 1995), 11–34.

2. Ibid. (1993), 129.

3. Ibid., 154.

4. Louis Marin, "Introduction: L'être de l'image et son efficace," in Marin, *Des pouvoirs de l'image: Gloses* (Paris: Editions du Seuil, 1993), 9–22, quotations 18, 19.

5. Ibid., 14.

6. Louis Marin, *La critique du discours: Sur la "Logique de Port-Royal" et les "Pensées" de Pascal* (Paris: Editions de Minuit, 1975).

7. Louis Marin, *L'opacité de la peinture: Essais sur la représentation au Quattrocento* (Paris: Editions Usher, 1989), esp. "Paolo Uccello au Chiostro Verde de Santa Maria Novella à Florence," 73–98, quotation 73.

8. Ibid., "Introduction," 9–12, quotations 10.

9. Louis Marin, in Marin, "Introduction: Les trois formules," *Le portrait du roi* (Paris: Editions de Minuit, 1981), 7–22, esp. 18–19, available in English as

Portrait of the King, trans. Martha M. Houle, foreword by Tom Conley, Theory and History of Literature 57 (Minneapolis: University of Minnesota Press, 1988).

10. Louis Marin "La parole mangée, ou le corps divin saisi par les signes," in Marin, *La parole mangée et autres essais théologico-politiques* (Paris: Méridiens Klincksieck, 1986), 11–35, available in English as *Food for Thought,* trans. with afterword by Mette Hjort (Baltimore: Johns Hopkins University Press, 1989).

11. Marin, *La parole mangée,* 35; *Food for Thought,* 25.

12. Marin, introduction to *L'opacité de la peinture,* 10.

13. Two examples of this interest are Louis Marin, "Pinturicchio à Spello" and "Paolo Uccello au Chiostro Verde de Santa Maria Novella à Florence," in Marin, *L'opacité de la peinture,* 1–72 and 73–98, respectively.

14. For examples, see Louis Marin, "Le pouvoir du récit," in Marin, *Le récit est un piège* (Paris: Editions de Minuit, 1978), 16–34 (on the fable of La Fontaine, "Le pouvoir des fables"), and Marin, "Une lisière de lecture," in Marin, *Lectures traversières* (Paris: Albin Michel, 1992), 17–25 (on the frontispiece of the 1697 edition of Charles Perrault's *Histoires, ou Contes du temps passé*).

15. Marin, "Introduction: L'être de l'image et son efficace," 14.

16. Marin, "Introduction: Les trois formules," 11; "Introduction: The Three Formulas," 6.

17. Blaise Pascal, *Pensées,* Lafuma edition, 44; Brunschvicg edition, 82, quoted here from Marin, *Portrait of the King,* 31, 32.

18. Pascal quoted from *Pensées: Thoughts on Religion and Other Subjects,* trans. William Finlayson Trotter, ed. H. S. Thayer and Elisabeth B. Thayer (New York: Washington Square Press, 1965), no. 12; Marin, *Le portrait du roi,* 11; *Portrait of the King,* 7.

19. Pascal, *Pensées,* Lafuma edition, 25; Brunschvicg edition, 308; quoted from Marin, *Portrait of the King,* 14.

20. Michel de Certeau, *L'invention du quotidien,* vol. 1 of *Arts de faire* (1980), new ed., ed. Luce Giard (Paris: Gallimard, 1990), 260, quoted from *The Practice of Everyday Life,* trans. Steven F. Rendall (Berkeley: University of California Press, 1984), 178.

21. Louis Marin, "Pour une théorie baroque de l'action politique: Lectures des *Considérations sur les coups d'état* de Gabriel Naudé" in Gabriel Naudé, *Considérations politiques sur les coups d'état,* notes, supplementary materials, and index by Frédérique Marin and Marie-Odile Perulli (Paris: Editions de Paris, 1988), 7–65, quotation 31.

22. Louis Marin, "Le récit du roi ou comment écrire l'histoire," in Marin, *Le portrait du roi,* 49–107, quotation 95, quoted from "The King's Narrative, or How to Write History," in Marin, *Portrait of the King,* 39–88, quotation 78.

23. Marin, "Introduction: L'être de l'image et son efficace," 21.

24. Louis Marin, "Le descripteur fantaisiste: Diderot, *Salon de 1765, Casanove, N° 94, "Une marche d'armée,"* description," in Marin, *Des pouvoirs de l'image,* 72–101, quotation 72.

25. Marin, "Introduction: Les trois formules," 7; *Portrait of the King,* 3.

26. Pierre Bourdieu, *La distinction: Critique sociale du jugement* (Paris: Editions de Minuit, 1979), 563–64, quoted from *Distinction: A Social Critique of the Judgement of Taste,* trans. Richard Nice (Cambridge: Harvard University Press, 1984), 483.

27. Jean de La Bruyère, *Les Caractères de Théophraste traduits du grec, avec les Caractères ou les moeurs de ce siècle* (1688), "Du mérite personnel."

28. Louis Marin, "Sémantique des systèmes de représentation," in Ecole des Hautes Etudes en Sciences Sociales, *Annuaire: Comptes rendus des cours et conférences, 1990–1991*, 400–401. Louis Marin's seminar, which began in 1978–79, was titled "Sémantique des systèmes représentatifs" until 1988–89; in its last year, 1991–92, it was called "Systèmes de représentations à l'âge moderne."

29. Louis Marin, "Le portrait-du-roi en auteur: Jacques Ier d'Angleterre, le *Basilikon Dōron*, sonnet, 1599–1603," and "Le portrait du poète en roi: William Shakespeare, *La Tempête*, acte I, scènes 1 et 2 (1611)," in Marin, *Des pouvoirs de l'image*, 159–68 and 169–85, respectively.

30. Louis Marin, "Rue Traversière," in Marin, *Lectures traversières*, 9–15, quotation 14–15.

Chapter 8. Self-consciousness and the Social Bond

1. Norbert Elias, *Die Gesellschaft der Individuen* (Frankfurt am Main: Suhrkamp, 1987), available in French as *La société des individus*, trans. Jeanne Etoré, preface by Roger Chartier (Paris: Fayard, 1991), and in English as *The Society of Individuals*, ed. Michael Schröter, trans. Edmund Jephcott (Oxford: Basil Blackwell, 1991).

2. Norbert Elias, *Über den Prozess der Zivilisation: Soziogenetische und psychogenetische Untersuchungen*, 2 vols. (Basel: Haus zum Falken, 1939); new edition, with a new introduction, 2 vols. (Berne: Francke AG, 1969); paperback edition, 2 vols., Suhrkamp Taschenbuch (Frankfurt am Main: Suhrkamp, 1976). The work is available in French, abridged, in two publications: Elias, *La civilisation des moeurs*, trans. Pierre Kamnitzer (Paris: Calmann-Lévy, 1973, 1991) and Elias *La dynamique de l'Occident*, trans. Pierre Kamnitzer (Paris: Calmann-Lévy, 1975, 1991). The most recent English edition is Elias, *The Civilizing Process: The History of Manners and State Formation and Civilization*, trans. Edmund Jephcott (Oxford: Basil Blackwell, 1994).

3. Norbert Elias, *Über sich selbst* (Frankfurt am Main: Suhrkamp, 1990), 71, consulted in French translation as *Norbert Elias par lui-même* (Paris: Fayard, 1991), 71, quoted from A. J. Heerma van Voss and A. van Stolk, "Biographical Interview with Norbert Elias," in Elias, *Reflections on a Life*, trans. Edmund Jehpcott (Cambridge: Polity Press, 1994), 1–80, quotation 54.

4. Elias, *Über sich selbst*, 79–80; van Voss and van Stalk, "Biographical Interview," 61. On the history of the publication of *The Civilizing Process* in 1939, see Hermann Korte, *Über Norbert Elias: Das Werden eines Menschenwissenschaftlers* (Frankfurt am Main: Suhrkamp, 1988), 13–34.

5. An inventory of reviews of this work can be found in *Materialen zu Norbert Elias' Zivilisationstheorie*, ed. Peter R. Gleichmann, Johan Goudsblom, and Hermann Korte (Frankfurt am Main: Suhrkamp, 1979), completed in *Macht und Zivilisation: Materialen zu Norbert Elias' Zivilisationstheorie 2*, ed. Gleichmann, Goudsblom, and Korte (Frankfurt am Main: Suhrkamp, 1984), 316–18.

6. Stephen Mennell, *Norbert Elias: Civilization and the Human Self-Image* (Oxford: Basil Blackwell, 1989), 20.

7. Norbert Elias and John L. Scotson, *The Established and the Outsiders: A*

Sociological Enquiry into Community Problems (London: Frank Cass; New York: Humanities Press, 1965). Elias added a theoretical introduction in the form of a preface to the Dutch translation of this work, Norbert Elias and J. L. Scotson, "Een theoretisch essay over gevestigden en buitenstaanders," in *De gevestigden en de buitenstaanders: Een studie van de spanningen en machtsverhoudingen tussen twee arbeidersbuurten* (Utrecht: Spectrum, 1976), 7–46, available in English as "Introduction: A Theoretical Essay on Established and Outsider Relations," in Elias and Scotson, *The Established and the Outsiders: A Sociological Enquiry into Community Problems,* 2d ed. (London: Thousand Oaks; New Delhi: Sage, 1994), xv–lii.

8. Elias, *Über sich selbst,* 158–70; Elias, "Notes on a Lifetime," in Elias, *Reflections on a Life,* 81–154, esp. 121–30.

9. On this question, see Norbert Elias, *Engagement und Distanzierung,* ed. Michael Schröter, Arbeiten zur Wissensoziologie 1 (Frankfurt am Main: Suhrkamp, 1983), available in French as *Engagement et distanciation: Contributions à la sociologie de la connaissance,* trans. Michèle Hulin, foreword by Roger Chartier (Paris: Fayard, 1993), and in English as *Involvement and Detachment: Contributions to the Sociology of Knowledge* (Oxford: Basil Blackwell, 1985).

10. Elias, *Die Gesellschaft der Individuen,* 38–39; *Society of Individuals,* 19–20.

11. Norbert Elias, *Die höfische Gesellschaft: Untersuchungen zur Soziologie des Königtums und der höfischen Aristokratie mit einer Enleitung: Soziologie und Geschichtswissenschaft* (Darmstadt: Luchterhand, 1969, 1979), 219, available in French as *La société de cour,* foreword by Roger Chartier (Paris: Flammarion, 1985), quotation 152–53; quoted here from Elias, *The Court Society,* trans. Edmund Jephcott (Oxford: Basil Blackwell, 1983), 144.

12. Norbert Elias, *Was ist Soziologie?* Grundfragen der Soziologie 1 (Munich: Juventa, 1970), available in French as *Qu'est-ce que la sociologie?* trans. Yasmin Hoffman (Paris: Pandora, 1981), and in English as *What Is Sociology?* trans. Stephen Mennell and Grace Morrissey, foreword by Reinhard Bendix (New York: Columbia University Press, 1978).

13. Elias, *Was ist Soziologie?* quoted from *What Is Sociology?* 130.

14. Elias, *Die Gesellschaft der Individuen,* 54; *Society of Individuals,* 32.

15. Elias, *Die höfische Gesellschaft,* 178–221; *La societe société de cour,* 115–54; *Court Society,* 117–45.

16. Elias, *Über den Prozess der Zivilisation* (1979), 2:320; *La dynamique de l'Occident,* 193–94; *Civilizing Process,* 447. On Elias's fundamental concepts, see Roger Chartier, "Social Figuration and Habitus," in Chartier, *Cultural History: Between Practices and Representations,* trans. Lydia G. Cochrane (Cambridge: Polity Press; Ithaca: Cornell University Press, 1988), 71–94.

17. Elias, *Die Gesellschaft der Individuen,* 157; *Society of Individuals,* 113.

18. Elias, *Über sich selbst,* 120; "Notes on a Lifetime," 91. On relations between Elias and Hönigswald and Elias's 1924 dissertation, see Korte, *Über Norbert Elias,* 72–78.

19. Norbert Elias, "Idee und Individuum: Ein Beitrag zur Philosophie der Geschichte" (Auszug aus einer Schrift zur Erlangung der Doctorwürde der Hohen Philosophischen Fakultät der Schles. Friedrich-Wilhelms-Universität zu Breslau, 1924). On Elias's own rediscovery and rereading of his dissertation fifty-six years

after its defense, see the long note in Elias, *Über sich selbst,* 132–34; "Notes on a Lifetime," 151–53 n. 4.

20. Elias, *Über sich selbst,* 131–32; "Notes on a Lifetime," 101.

21. Elias, *Über sich selbst,* 116: "Notes on a Lifetime," 87–89.

22. "Norbert Elias ou la sociologie des continuités," interview with Roger Chartier, *Libération,* 5 December 1985, 29.

23. Elias, *Die Gesellschaft der Individuen,* 184; *Society of Individuals,* 138–39.

24. On the theory of personal pronouns, see the chapter "The Personal Pronouns as a Figurational Model," in Elias, *What Is Sociology?* 122–28.

25. Elias, *Die Gesellschaft der Individuen,* 299; *Society of Individuals,* 224–25.

26. Elias, *Die Gesellschaft der Individuen,* 184; *Society of Individuals,* 134–135.

27. On critiques of Elias's work, see Mennell, *Norbert Elias: Civilization and the Human Self-Image,* chap. 10, "Civilization and Decivilization," 227–50.

28. On this problem, see the articles of the Dutch sociologist Cas Wouters: "Formalization and Informalization: Changing Tension Balances in Civilizing Processes," *Theory, Culture and Society* 3, 2 (1986): 1–18; Wouters, "Development in the Behavioural Codes between the Sexes: The Formation of Informalization in the Netherlands, 1930–85," *Theory, Culture and Society* 4, 2–3 (1987): 405–27. For an overall view of the many studies carried out in the Low Countries based on Elias's theses and concepts, see Willem H. Kranendonk, ed., *Society as Process: A Bibliography of Figurational Sociology in the Netherlands (up to 1989): Sociogenetic and Psychogenetic Studies* (Amsterdam: Publikatiereeks Sociologisch Instituut, Universiteit van Amsterdam, 1990).

29. See Norbert Elias, introduction to Norbert Elias and Eric Dunning, *Quest for Excitement: Sport and Leisure in the Civilizing Process* (Oxford: Basil Blackwell, 1986), 19–62. On that text, see chapter 10 below.

30. For two witnesses to the machinery of extermination, founded in an implacable administrative rationality and in the elimination of all individual emotion in the executioners, see the accounts in Claude Lanzmann, *Shoah,* preface by Simone de Beauvoir (Paris: Fayard, 1985), of the historian Raul Hilberg (pp. 92–97) and of the *Untersturmführer* SS Franz Suchomel (135–41), available in English as *Shoah: An Oral History of the Holocaust,* film substitles by A. Whitelaw and W. Byron (New York: Pantheon, 1985).

31. Elias, *Die Gesellschaft der Individuen,* 58; *Society of Individuals,* 35.

32. Norbert Elias, "The Retreat of Sociologists into the Present," special issue, "Norbert Elias and Figurational Sociology," *Theory, Culture and Society* 4, 2–3 (1987): 223–47.

Chapter 9. The Double Bind and Detachment

1. Norbert Elias, *Engagement und Distanzierung,* ed. Michael Schröter, Arbeiten zur Wissensoziologie 1 (Frankfurt am Main: Suhrkamp, 1983), available in French as *Engagement et distanciation: Contributions à la sociologie de la connaissance,* trans. Michèle Hulin, foreword by Roger Chartier (Paris: Fayard, 1993), and in English as *Involvement and Detachment: Contributions to the Sociology of Knowledge* (Oxford: Basil Blackwell, 1985), the edition to which page citations for quotations refer.

2. Carlo Ginzburg, "Spie: Radici di un paradigma indiziario," in Ginzburg,

Miti, emblemi, spie: Morfologia e storia (Turin: Einaudi, 1986), 158–209, available in French as "Traces: Racines d'un paradigme indiciaire," in Ginzburg, *Mythes, emblèmes, traces: Morphologie et histoire* (Paris: Flammarion, 1989), 139–80, and in English as "Clues: Roots of an Evidential Paradigm," in Ginzburg, *Clues, Myths, and the Historical Method,* trans. John Tedeschi and Anne Tedeschi (Baltimore: Johns Hopkins University Press, 1989), 96–125.

3. Norbert Elias, *Die Gesellschaft der Individuen* (Frankfurt am Main: Suhrkamp, 1987), available in French as *La société des individus,* trans. Jeanne Etoré, preface by Roger Chartier (Paris: Fayard, 1991), and in English as *The Society of Individuals,* ed. Michael Schröter, trans. Edmund Jephcott (Oxford: Basil Blackwood, 1991).

4. Giovanni Levi, *L'eredità immateriale: Carriera di un esorcista nel Piemonte del Seicento* (Turin: Einaudi, 1985), available in English as *Inheriting Power: The Story of an Exorcist,* trans. Lydia G. Cochrane (Chicago: University of Chicago Press, 1988); Jaime Contreras, *Sotos contra Riquelmes: Regidores, inquisidores y criptojudíos* (Madrid: Anaya/Mario Muchnik, 1922).

5. On the work of Gregory Bateson, see *Bateson, premier état d'un héritage,* ed. Yves Winkin (Paris: Editions du Seuil, 1988). The concept of the "double bind" comes from Gregory Bateson, "Toward a Theory of Schizophrenia," in Bateson, *Steps to an Ecology of Mind* (San Francisco: Chandler, 1972; reprint, Northvale, N.J.: Aronson, 1987), 201–27, consulted in French translation as "Vers une théorie de la schizophrénie," in Bateson, *Vers une écologie de l'esprit,* 2 vols. (Paris: Editions du Seuil, 1980), 2:3–34.

6. Constant Piqueray, ". . . et le double lien un fonctionnement inverse du principe de complexité par le bruit," in *Bateson, premier état d'un héritage,* 320–30, quotation 320.

7. Norbert Elias, *Die höfische Gesellschaft: Untersuchungen zur Soziologie des Königtums und der höfischen Aristokratie mit einer Enleitung: Soziologie und Geschichtswissenschaft* (Darmstadt: Luchterhand, 1969, 1979), available in French as *La société de cour,* foreword by Roger Chartier (Paris: Flammarion, 1985), and in English as Elias, *The Court Society,* trans. Edmund Jephcott (Oxford: Basil Blackwell, 1983).

Chapter 10. Sports

1. Norbert Elias and Eric Dunning, *Quest for Excitement: Sport and Leisure in the Civilizing Process* (Oxford: Basil Blackwell, 1986).

2. Norbert Elias, *Über den Prozess der Zivilisation: Soziogenetische und psychogenetische Untersuchungen,* 2 vols. (Basel: Haus zum Falken, 1939); new edition, with a new introduction, 2 vols. (Berne: Francke AG, 1969); paperback edition, 2 vols., Suhrkamp Taschenbuch (Frankfurt am Main: Suhrkamp, 1976). This work is available in French, abridged, as *La civilisation des moeurs,* trans. Pierre Kamnitzer (Paris: Calmann-Lévy, 1973, 1991) and *La dynamique de l'Occident,* trans. Pierre Kamnitzer (Paris: Calmann-Lévy, 1975, 1991), and in English as *The Civilizing Process: The History of Manners and States Formation and Civilization,* trans. Edmund Jephcott (Oxford: Basil Blackwell, 1994). On the history of this book, see Hermann Korte, *Über Norbert Elias: Das Werden eines Menschenwissenschaftlers* (Frankfurt am Main: Suhrkamp, 1988), 13–34. On its re-

ception, see Johan Goudsblom, "Responses to Norbert Elias' Work in England, Germany, the Netherlands and France," in Goudsblom, *Human Figurations: Essays for/Aufsätze für Norbert Elias* (Amsterdam: Amsterdams Sociologisch Tijdschrift, 1977), 37–97, in German translation as Johan Goudsblom, "Aufnahme und Kritik der Arbeiten von Norbert Elias in England, Deutschland, den Niederlanden und Frankreich," in *Materialien zu Norbert Elias' Zivilisationstheorie,* ed. Peter R. Gleichmann, Johan Goudsblom, and Hermann Korte (Frankfurt am Main: Suhrkamp, 1979), 17–100, completed by Johan Goudsblom, "Aufnahme und Kritik der Arbeiten von Norbert Elias," in *Macht und Zivilisation: Materialien zu Norbert Elias' Zivilisationstheorie 2,* ed. Peter R. Gleichmann, Johan Goudsblom, and Hermann Korte (Frankfurt am Main: Suhrkamp, 1984), 305–22. On the major theses of the book compared with two other works of Elias, see Roger Chartier, "Formation sociale et économie psychique: La société de cour dans le procès de civilisation," foreword to Norbert Elias, *La société de cour* (Paris: Flammarion, 1985), i–xxviii, available in English as "Social Figuration and Habitus," in Chartier, *Cultural History: Between Practices and Representations,* trans. Lydia G. Cochrane (Cambridge: Polity Press; Ithaca: Cornell University Press, 1988), 71–94; Chartier, "Avant-propos: Conscience de soi et lien social," foreword to Elias, *La société des individus,* trans. Jeanne Etoré (Paris: Fayard, 1991), i–xxviii, translated above as chapter 8.

3. A. J. Heerma van Voss and A. van Stolk, "Interview biographique de Norbert Elias," in *Norbert Elias par lui-même* (Paris: Fayard, 1991), 9–100, quotation 84, the French translation of Norbert Elias, *Über sich selbst* (Frankfurt am Main: Suhrkamp, 1990); quoted here from van Voss and van Stolk, "Biographical Interview with Norbert Elias," in Elias, *Reflections on a Life,* trans. Edmund Jephcott (Cambridge: Polity Press, 1994), 1–80, quotation 65.

4. Richard Brown, "Norbert Elias in Leicester," special issue, "Norbert Elias and Figurational Sociology," *Theory, Culture and Society,* 4, 2–3 (1987): 533–39, quotation 537. The Elias articles Richard Brown mentions are "Studies in the Genesis of the Naval Profession," *British Journal of Sociology* 1, 4 (1950): 291–309 (the only article Elias published before he entered the University of Leicester, with the exception of two articles in German that had appeared in 1935 in German in reviews publishing the works of German emigrants, *Die Sammlung* and *Der Auswig*), and "Problems of Involvement and Detachment," *British Journal of Sociology* 7, 3 (1956): 226–52. He had also published *Die öffentliche Meinung in England,* Vortrag, gehalten am 23. April 1959 bei den Hochschulwochen für Staatswissenschaftliche Fortbildung in Bad Wildungen (Bad Homburg: Max Gehlen, 1959). In this connection a strong continuity marks Elias's works: he returned to the questions discussed in the article "Problems of Involvement and Detachment," in his *Engagement und Distanzierung,* ed. Michael Schröter, Arbeiten zur Wissensoziologie 1 (Frankfurt am Main: Suhrkamp, 1983), available in French as Elias, *Engagement et distanciation: Contributions à la sociologie de la connaissance,* trans. Michèle Hulin, foreword by Roger Chartier (Paris: Fayard, 1993), and in English as *Involvement and Detachment: Contributions to the Sociology of Knowledge* (Oxford: Basil Blackwell, 1985). Moreover, when Elias was invited to the Ecole des Hautes Etudes en Sciences Sociales in 1983, he used material from his history of the naval officers' corps in a lecture in which he compared the structure of power and the balance of social tensions in ancien régime France and En-

gland of the same period (see Roger Chartier, "Le vieil Elias et la mer," *Libéra-tion*, 24 March 1983, 30).

5. Van Voss and van Stolk, "Biographical Interview," 66.

6. Norbert Elias and John L. Scotson, *The Established and the Outsiders: A Sociological Enquiry into Community Problems* (London: Frank Cass; New York: Humanities Press, 1965). Elias outlined the general thrust of the book's theoretical model in a preface, "Een theoretisch essay over gevestigden en buitenstaanders," to the Dutch translation of this work, Elias and Scotson, *De gevestigden en de buitenstaanders: Ein studie van de spanningen en machts verhoudingen tussen twee arbeidersbuurten* (Utrecht: Spectrum, 1976), 7–46, available in English as "Introduction: A Theoretical Essay on Established and Outsider Relations," in Elias and Scotson, *The Established and the Outsiders: A Sociological Enquiry into Community Problems*, 2d ed. (London: Thousand Oaks; New Delhi: Sage, 1994), xv–lii.

7. See the "Notes biographiques" in *Norbert Elias par lui-même*, 101–83, in particular 150–60, "Notes sur les juifs en tant que participant à une relation établis-marginaux." This text was first published under the title "Notizen zum Lebenslauf," in Gleichman, Goudsblom, and Korte, *Macht und Zivilisation: Materialien zu Norbert Elias' Zivilisationstheorie 2*, 9–82.

8. Elias and Dunning, *Quest for Excitement*, 19.

9. In chronological order, these articles are Norbert Elias and Eric Dunning, "Dynamics of Sport Groups with Special Reference to Football," *British Journal of Sociology* 8, 4 (1957): 388–402; Elias and Dunning, "The Quest for Excitement in Leisure," *Society and Leisure: Bulletin for the European Centre for Leisure and Education* (Prague) 2 (1969): 50–85, also published as "The Quest for Excitement in an Unexciting Society," in *The Cross-Cultural Analysis of Sport and Games*, ed. Gunther Lüschen (Champaign: University of Illinois Press, 1970), 31–51; Norbert Elias and Eric Dunning, "Leisure in the Sparetime Spectrum," in *Soziologie des Sports: Theoretische und methodische Grundlagen/Sociology of Sport: Theoretical Foundations and Research Methods*, ed. Rolf Albonico and Katherina Pfister-Binz, tenth Magglinger symposium, 7–13 September 1969 (Basel: Birkäuser, 1971), 27–34; Norbert Elias, "The Genesis of Sport as a Sociological Problem," and Norbert Elias and Eric Dunning, "Folk Football in Medieval and Early Modern Britain," in *The Sociology of Sport: A Selection of Readings, with a Foreword by Norbert Elias*, ed. Eric Dunning (London: Frank Cass, 1971), 88–115 and 116–32, respectively.

10. Eric Dunning and Kenneth Sheard, *Barbarians, Gentlemen, and Players: A Sociological Study of the Development of Rugby Football* (Oxford: Martin Robertson; New York: New York University Press, 1979). During the 1970s and 1980s, Eric Dunning continued his research on sports at Leicester, becoming in 1986 director of the Sir Norman Chester Centre for Football Reasearch at that university. Among the works put out by that group, cosigned by Dunning and faithful to the inspiration of Elias, one might mention John Williams, Eric Dunning, and Patrick Murphy, *Hooligans Abroad: The Behaviour and Control of English Fans in Continental Europe* (London: Routledge and Kegan Paul, 1984); Eric Dunning, Patrick Murphy, and John Williams, *The Roots of Football Hooliganism: An Historical and Sociological Study* (London: Routledge and Kegan Paul, 1988).

11. Norbert Elias and Eric Dunning, *Sport in Zivilisationsprozess: Studien zur Figurationssoziologie,* ed. Wilhelm Hopf (Münster: Lit, 1982).

12. One of the works that best illustrate the views Elias and Dunning attacked in *Quest for Excitement* is Johan Huizinga, *Homo ludens: Versuch einer bestimmung des spielelements der Kultur* (1938), available in French as *Homo ludens: Essai sur la fonction sociale du jeu* (Paris: Gallimard, 1988) and in English as *Homo Ludens: A Study of the Play-Element in Culture* (Boston: Beacon Press, 1950, 1955). (On Huizinga, see the biographical note of E. H. Kossmann, "Huizinga and Geyl: A Portrait of Two Dutch Historians," in *The Low Countries: Arts and Society in Flanders and in the Netherlands: A Yearbook, 1993–94* [Rekkem: Flemish Netherlands Foundation "Stichting Ons Erfdeel," 1993], 130–36.) Included among such works are Roger Caillois, *Les jeux et les hommes: Le masque et le vertige* (Paris: Gallimard, 1967), available in English as *Man, Play, and Games,* trans. Meyer Barash (Glencoe, Ill.: Free Press of Glencoe, 1961; New York: Schocken Books, 1979); and Caillois, *Jeux et sports,* Bibliothèque de la Pléiade (Paris: Gallimard, 1968).

13. Cas Wouters, "Ja, ja, ik was nog niet zoo'n beroerde kerel, die zoo'n vrind had (Nescio)," in *Over Elias: Herinneringen en anekdotes,* ed. Hans Israëls, Mieke Komen, and Abram de Swaan (Amsterdam: Spinhuis, 1993), 7–19, quotations 13–15.

14. See "Sport, religion et violence: Débat entre Alain Ehrenberg, Roger Chartier et Marc Augé," *Esprit* 4 (1987): 63–70.

15. For an overview of investigation on this topic in France, see *Sciences sociales et sports: Etats et perspectives,* ed. Bernard Michon with the aid of Claude Faber, Acts of the Journées d'Etudes, Strasbourg, 13–14 November (Strasbourg: Université des Sciences Humaines de Strasbourg, Laboratoire APS et Sciences Sociales, UFR STAPS, 1988).

16. Pierre Bourdieu, "Comment peut-on être sportif?" in Bourdieu, *Questions de sociologie* (Paris: Editions de Minuit, 1980), 173–95, quotation 176, quoted from Bourdieu, "How Can One Be a Sportsman?" in Bourdieu, *Sociology in Question,* trans. Richard Nice (London: Sage, 1993), 117–31, quotation 119.

Epilogue

1. Philippe Ariès, *Le temps de l'histoire,* 2d ed. (Paris: Editions du Seuil, 1986).

2. Fernand Braudel, "Histoire et sciences sociales: La longue durée," *Annales ESC* 13 (1958): 725–53, esp. 737; Micheline Johnson, "Le concept de temps dans l'enseignement de l'histoire," *Revue d'Histoire de l'Amérique Française* 28, 4 (1975): 483–516, esp. 493–94.

3. Gabrielle M. Spiegel, "Political Utility in Medieval Historiography: A Sketch," *History and Theory* 14, 3 (1975): 314–25 nn. 2, 41; Orest A. Ranum, *Artisans of Glory: Writers and Historical Thought in Seventeenth-Century France* (Chapel Hill: University of North Carolina Press, 1980), 4; Erica Harth, *Ideology and Culture in Seventeenth-Century France* (Ithaca: Cornell University Press, 1983), 132, 133, 139. *Le temps de l'histoire* was also used and cited in Emmanuel Le Roy Ladurie, *Montaillou, village occitan de 1294 à 1324* (Paris: Gallimard, 1975), chap. 18, "Outillage mental: Le temps et l'espace"; available in English as *Montaillou, the Promised Land of Error,* trans. Barbara Bray (New York: G. Braziller, 1978; Vintage Books, 1979), chap. 17, "Concepts of Time and Space."

4. William R. Keylor, *Jacques Bainville and the Renaissance of Royalist History in Twentieth-Century France* (Baton Rouge: Louisiana State University Press, 1979), 202–3 and 214–18.

5. This essay by Philippe Ariès has been republished in Ariès, *Essais de mémoire (1943–1983)*, foreword by Roger Chartier (Paris: Editions du Seuil, 1993), 91–187.

6. Philippe Ariès, with Michel Winock, *Un historien du dimanche* (Paris: Editions du Seuil, 1980), 111.

7. Ibid., 122.

8. Ibid., 111.

9. William R. Keylor notes that between 1924 and 1947, the date of Ariès's study "L'histoire marxiste et l'histoire conservatrice," Fayard printed 260,300 copies of Bainville's *Histoire de France* (and 167,950 copies of his *Napoléon* between 1931 and 1947): Keylor, *Jacques Bainville*, 327–28.

10. Ariès, *Un historien du dimanche*, 81.

11. Ibid., 118.

12. I am indebted to Marie-Rose Ariès for her kindness in sharing this dossier, which includes press clippings and letters of thanks gathered by Philippe Ariès's wife, Primerose.

13. André Armengaud, "Les débuts de la dépopulation dans les campagnes toulousaines," *Annales ESC* 6 (1951): 172–78.

14. Jean-Louis Flandrin, "Enfance et société," *Annales ESC* 19 (1964): 322–29.

15. For example, *Historiography: A Bibliography*, comp. and ed. Lester D. Stephens (Metuchen, N.J.: Scarecrow Press, 1975).

16. Bernard Guenée, *Histoire et culture historique dans l'Occident médiéval* (Paris: Aubier Montaigne, 1980), 52. This book, enhanced by a bibliography of 829 entries, is the best synthesis on the writing of history in the Middle Ages. See also Guenée, ed., *Le métier d'historien au Moyen Age: Etudes sur l'historiographie médiévale*, Publications de la Sorbonne, série Etudes 13 (Paris: Université de Paris I Panthéon-Sorbonne, Centre de Recherches sur l'Histoire de l'Occident Médiéval, 1977).

17. Guenée, *Histoire et culture historique*, 63.

18. Ibid., 345, 323.

19. Ariés, *Un historien du dimanche*, 121–23.

20. George Huppert, *The Idea of Perfect History: Historical Erudition and Historical Philosophy in Renaissance France* (Urbana: University of Illinois Press, 1970); Donald R. Kelley, *Foundations of Modern Historical Scholarship: Language, Law and History in the French Renaissance* (New York: Columbia University Press, 1970); Roger Chartier, "Comment on écrivait l'histoire au temps des guerres de religion," *Annales ESC* 29 (1974): 883–87.

21. Michel Tyvaert, "Erudition et synthèse: Les sources utilisées par les histoires générales de la France au XVIIᵉ siècle," *Revue Française d'Histoire du Livre* 8 (1974): 249–66. This article, as well as Tyvaert, "L'image du roi: Légitimité et moralités royales dans les histoires de France au XVIIᵉ siècle," *Revue d'Histoire Moderne et Contemporaine* 21 (1974): 521–47, is an extract from Tyvaert's thèse de troisième cycle, "Recherches sur les histoires générales de la France au XVIIᵉ siècle (Domaine française)" (Université de Paris I, 1973).

22. On Mézeray, see Alain Viala, *Naissance de l'écrivain: Sociologie de la littérature à l'âge classique* (Paris: Editions de Minuit, 1985), 205–12.

23. Ranum, *Artisans of Glory.*

24. Paul Pellisson-Fontanier's project for a history of Louis XIV is analyzed by Louis Marin, "Le récit du roi ou comment écrire l'histoire," in Marin, *Le portrait du roi* (Paris: Editions de Minuit, 1981), 49–107, available in English as *Portrait of the King,* trans. Martha M. Houle, foreword by Tom Conley, Theory and History of Literature 57 (Minneapolis: University of Minnesota Press, 1988), 39–88, quotation 40. See chapter 7 above.

Index

Library of Congress Cataloging-in-Publication Data

Chartier, Roger, 1945–
    On the edge of the cliff : history, language, and practices / Roger Chartier : translated by
Lydia G. Cochrane.
        p.   cm. — (Parallax)
Collection of previously published (1983–1994) essays, articles, etc. translated from the
French.
    Includes bibliographical references and index.
    Contents: History between narrative and knowledge — Four questions for Hayden
White — Michel de Certeau : history, or knowledge of the other — The chimera of the ori-
gin : archaeology of knowledge, cultural history, and the French Revolution — Discourses
and practices : on the origins of the French Revolution — Texts, forms, and interpretations —
The powers and limits of representation — Self-consciousness and the social bond —
The double bind and detachment — Sports, or the controlled decontrolling of emotions —
Epilogue : friendship with history : Philippe Ariès.
    ISBN 0-8018-5435-0 (alk. paper). — ISBN 0-8018-5436-9 (pbk : alk. paper)
    1. History—Philosophy.   2. Language and history.   I. Title.   II. Series: Parallax
(Baltimore, Md.)
    D16.9.C45375   1997
    901—dc20   96-18980